From Mutiny to Revolt

Why did the nonviolent Meerut mutiny of 1857 in India explode into a violent military revolt? Breaking new ground on the events of May 10, William Pinch reexamines the evidence, shifting our focus toward the identity of female participants and their actions in the hours before the revolt began. Drawing upon a wide range of sources, including Hindi folksongs, military records, police reports, literary fiction, and Urdu memoir, he creates snapshots from the perspective of key figures to uncover the social and emotional world of the military "cantonment" and its rural hinterland. By foregrounding the lives of ordinary "military women" and "their men" – the Indian sepoys who peopled the revolt – Pinch challenges conventional narratives and guides readers through the literary and historiographical echoes of the fateful decision to take up arms against the British.

William R. Pinch is Professor of History and Global South Asian Studies at Wesleyan University.

From Mutiny to Revolt
Women and the Beginning of 1857

William R. Pinch
Wesleyan University

CAMBRIDGE
UNIVERSITY PRESS

Shaftesbury Road, Cambridge CB2 8EA, United Kingdom

One Liberty Plaza, 20th Floor, New York, NY 10006, USA

477 Williamstown Road, Port Melbourne, VIC 3207, Australia

314–321, 3rd Floor, Plot 3, Splendor Forum, Jasola District Centre,
New Delhi – 110025, India

103 Penang Road, #05-06/07, Visioncrest Commercial, Singapore 238467

Cambridge University Press is part of Cambridge University Press & Assessment, a department of the University of Cambridge.

We share the University's mission to contribute to society through the pursuit of education, learning and research at the highest international levels of excellence.

www.cambridge.org
Information on this title: www.cambridge.org/9780521885317

DOI: 10.1017/9781139029971

© William R. Pinch 2026

This publication is in copyright. Subject to statutory exception and to the provisions of relevant collective licensing agreements, no reproduction of any part may take place without the written permission of Cambridge University Press & Assessment.

When citing this work, please include a reference to the
DOI 10.1017/9781139029971

First published 2026

Cover: "A sepoy in the service of the East India Company, with a woman (courtesan?) on the right. Gouache, 18–". Wellcome Collection, London.

A catalogue record for this publication is available from the British Library

A Cataloging-in-Publication data record for this book is available from the Library of Congress

ISBN 978-0-521-88531-7 Hardback
ISBN 978-1-009-68242-8 Paperback

Cambridge University Press & Assessment has no responsibility for the persistence or accuracy of URLs for external or third-party internet websites referred to in this publication and does not guarantee that any content on such websites is, or will remain, accurate or appropriate.

For EU product safety concerns, contact us at Calle de José Abascal, 56, 1°, 28003 Madrid, Spain, or email eugpsr@cambridge.org

Contents

	List of Figures and Tables	*page* vi
	Acknowledgments	viii
	Introduction	1
1	Finding Uncommon Ground	9
2	Humiliation	50
3	Frail Ones	82
	Entr'acte: Zahir Dehlvi's *Tale of Treachery*	116
4	... Women Whose Men	125
5	Conclusions, Reflections	179

Appendices
1 Prostitutes in Criminal Judicial Proceedings, Oriental and India Office Collection, London ... 194
2 Pension Fraud Cases, 1850–1857 (a Selection) ... 197
Bibliography ... 206
Index ... 215

Figures and Tables

FIGURES

1.1 Map of Meerut cantonment, sadr bazaar, and Meerut City *page* 12
1.2 "Shops for colours and flowers used at festivals, Sadr bazaar, Pune" 27
1.3 "Painting [of shops selling liquor and paan, with moneylender between]" 28
1.4 "Bazaar in Cantonment, Meerut (U.P.)" 29
1.5 "Sudder Bazaar, Meerut" 30
2.1 Placard on display in the garden at the Gandhi Memorial Museum, Birla House, Tees January Marg, New Delhi, 2013 54
2.2 The shrine marking the site of Gandhi's assassination in the garden of the Birla House, Tees January Marg, New Delhi, 2013 55
3.1 "Wuzeerun. Bazar Woman. Mahomedan. Saharunpoor," 1868–1875 84
3.2 "Diljan. Bazar Woman. Saharanpoor," 1868–1875 85
3.3 "Beswā" (prostitute), Hansi Cantonment, 1825 86
3.4 (Untitled) a "nautch" scene, Hansi Cantonment, 1825 87
3.5 "Nách Girl. Aurat-e barqāz," Lucknow, 1815–1820 88
3.6 "Aurat-e barqāz. A Nátch Girl. Zan-e Katarānīh. A Khutteranee woman," Lucknow, 1815–1820 89
3.7 "Bengal Troops on the Line of March," 1835 96
3.8 "Cart in which Native Females ride," detail of "Bengal Troops on the Line of March," 1835 (?) 96
4.1 "An old pensioned sepoy, wearing a medal," Calcutta (?), 1840 127

4.2 "A pensioned sepoy who had distinguished himself in the time of Lord Lake, and one of the police Chaprassees at Moradabad," North India, 1836–1842   128
4.3 "Two old women who stationed themselves near the entrance to the camp on each day's march and accompanied 'our' camp for three successive years," Simla (?), 1840   129
5.1 "Qr Mr Sergeant" and "Camp Followers"   191

TABLE

3.1 Percentages of select bazaar "professions" in eight cantonments, 1855   *page* 90
3.2 Major Meerut District crimes, 1855   100

Acknowledgments

The research for this book was supported by a Fulbright-Nehru senior research fellowship, administered by the United States – India Educational Foundation (USIEF) in New Delhi. Additional support was provided by the Wesleyan History department's Colonel Return Jonathan Meigs First (1740–1823) Fund, created by Dorothy Mix Meigs and Fielding Pope Meigs, Jr. of Rosemont, Pennsylvania in memory of that soldier of the revolution, whose home was in Middletown, Connecticut from 1740 to 1787. Colonel Meigs would be pleased, I hope, that funds endowed in his name have supported a book on India's own rebellion against the British Empire. Several Wesleyan "project grants" were also crucial in advancing my research, as were two sabbaticals.

I have been fortunate to be able to share this work in progress with many students over the past decade. Their names are too numerous to list in their entirety, but I will single out those in my most recent "Raj" class, in spring 2024: Sajid Aziz, Miles Craven, Rafay Khan, Spencer Landers, Oliver Meier, Joshua Silbert, Maggie Smith, and Stella Tannen. Friends and colleagues – alas, too many to name here – have helped shape this work with comments, criticisms, and invitations to speak. They know who they are. I thank them all.

This book would not be possible without the love and support of Kailash and Abha Jha, and most of all Jennifer Saines. This book is for Jennifer.

Introduction

> When it was dusk, I went to the lines of my regiment. I saw the sepoys weeping, they were very sad and said the recruits had ruined them, but they had killed the sepoy who fired the first shot. I then secreted myself with my wife and family, but lost all my property.
>
> Sheikh Moulla Buksh, havildar, 20th Regiment, Native Infantry, describing the events at Meerut cantonment on May 10, 1857[1]

Imagine the following scenario: in 2021 the US armed forces, in its wisdom, decides to introduce a new technology said to afford its fighting men and women a key advantage on a rapidly evolving battlefield. This new technology entails ingesting a substance rumored to be controversial. Many soldiers resist for both medical and religious reasons, and soon this resistance swells into a wholesale refusal to ingest the substance by entire regiments. As a result, the military authorities decide to make an example of the dissenters, whom they accuse of mutiny – the refusal to obey a direct order – and subject to a series of courts martial. Entire regiments are, one after another, convicted and dishonorably discharged, and the more outspoken "ringleaders" are sent to prison. Reeling from this dramatic turn of events and furious at the ill-treatment of their recently punished brothers and sisters in arms, two special forces battalions stationed at Fort Bragg, North Carolina, rise up in revolt. The resulting mayhem, in which not just key commanding officers but also members of their families are killed, sends shock waves across the nation. Meanwhile the military revolt quickly spreads from base to base throughout the South. Soon the violence crosses the civil–military divide, as anxieties about the controversial substance link up with simmering discontent with government among the public at large. The ensuing "civil rebellion" is eventually put down, but not before many hundreds of thousands innocent civilians are killed in brutal counter-insurgency operations.

---

[1] *Depositions Taken at Meerut*, by Major G. W. Williams, Superintendent of Police, North Western Province, 1858 (British Library, London), p. 13.

Had there been a mutiny-revolt-rebellion like the one counterfactually posed here, there is no doubt that a swarm of officials, journalists, policy analysts, and – eventually – historians would want to know why it occurred and what lessons might be drawn from it.[2] They would doubtless examine all factors, including the decision to introduce the controversial substance in the first place. They also would look for patterns – why some battalions or branches of the service revolted while others did not; whether there was geographic or sociocultural variation to the mutiny-revolt-rebellion; and whether there were warning signs that went unheeded. Of particular interest would be why, and how, what began as simply a refusal to ingest a substance quickly exploded into a revolt at a specific military base – in other words, whether there were particular circumstances or developments in and around Fort Bragg that turned an essentially nonviolent mutiny into a violent revolt.

As it happens, a process of mutiny → revolt → rebellion like the one counterfactually described here did occur in British India in 1857. As with the US army today, Britain's Indian (or "native") army was one of the largest volunteer forces of its time, with about a quarter of a million men stationed in bases (called "cantonments") across the subcontinent. And like its American counterpart, service in the Company Army was voluntary, highly sought after, and considered a mark of distinction. The controversial substance imposed upon the soldiery was a greased cartridge, introduced in the early months of 1857, as part of a plan to replace the old "Brown Bess" musket with the Pattern 1853 Enfield. The original drill for loading the new weapon involved tearing the top of the paper cartridge with the teeth. (This process, as well as its slight alteration in April of 1857 that involved tearing the cartridge with the fingers instead of teeth, is described in greater detail in Chapter 1.) Because the grease for some of the original cartridges was rendered from cow and pig fat, the prospect of touching,

---

[2] To extend the counterfactual history onto historiography, one can further imagine the following: Almost immediately the history of the insurgency begins to emerge, and it is written in such a way as to position the insurgency – whether military or civilian – as a betrayal of the common good, a mutiny not simply against military command but American society and the American way of life. Some particularly imaginative authors explore the possibility that the insurgency was the result of a preconcerted conspiracy, designed to overthrow the legitimate government. The losers, shamed and terrorized into submission, are unable to openly express their understanding of the mutiny-revolt-rebellion. Over time, however, their descendants begin to turn the historiographical tables on the conspiracy narrative: They craft a new historical understanding of the events of 2021–2022 as a (Second) War of American Independence. This insurgent historical narrative begins to gain a purchase on the political imaginary of the public at large and leads to the rise of a new political order, the Second American Republic.

let alone biting, the ammunition was scandalous for both Hindus and Muslims. This led to a series of "mutinies" across north India, as regiment after regiment in the Bengal Army refused to perform routine "firing drills" in preparation for the issuing of the new weapon. The military trials (courts martial) for these mutinies invariably resulted in guilty verdicts, dishonorable discharges, and even imprisonment for some men. Remarkably, save for one famous episode in March 1857, in which a soldier attacked his British officers in a failed bid to spark a regimental revolt,[3] the refusal of the cartridges and the "reduction" and dismissal of the mutinous regiments was a nonviolent process.

Until May 10, 1857.

In the late afternoon and evening of May 10, Meerut cantonment, a major military garrison about forty miles north of Delhi, was rocked by violence. Nearly the entirety of the Bengal 3rd Light Cavalry and 20th Native Infantry, joined by a large portion of the 11th Native Infantry, rose up in revolt and began attacking their officers, killing several. A mob from the cantonment bazaar quickly joined in the mayhem and began an indiscriminate killing of British military and civilian residents, including some women and children. A day earlier, the native regiments had been forced to watch while eighty-five "skirmishers" of the 3rd Light Cavalry, who in late April had refused to perform the firing drill and were subsequently court-martialed, were stripped of their uniforms, placed in irons, and marched off to prison. For reasons that, to my mind, have never been made entirely clear, the remaining men of the 3rd Light Cavalry plus the men of the 20th Native Infantry and most men of the 11th Native Infantry, decided to revolt. This book is, in part, about that decision. But it is also about the social and emotional world of the cantonment upon which the circumstances of that decision necessarily cast light.

Much has been written about 1857. Much less about the events at Meerut. This is because the Meerut rebels quickly abandoned the cantonment and rode south to Delhi, turning the old Mughal capital into the epicenter of the rebellion. Aside from the ignominy associated with the failure to pursue the rebels as they galloped to Delhi, Meerut quickly recedes into the background in the emerging 1857 historiography.[4] As is detailed in Chapters 1 and 2, insofar as Meerut cantonment appears in the history, it does so mainly as the site of the initial revolt – little more than a narrative point of departure. There are three main exceptions to this rule.

---

[3] The soldier was, of course, Mangal Pandey. The failure of his comrades to join in his revolt led him to attempt suicide. He was quickly tried, convicted, and hanged.

[4] As I note later, Meerut also becomes a staging ground for the post-revolt pacification of the countryside north of Delhi in what is now Haryana and northwestern Uttar Pradesh.

4   Introduction

The first is a study of the Meerut revolt by J. A. B. Palmer, entitled *Mutiny Outbreak at Meerut in 1857* (1966). Palmer was interested in the question of whether the revolt was premeditated, as was often alleged – especially in nationalist narratives. He ultimately concluded that while there was some local premeditation, there was no widespread conspiracy.

The second exception is the work of Eric Stokes, especially his posthumous *The Peasant Armed: The Indian Rebellion of 1857* (1986), whose focus was less on Meerut cantonment itself than on the rebellion in the Meerut Division – especially with an eye to whether an overarching logic, whether class, caste, or religious, might be discerned in the agrarian uprisings that accompanied the insurgency and gave it the character of a broad-based civil rebellion.[5] His answer, ultimately, was in the negative, or more precisely that insofar as there was an agrarian logic to the revolt, it was whether local actors could benefit vis-à-vis their enemies in the locality by remaining "loyal" or by joining the rebellion. There is some early attention to events in Meerut cantonment, but Stokes is mainly focused on the loss-of-caste fears attendant on the greased cartridges and how those connected to the precarious economic conditions in the countryside.

The third and most important exception is the painstaking narrative reconstruction by Kim Wagner, *The Great Fear of 1857: Rumours, Conspiracies and the Making of the Indian Uprising*, (2010), which devotes several chapters to Meerut. Both Palmer and Wagner offer a close examination of the unfolding events in the cantonment and both point to the importance of developments in the cantonment bazaar (called "sudder" [*sadr* or main] bazaar in the military argot of the time) and key bazaar inhabitants in initiating the soldiers' turn to violence. Curiously, however, Palmer had provided no information about the bazaar, to say nothing of the people that worked and lived there. This deficiency is admirably remedied by Wagner, who introduces the reader to the array of bazaar characters that took part in the mayhem that erupted on May 10, 1857. In Chapter 1, building on Wagner's account, I undertake a more synchronic investigation of the cantonment bazaar, in Meerut and beyond. One important class of characters involved in the precipitation of the revolt was, according to a major source,

---

[5] Gautam Bhadra, "Four Rebels of 1857," in Ranajit Guha (ed.), *Subaltern Studies 4* (Delhi: Oxford University Press, 1984), pp. 276–329, also includes (in part 1) an analysis of the rebel leader Shah Mal, a small landlord of Meerut District. His goal, not wholly inconsistent with Stokes', was to shed light on the "ordinary rebels," the non-elite "active spirits" of resistance to British rule – mainly to contest the notion that the popular rebellion was a result of simply the disaffection of the landed magnates, the "natural leaders" of rural society.

Introduction 5

"prostitutes". Indeed, the allegedly catalytic role of the prostitutes of the Meerut bazaar in sparking the soldiers' revolt quickly became a staple of Mutiny historiography. Chapter 2 is devoted to this theme – that is, to the origin of the prostitute narrative, the manner in which it became embedded in the story of 1857, and the twists and turns of that narrative as it underwent considerable evolution over the course of the following century and more. Indeed, the entire book may be read as a commentary on the degree to which the blanket term "prostitute" is something of a blunt instrument that conceals more than it reveals – a reflection of which point are the many and varied terms and euphemisms that were used in the mid nineteenth century (and not only in India) to reference women who provided sexual service and companionship. As such, scare quotes may be presumed around my usage of the term henceforth.

Especially surprising, given the prominence and longevity of Meerut prostitutes in the narrative of 1857, to say nothing of the question of their actual identity (questions that took on greater intrigue in the wake of discoveries about the mysterious figure of "Mees Dolly" in the early twentieth century, recounted in Chapter 2, as well as the roughly concurrent emergence of Zahir Dehlvi's Urdu account of the mutiny-revolt in Meerut, discussed in the Entr'acte between Chapters 3 and 4), is the fact that no one has bothered to actually investigate the quality of the source material concerning the prostitute narrative, to say nothing of the precariously influential position of prostitutes in the world of the mid-century cantonment that the narrative implies. Chapter 3 investigates this latter issue, relying mainly on heretofore ignored police and judicial records – much of which were generated by the new hybrid office of the "Cantonment Joint Magistrate" in the 1850s. While post-1860s prostitutes in Britain and the British Empire have been the subject of much detailed analysis, due in large part to the generation of massive "lock hospital" documentation in the wake of the "Contagious Diseases Acts," a body of 1860s legislation that subjected prostitutes to hostile official attention and unprecedented imperial medical control,[6] there has been comparatively little analysis of pre-1860 prostitution in India – and that which does exist tends to fall back on generalities concerning a largely benign and nostalgic image of pre-colonial (mainly Mughal, late Mughal, and early Company) courtesanship and the glamorous, if

---

[6] See especially the work of Philippa Levine, Ashwini Tambe, Stephen Legg, and, more recently, Durba Mitra. Mitra argues that exploding official anxiety about the prostitute in the latter half of the nineteenth century produced an "incitement to discourse" that shaped scientific (including social scientific) understanding of India.

ontologically challenging, figure of the *tawāif*.⁷ One contribution of this book is the focus on the cantonment world of entertainment, prostitution, and "domestic sociality"⁸ that links (and served as a transitional space between) the world of the "common prostitute" with the world of the *tawāif*.

Without giving away too much, as I wish for the reader to experience the excitement of discovery that I enjoyed in the archives over the past decade or more while conducting the research for this book, let me add (as I have already hinted) that the publication of Zahir Dehlvi's memoir of the mutiny, *Dāstān-e-Ghadr*, in 1914 raised wholly new and intriguing questions about the identity of the Meerut prostitute – or more precisely, whether the women who played a key role in prompting the men of the 3rd Light Cavalry, 20th Native Infantry, and 11th Native Infantry to rise in revolt were, in fact, prostitutes. The key passage in Dehlvi's account has been available in English translation since 1957, but almost no historians have made actual analytical recourse to it.⁹ I examine the account anew in the Entr'acte (between Chapters 3 and 4) and offer a new and more detailed translation there of the key passage concerning the women of Meerut and their catalytic role in the revolt. The startling implications of my close reading of Dehlvi's account are played out in Chapter 4, entitled "… Women Whose Men," which relies upon heretofore untapped military pension records and "fraudulent wife" controversies in the 1850s. In addition to helping to resolve the question of the Meerut women/prostitutes conundrum, Chapter 4 also affords unprecedented access to the social and emotional world of the Indian soldier in the Company Army – an army that, as Seema Alavi noted in her pioneering work three decades ago, was the main source of legitimacy for British sovereignty from the late eighteenth to the mid nineteenth century.¹⁰ Chapter 4 also suggests a possible new source of sepoy disaffection that led to the explosion of 1857.

This book is, then, both a microhistory of 1857 – and the world that made 1857 – as well as a new military history of the Company Army.

---

⁷ Key exceptions are Douglas Peers, "Privates on Parade"; and Indrani Chatterjee, *Gender, Slavery, and Law in Colonial India* (Delhi: Oxford University Press, 1999). For more discussion, see Chapter 2.
⁸ To draw upon Luise White; see esp. her pioneering work, *The Comforts of Home: Prostitution in Colonial Nairobi* (Chicago: University of Chicago Press, 1990). In many ways, I have taken inspiration from White's oeuvre and am grateful to my colleague Laura Ann Twagira for bringing her to my attention.
⁹ The exception is Rajat Ray, whose work I discuss in Conclusions, Reflections.
¹⁰ And, as she points out, pensions were central to the Company's appropriation of late Mughal authority; Seema Alavi, "The Company Army and Rural Society: The Invalid Thanah 1780–1830," *Modern Asian Studies* 27, 1, (1993): esp. 149–155.

The "new military history" promised, decades ago, to reinvigorate the study of military history by connecting transformations in the army to changes taking place in society – either as a stimulant or a response, or both simultaneously in true auto-catalytic fashion. (This is as true for armies in the mid nineteenth century as it is for armies today.) As noted earlier, I rely in part on military and police/judicial records – particularly in the more social-history-oriented Chapters 3 and 4. However, I also make recourse to Hindi and Urdu materials throughout. Zahir Dehlvi's *Dāstān* has already been mentioned. Also crucial are Hindi songs sung in the wake of 1857, which afford a sense of what 1857 meant to the largely agrarian society in which it occurred. This is in marked contrast to Dehlvi's point of view, which is decidedly more urbane and elite.

The pursuit of microhistory is predicated on the idea, for me at any rate, that the closer we look at the past, the stranger (and more interesting) it becomes. Certainly 1857 looks different when we examine it up close and personal, and so does the world of the military cantonment. While this may not overturn long-standing arguments about the ultimate causes of 1857, it will, I hope, help us understand not only what motivated the sepoys (and *sawār*s, cavalrymen) to take the unprecedented step of attacking their British commanders, but appreciate how profoundly difficult a decision – a dizzying leap into an unknown, perilous future – that was. (A measure of that difficulty is that even as they turned against their officers, some and perhaps many of the rebel sepoys sought to protect them, their wives, and their children.)[11] Another virtue of microhistory is that it prompts the historian to pay closer attention to how it is that we arrive at knowledge of the past. As such, it brings us face to face with history as ontology. As will be evident in the following pages, what historians came to believe about the "fact" of the prostitutes of Meerut was constituted by a long process of narrative unfolding, a process that began in the immediate wake of the moment of revolt and concludes, in the early twenty-first century, with an interweaving of historical fact and literary fiction. What, then, does this say about history as a domain of truth? Are we to conclude that the Meerut narrative about women is not true, that it is merely a form of literary representation that has infected

---

[11] See e.g. Palmer, *Mutiny Outbreak at Meerut*, 89; G. W. Williams, "Narrative of events connected with the outbreak in 1857," Appendix II (India Office Records, British Library, London), p. 22, describing "a few instances in a well-disposed Corps that mutinied, to show that the men of the Regiment held no ill-feeling against, or any wish to harm or injure their Officers." (Note that as was increasingly common in subsequent years, the term "mutiny" and "revolt" became synonymous.)

the discourse of history? And to what degree is this a subset of a larger philosophical issue, about the nature of the history itself – as both the past as well as the story about the past?[12]

Read on and decide for yourself.

---

[12] On the doubleness of history, see Reinhart Koselleck, *Futures Past: On the Semantics of Historical Time*, trans. Keith Tribe (New York: Columbia University Press, 2004), p. 32, beautifully illuminated by Ritwik Ranjan, "Postcoloniality and the Two Sites of Historicity," *History and Theory* 56, 1 (2017): esp. 42–43.

1 Finding Uncommon Ground

Mutiny, Revolt, Rebellion, War

The violence that engulfed northern India in 1857–1858 began with a series of regimental mutinies in the cantonments of the Honorable East India Company's Bengal Army. Strictly speaking, these mutinies consisted of groups of soldiers and sometimes entire regiments refusing to carry out a new "firing drill" that was being introduced in late 1856 and early 1857 *in anticipation of* the general issue of the Pattern 53 Enfield rifled musket, which was slated to replace the old "Brown Bess" smooth-bore musket in the Company regiments. The Brown Bess had been in use for over a century and was, indeed, still in widespread use in India in the months leading up to and during the revolt.[1] Because the Enfield employed a "rifled" barrel, which necessitated a tighter fit for the "ball" (the "Minie ball," actually a bullet, named after one of the French inventors, Captain Claude-Etienne Minié) so as to produce the trajectory-improving spin, the bottom third of the paper exterior of the cartridge received a layer of grease to ease the muzzle-loading action. It was the nature of this grease that became the focus of much discussion and controversy among the ranks from January of 1857, as rumors – originating at Dum Dum cantonment, near Calcutta – began circulating among the Company regiments that Indian soldiers would soon be ordered to handle and even touch to their lips and teeth (for the purpose of tearing the cartridge in order to empty the contents into the barrel) forbidden substances, namely, tallow made in part with fat rendered from slaughtered cows and pigs.

---

[1] David Harding, "Arming the East India Company's Forces," in Alan J. Guy and Peter B. Boyden (Eds.), *Soldiers of the Raj: The Indian Army, 1600–1947* (London: National Army Museum, 1997), pp. 145–146; and Danield R. LeClair, "The 'Greased Cartridge Affair': Re-examining the Pattern 1853 Enfield Cartridge and Its Role in the Indian Mutiny of 1857," *International Ammunition Association Journal* 504 (July/August 2015): 104. This and the following paragraph also rely on Julian Saul Markham David, "The Bengal Army and the Outbreak of the Indian Mutiny" (PhD thesis, Department of History, University of Glasgow, 2001), chapter 6, entitled, "Mutiny: the Cartridge Question," pp. 168–196.

By late January of 1857, after official inquiries into the composition of the tallow were unable to confirm or refute the rumors, the military authorities removed all new cartridges from use. In any case, only one British rifle regiment, the 60th Queen's Royal Rifles, stationed at Meerut, had been issued Enfields. Some were sent to the musketry depots at Ambala, Sialkot, and Dum Dum for the use of small groups of trainee detachments from the "native regiments"; the remainder were kept in storage.[2] By the end of January any Indian soldiers undergoing training with the new weapons at the musketry depots were authorized to purchase their own ingredients – usually a combination of ghee and beeswax – from the local market in order to grease the cartridges themselves.[3] Other than these select men, all Indian soldiers performing (or refusing to perform, as the case may be) firing drills were using their old smooth-bore muskets and the cartridges designed for them. Some, as we shall see, were being instructed in the mechanics of the new drill but while using the old weapons and cartridges. By February, however, doubts about the quality of the paper had shifted to the Brown Bess cartridges (known as Pattern 1842 cartridges).[4]

On April 24, 1857 eighty-five "skirmishers" of the Bengal 3rd Light Cavalry, stationed at Meerut, refused to load their Brown Bess weapons according to the new firing drill.[5] They were immediately charged with

---

[2] According to J. A. B. Palmer, *Mutiny Outbreak at Meerut in 1857* (Cambridge: Cambridge University Press, 1966), p. 14, the depot at nearby Ambala cantonment was visited by detachments from forty-four native regiments in the first quarter of 1857. Palmer also mentions that training in the Enfield rifles was also undertaken at the Artillery School in Meerut, but that was restricted to recruits for the Bengal Artillery. Until April 17, all musketry training focused on the mechanism and care of the weapon and did not include loading and firing. See also David Saul, *The Bengal Army and the Outbreak of the Indian Mutiny* (New Delhi: Manohar Publishers & Distributors, 2009), p. 86 (cited in LeClair, "The 'Greased Cartridge Affair'," p. 104). By May 1857 there were only 12,000 Enfield rifled muskets in the Bengal Presidency. The vast majority were in storage at the arsenals.

[3] David, "The Bengal Army and the Outbreak of the Indian Mutiny," p. 172; LeClair, "The 'Greased Cartridge Affair'," p. 104.

[4] The reasons for this are unclear. David Saul argues that a concerted conspiracy among Muslim soldiers was behind the persistent unease over the grease for the Enfield cartridges and then even the "ungreased" Brown Bess cartridge paper. A contributing factor may have been that the Bengal Army had begun, either in 1853 or in 1855, introducing an "improved 'country paper'" for the Brown Bess from the Serampore Paper Mills, and that this had a slightly darker hue. See David Harding, "Arming the East India Company's Forces," p. 145; and D. F. Harding, *Smallarms of the East India Company*, vol. 3, *Ammunition and Performance* (London: Foresight Books, 1999), pp. 137, 145–146.

[5] As David Harding pointed out on the 150th anniversary of the revolt ("Arming the East India Company's Forces," p. 145), "[t]he cartridges refused by so many of the sepoys, including momentously the skirmishers of the 3rd Bengal Light Cavalry at Meerut on May 10, 1857, were in fact not for the Enfield rifle, but for the smooth-bore weapons so long in use."

"disobeying a lawful command" and, after a court of inquiry on April 25 and court-martial on May 6–8, found guilty of mutiny. Most were sentenced to ten years' imprisonment with hard labor; a few of the younger men had their sentences halved. On May 9 they were marched from their temporary confinement to the British infantry parade ground where, surrounded by fully armed British artillery, infantry, and cavalry regiments, and in full view of their own native cavalry regiment and two additional native infantry regiments (all lacking live ammunition), they were stripped of their uniforms, shackled in irons, and marched off to the civil jail. This ritual dishonoring and humiliation was known in military circles as an "ironing parade" and was intended as an object lesson to the remainder of the corps.

It was a lesson that produced unexpected results. The next day, around 5 pm, almost the entirety of the 20th Native Infantry and 3rd Light Cavalry, and most of the 11th Native Infantry, rose up in revolt. The first British officer to be killed was Colonel John Finnis of the 11th Native Infantry, shot by someone from the 20th Native Infantry while trying to restore order in the ranks. All told, between forty and fifty Britons were killed in Meerut during the evening and night of May 10, including eight officers, four officers' wives, and four children. The remainder of the dead were either rank-and-file British soldiers or Britons of nonofficial status (veterans and pensioners, merchants, etc.). Much of the violence occurred in the sadr bazaar on the southwest edge of the cantonment (see Figure 1.1 for a map of Meerut). In the months that followed, India would witness a paroxysm of violence that has been deemed "the single most serious armed challenge any Western empire would face, anywhere in the world, in the entire course of the nineteenth century."[6]

We return to the events at Meerut, and especially the court-martial, in the pages that follow. For now, let us jump fifty-four years into the future. In 1911, the retired Indian civil service officer and noted folklorist William Crooke published a two-part article in *The Indian Antiquary* entitled "Songs of the Mutiny."[7] Crooke began by noting that the songs, "collected some time ago chiefly by Râmgharîb Chaube [and] found all over Northern India," were "still upon the lips of the people." According to Crooke, Chaube held that the songs were "an indication of the real

---

[6] William Dalrymple, *The Last Mughal: The Fall of a Dynasty, Delhi, 1857* (London: Penguin Viking, 2007), p. 192. For a detailed examination of the firing drill, the court of inquiry and court-martial, the ironing parade, and the military revolt, see Palmer, *The Mutiny Outbreak at Meerut in 1857*, esp. pp. 58–87.
[7] William Crooke, "Songs of the Mutiny," *The Indian Antiquary*, part I (April 1911), pp. 123–124, and part II (June 1911), pp. 165–169.

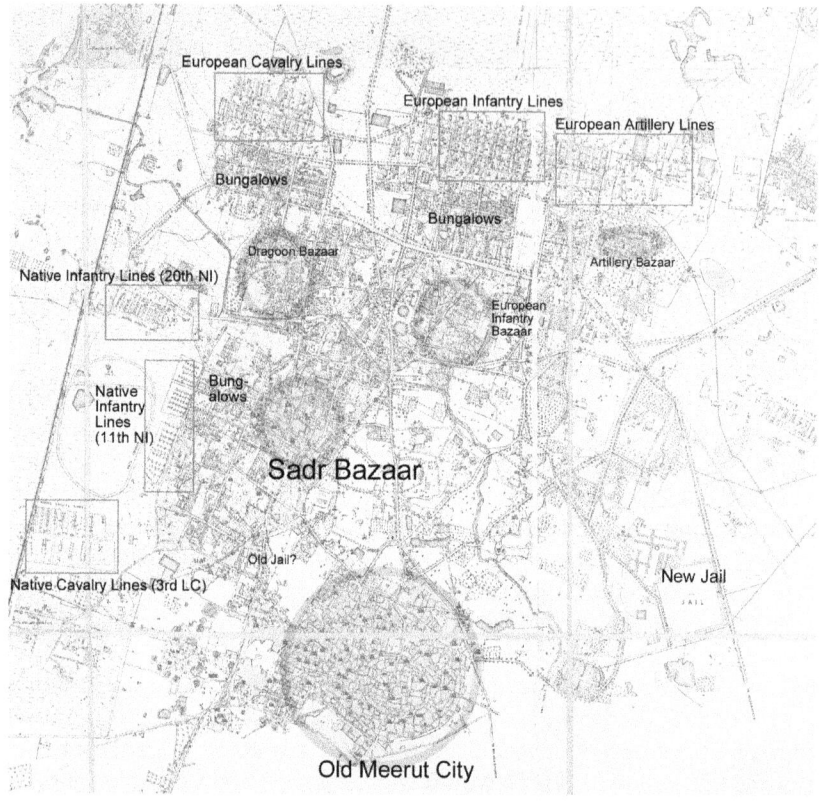

Figure 1.1 Map of Meerut cantonment, sadr bazaar, and Meerut City
Source: The base map is the map entitled "Cantonment and Environs of Meerut ... 1867–68" (Calcutta, 1871). Shelfmark: Cartographic Items Maps I.S.112. British Library, London. Additional labels are by the author.

feeling of the people on the subject [of the Mutiny] fifty years after the occurrence." What was that *real feeling*? Chaube (again, according to Crooke): "[T]he Mutiny had very deeply impressed the overwhelming power of the English on the whole of the population of the districts affected by it," and that "[t]he higher classes hid this impression, but the lower orders had no compunction in composing verses in honour of the British victories."[8]

---

[8] Crooke, "Songs of the Mutiny," part I, p. 123. On the Crooke–Chaube relationship, see Sadhana Naithani, *In Quest of Indian Folktales: Pandit Ram Gharib Chaube and William Crooke* (Bloomington: Indiana University Press, 2006).

These assertions notwithstanding, there was little in the songs themselves that reflected a desire to honor British victories in 1857. Of the seven songs in the collection, only one (no. 7, the longest) actually celebrated the British. It employed the refrain, "entrenching themselves all round, the white warriors fought well" (*chāroṇ taraf se bāndhī morchā, laṛe khūb jaṅgī gorā* / चारों तरफ़ से बांधी मोर्चा, लड़े ख़ूब जंगी गोरा), and offered much additional praise for the martial skill of both the British soldiers and Indian sepoys.[9] Only two other songs (nos. 2 and 5) alluded to the British victory, but they did so in the form of a lamentation. Indeed, Crooke referred to one of these (no. 5) as a "dirge." The other, no. 2, described how a rebel chieftain was betrayed by his fellow landholder-aristocrats in Awadh ("Oudh") who had joined the British. Three of the remaining four songs (nos. 1, 3, and 6) made no explicit mention of the British. In two of these the British were the unnamed opponents of the Indian commanders being celebrated (no. 3 about one Gulab Thakur of Barwa Batola and no. 6 about the Rani of Jhansi). In the third (no. 1, discussed later), a woman criticizes her lover for the paltry amount of loot he managed to plunder during the post-revolt mayhem in the cantonment bazaar at Meerut. The final song (no. 4), however, was in many ways the most interesting of the collection: Like nos. 2, 5, and 7, this song mentioned the British, but it celebrated their *defeat* in 1857. We return to this song in due course.

Much has been written about 1857 – especially in the decades immediately following that cataclysmic year. In the heated aftermath of the conflict, Britons debated both the nature and the causes of the revolt. Foremost among their concerns was whether it was a spontaneous uprising or the result of a long-planned conspiracy. If the latter, did the conspiracy extend beyond the Indian soldiery to include key Indian elites, particularly members of royal families long considered either loyal or supine? Another topic of abiding interest was the role of religion and caste, particularly (as we have seen) when it came to what substances the soldiery was willing to ingest. Britons were also gripped by the sudden explosion of the violence, and especially the willingness of the rebels to kill women and children. The question of rape was hotly debated, prompting official inquiries. A few European observers, such as W. H. Russell of *The Times*, noted the brutality of British reprisals. Looming behind these discussions was the larger question of whom – on the British side – to blame for the revolt? Was it the result of the aggressive annexations of Indian states under the infamous "Doctrine of Lapse,"

---

[9] Crooke, "Songs of the Mutiny," part II, pp. 166–169 (vv. 1, 4, 7, 10, 13, 16, 19, and 22.)

and especially the high-handed 1856 decision to depose Nawab Wajid Ali Shah of Awadh? What role did official attitudes play, particularly around issues such as Christian missionary activity, education, and social reform? To what degree were the military authorities to blame? After all, it was a cliché (in naval circles, at any rate) that "a captain was the cause of his own mutiny."[10] As we have seen, much attention, naturally, was given over to the vexed issue of the cartridges required by the new Enfield rifle – adopted to good effect in Crimea in 1855 – and the composition of the grease that covered those, and ultimately all, cartridges.

These were the questions that dominated the newspapers and other public media, in Britain as well as British India. In the end, Parliament blamed the anomaly of the Company itself, abolished it, and instituted direct Crown Rule. Not surprisingly, very few Indian voices were heard in these early years. Initially the few that did dare to speak out made it a point to insist on their loyalty to the Empire, and the first and most famous of these, "Sir Syed" (Sayyad Ahmad Khan), argued that the cause of the revolt was not religious hostility to the British – at least not on the part of Muslims. Rather, the rebellion was due to misguided policy, especially when it came to the annexation of Indian states, ignorance about Indian culture on the part of British leaders, and an insufficient attention to and reliance upon elite "native opinion" – especially that of the Muslim gentry, the "natural rulers" of India prior to the rise of the British. Over time cautiously critical Hindu opinion also began to be heard, sometimes without invoking 1857 directly. Most famous was Bankim Chandra Chatterjee's 1882 argument, scaffolded onto the history of a sprung-from-the-soil rebellion a century earlier (the so-called Sannyasi and Fakir Rebellion), that even though Britons in India were callous and profit-driven, continued British rule was necessary if Indians – or rather, Hindus (Bankim positioned Muslims as scapegoats) – were fully to imbibe the secrets of enlightened governance.

By the early twentieth century, the cautious Indian loyalist tone was being dispensed with. Writing from the heart of the Empire in London, the young firebrand V. D. Savarkar marked the fifty-year anniversary of the rebellion with a history that celebrated it as a patriotic "war of independence." First published in Marathi (and promptly banned by the India Office) in 1908, Savarkar's nationalist interpretation of 1857 attracted attention among the slowly radicalizing ranks of Indian

---

[10] Attributed to Admiral Lord Collingwood; see Greg Dening, *Mr. Bligh's Bad Language: Passion, Power, and Theatre on the Bounty* (Cambridge: Cambridge University Press, 1992), p. 115.

nationalists who, at the time, were mostly English-educated elites – in other words, the "higher classes" dismissively invoked by Chaube or, at the very least, Crooke ventriloquizing Chaube. Underscoring the publicity surrounding Savarkar's book was the fact that in the very year it was published the author was implicated in the assassination of William Hutt Curzon Wylie in London by an Indian student, Madan Lal Dhingra. In 1910 Savarkar was arrested, tried, and convicted of waging war against the King Emperor and sentenced to fifty years' imprisonment.[11]

Thus, in presenting the "Mutiny songs" to the British and Indian public, Crooke (via Chaube) was implicitly contesting a radical interpretation of 1857 that was attracting a younger generation of nationalists. We might even suggest that Crooke opted to deploy Chaube's voice, the voice of a "native," to expose Indian nationalism as elitist and out of touch with the real India of the thousands of villages and towns that dotted the countryside. According to this line of reasoning, Savarkar and his class might want to believe that the emerging Indian nation stood united in rejecting British rule, but the people of India – the "lower orders," including, crucially, the peasantry – were immune to the ideology of nationalism and not only recognized the supremacy of British arms but celebrated it.

Interest in 1857 waned in the wake of the nationalist movement and independence. The attention of most historians interested in patriotic resistance to British imperialism were drawn instead to the study of the Indian National Congress and, especially, Gandhi, whose legacy of effective nonviolence made for an awkward narrative fit with the failed violence of 1857. (Only more recently have historians come around to the idea that there was, indeed, the potential for much *hiṁsā* beneath the veneer of Gandhian *ahiṁsā*, of which Gandhi himself was all too aware.) Insofar as historians attempted new approaches to 1857, they explored how and whether larger structural contradictions in Indian society figured in the unfolding of the uprising. Most concluded that while the military mutiny and revolt possessed a clear pattern, the "civil rebellion" that tore across north India was more of a piecemeal, context-specific affair – that the individual decisions to join in the revolt or remain loyal to the Raj depended more on local animosities and circumstances than on some overarching theory of nationhood or economic grievance. Whether or not 1857 should be seen as *The Indian*

---

[11] Savarkar has been experiencing renewed, and deserved, historiographical interest. See esp. Vinayak Chaturvedi, *Hindutva and Violence: V. D. Savarkar and the Politics of History* (New Delhi: Permanent Black, 2022), and Janaki Bakhle, *Savarkar and the Making of Hindutva* (Princeton, NJ: Princeton University Press, 2024).

War of Independence, as Savarkar had put it, it did not bear the hallmarks of a class war, as indeed Marx and Engels had made clear in their contemporary commentary in the pages of the *New-York Daily Tribune*. As scholars encountered local narratives in 1857, however, some wished to know more about the people on the margins, whether in terms of caste or religion or class – and occasionally, though less frequently, gender – and how they responded to the turmoil, and what their actions and thoughts, insofar as they could be accessed, revealed about Indian society in general. Increasingly in the 1980s and 1990s the goal was to perceive a "subaltern" uniformity if not unity in the insurgency. Others looked to local manifestations of leadership among the rebels to understand how and whether older loyalties were recalibrated to meet new circumstances, and whether a theory of "subalternity" could be applied to the elite. Others still, most famously Ranajit Guha, argued for the existence of core discursive elements to anti-colonial resistance (by now, India was being regarded, historiographically, as a colonial setting even if it was not a destination of significant demographic colonial settlement), situating 1857 in a longer nineteenth-century history of resistance to the Raj.[12]

Given this literary outpouring, the reader may be forgiven for asking whether it is possible to say anything new about 1857. There are two answers to this question. First, yes: Historians have, I would argue, missed a key factor in the unfolding of the military revolt in Meerut, the site of the first serious "Mutiny" bloodletting. An effect of the voluminous telling and retelling of the story of 1857 is that the events of the military revolt itself have been taken for granted. This is nowhere more true than with regard to Meerut – and this despite the fact that an entire 1966 volume was dedicated to a study of the uprising there, itself substantially based on a detailed set of depositions given by seventy-plus witnesses in 1858.[13] Moreover, emphasis is often given to the distinction between the "military mutiny" of the soldiery and the "civil rebellion" of armed groups beyond the army proper, including local notables and royal lineages in league with sepoy regiments. What is often overlooked is the technical distinction between a military mutiny (the refusal to follow a direct order) and a military revolt (the decision to rise up in arms against the military leadership), which was a salient distinction in the cantonments and their immediate environs. Chapter 2 examines this

---

[12] The work generated under the aegis of "subaltern studies" was variously (and successively) influenced by the rise of social history, microhistory, postmodernism, and deconstruction in the social sciences and humanities.
[13] Palmer, *The Mutiny Outbreak at Meerut*.

issue in detail, and why it was that Indian infantrymen and cavalrymen – sepoys and sowars – decided to escalate a military mutiny into a full-blown revolt.

The second answer to the question is that, regardless of whether anything new might be said about 1857, the mutiny and revolt bring into view – or throw into relief – much about Indians' ability to navigate the institutional edifice of the Raj. The military was the largest and most important institutional manifestation of imperial authority, though it has not received a proper share of attention from historians interested in the British Empire in Asia – averse, as those historians have increasingly become in recent years, to military history.

This book seeks to remedy our understanding of 1857, then, on two levels. First, it seeks to retell the story of the revolt, with an eye to the Indian soldier's point of view. Second, it seeks to offer a reflection on how Indian society grappled with its new army in mid-century.

But first, let us attend to a song about Meerut.

The Sadr Bazaar: Uncommon Ground

The first of the songs featured in Crooke's 1911 article was titled simply "Meerut, 1857." Beneath the title Crooke added: "Sung by the Gûjar women of Sahâranpur."[14] The song described the looting of the Meerut cantonment's main or sadr bazaar, with an emphasis on a woman's hapless lover and his failure to acquire high-value goods:

>People stole all manner of shawls, my lover stole only kerchiefs
>>It's the sadr bazaar of Meerut, [but] my man knows not how to loot
>People stole metal plates and bowls, my lover stole only glassware
>>It's the sadr bazaar of Meerut, [but] my man knows not how to loot
>People stole coconuts and dates, my lover stole only almonds
>>It's the sadr bazaar of Meerut, [but] my man knows not how to loot
>People stole Ashrafi gold coins, my lover stole only coppers
>>It's the sadr bazaar of Meerut, [but] my man knows not how to loot

>*Logoṅ ne lūṭe śāl duśāl, mere pyāre ne lūṭe rumāl*
>>*Meraṭh kā sadar bazār hai, merā saiyāṇ lūṭ na jāne*
>*Logoṅ ne lūṭe thāl kaṭor, mere pyāre ne lūṭe gilās*
>>*Meraṭh kā sadar bazār hai, merā saiyāṇ lūṭ na jāne*

---

[14] William Crooke, "Songs of the Mutiny," part I, *Indian Antiquary* (April 1911), p. 123. Crooke provided the Hindi transliterated into Roman characters as well as a translation, which I have altered. The Devanagari is given in Bhagwan Das Mahaur, *1857 ke Swadhinta Sangram ka Hindi Sahitya par Prabhav* (The Impact of the 1857 War of Independence on Hindi Literature) (Ajmer: Krishna Brothers, 1976), p. 426. In 1857 Saharanpur District bordered Meerut District to the north.

Logoṅ ne lūṭe gole chhuhār, mere pyāre ne lūṭe bādām
  Meraṭh kā sadar bazār hai, merā saiyāṅ lūṭ na jāne
Logoṅ ne lūṭe muher asarfī, mere pyāre ne lūṭe chhaṭām
  Meraṭh kā sadar bazār hai, merā saiyāṅ lūṭ na jāne

लोगों ने लूटे शाल दुशाले, मेरे प्यारे ने लूटे रुमाल
  मेरठ का सदर बाज़ार है, मेरा सैयां लूट न जाने
लोगों ने लूटे थाल कटोर, मेरे प्यारे ने लूटे गिलास
  मेरठ का सदर बाज़ार है, मेरा सैयां लूट न जाने
लोगों ने लूटे गोले छुहारे, मेरे प्यारे ने लूटे बादाम
  मेरठ का सदर बाज़ार है, मेरा सैयां लूट न जाने
लोगों ने लूटे मुहर असर्फी, मेरे प्यारे ने लूटे छटाम
  मेरठ का सदर बाज़ारलूट न जाने

On first glance, it may seem odd today that Crooke labeled this as a "song of the Mutiny" – indeed, that he presented it as the *first* in the collection. The year 1857 is not mentioned, to say nothing of sepoys, the "Mutiny," or the British. But for many readers of the *Indian Antiquary* in 1911, Meerut's sadr bazaar would have been practically synonymous with the beginning of the revolt. Kaye's celebrated *History of the Sepoy War in India*, initially published between 1864 and 1876 and reissued many times during the late nineteenth and early twentieth century, emphasizes the centrality of the bazaar to the intensity of the violence enacted upon the British at Meerut. "Wheresoever a stray English soldier was to be found," Kaye wrote, "he was murdered without remorse" – adding, "[t]he Bazaars and the neighbouring villages were pouring forth their gangs of plunderers and incendiaries. From every street and alley, and from the noisome suburbs, they streamed forth, like wild beasts from their lairs, scenting the prey."[15]

The bazaar also figured prominently in an official report on the violence in Meerut by G. W. Williams, superintendent of police for the North-Western Provinces, completed in 1858. Williams had been tasked with investigating the behavior of the cantonment police force, staffed by local *Gūjar*s, which had played a significant part in the mayhem that unfolded on the evening and night of May 10 and, as suggested by the song of the Gūjar women of Saharanpur, in the looting of the bazaar in the following days. Williams announced at the outset of his report that the performance of the police had been found severely wanting and that

---

[15] John William Kaye, *A History of the Sepoy War in India*, vol. 2, (London: W. H. Allen & Co., 1874), p. 60. Kaye discusses Meerut on pp. 53–71. In a footnote, Kaye saw fit to add a passage by Victor Hugo comparing the "unclean" and "ugly" dens of urban crime to the "savage and grand" forest lairs, concluding, "Den for den, those of the beasts are preferable to those of men, and caverns are better than hiding-places."

they had been dismissed and punished.[16] More importantly, his narrative of the Meerut violence, pieced together from over seventy depositions, made clear that the sadr bazaar constituted what today would be called "ground zero" of the revolt.[17] Key for Williams were the rumors that ricocheted around the bazaar in the hours before 5 pm on that fateful Sunday, especially the unfounded report that the Artillery, supported by the Rifles (both British or "Queen's" regiments), were marching to disarm and imprison the Indian (or "native") regiments.

Williams later reported that he had since been informed that on Saturday afternoon or evening – that is, on May 9 and the day before the revolt – that "the men were taunted by the disreputable inhabitants of the Sudder Bazar for allowing their brethren to suffer on account of their religion."[18] He did not provide a source for this claim, however, and tended to discount it in favor of competing testimony that the spark for the uprising was not lit till the following day, Sunday, May 10. We return to this report – and competing versions of it, as well as the identity of these "disreputable inhabitants" – in the remainder of this book.

Williams was especially drawn to the testimony of Sheikh Moula Bux, havildar of the 20th Bengal Native Infantry. Havildar Bux reported that:

> On the 10th of May, about 5 o'clock, I went to the dyer's in the sudder, and whilst standing at a pedlar's shop, I was surprised at seeing sepoys of my own corps, and the 11th, running hastily to their lines. I stopt a musician named Darean, and asked him what was the matter? He said, he had just heard from a cook boy of the rifles, that the artillery and rifles were coming to take away the arms and ammunition of the native regiments. I immediately returned. The sudder bazar was then quiet, but the bad characters, with the butchers, pulladars, &c., followed the sepoys to their lines, calling out that the rifles and artillery were coming.[19]

---

[16] G. W. Williams, "Memorandum on the Mutiny and Outbreak at Meerut in May 1857," British Library, London, p. 1. On *Gūjars* in the police, see R. H. W. Dunlop, *Service and Adventure with the Khakee Resallah; or, Meerut Volunteer Horse, during the Mutinies of 1857–58* (London: Richard Bentley, 1858), p. 39. Dunlop considered them "inveterate robbers" (39) and "at heart plunderers and cattle stealers" (58). Prior to the revolt, Dunlop was the officiating magistrate for Meerut Division and in this capacity "strongly condemned" the policy of handing over the police force to "professional thieves." He added that "[a] reference on the subject was made last year to the Supdtt. of cantonment police of these provinces [Steele] who declined interfering in the matter." He added: "I must state that the power and influence for evil of Goojur members of the Cantonment Police is disgraceful in the extreme." See "Narrative of Crimes Committed, Meerut Division" (1855), no. 530 of September 22, 1856 (dated April 5, 1856), North Western Provinces Criminal Judicial Proceedings (hereafter NWPCJP), India Office Records, British Library, London. Dunlop's remarks on the *Gūjars* are given under the heading, "Theft of property valued at Rs. 500 and upward."

[17] Palmer, *The Mutiny Outbreak at Meerut*, esp. pp. 88–96, relying heavily on Williams, arrives at the same conclusion.

[18] Williams, "Memorandum," p. 5.

[19] "Depositions Taken at Meerut by Major G. W. Williams, Superintendent of Police, N.W.P.," 13.

Bux's account is populated by an array of characters: In addition to his fellow Indian sepoys and the British artillery and rifle regiments, he mentions a dyer, a pedlar (or peddler), a musician, a cook boy, and various "bad characters" – butchers and *palládárs* (load carriers) etc. The Hindustani term that appears repeatedly in the depositions for someone of "bad character" is "budmash" (*badmásh*). In many of the depositions, butchers and *palládárs*, along with milkmen, cobblers, and fruit and vegetable sellers, figured prominently as the *badmásh log* or roguish people of the bazaar. For example, one Boodh Singh, a shopkeeper and resident of the bazaar, when asked by Williams "where did these budmashes come from," replied: "The budmashes were chiefly pulladars, koonjras [from *kuñjrá*, vegetable sellers], butchers and cobblers of sudder bazar."[20] Similarly, Laik Ram, chowkidar, who was asked if he had "recognized any of the budmashes," named a dyer and two *palládárs* "amongst many," and added that he couldn't recall the names of them all "but [would] be able to recognize them, if I see them again."[21] Later, in his own deposition, Havildar Bux reported how he went with Major Taylor and the doctor of the regiment to the regimental magazine, where he "saw some 70 budmashes of the sudder bazar." He was ordered to take four sepoys and drive them away, but they only retreated a few paces. A trooper from the 3rd Bengal Light Cavalry soon galloped by the parade ground, shouting to the assembled infantrymen there that the Artillery and Rifles (both British regiments) were coming to "deprive the men of their arms and ammunition." Soon the "bad characters of the sudder took up the cry." Then one of the butchers "made a cut at Major Taylor," but the latter knocked him down. Bux grabbed the man's sword: "I would have killed the butcher, but the Major told me to let him go." Then, "seeing a number of bad characters about, I got the Major in to the baboo's house, and hid him there."

As the syntax of the previous quoted remarks makes clear, the terms *badmásh* and *sadr bázár* had become practically synonymous in 1857. In fact, cantonment sadr bazaars and the "bad characters" who seemed to haunt them had been a focus of British concern well before the mid-1850s. In 1852 the military and civil authorities attempted to hammer out a new set of rules for the policing of sadr bazaars in the North-Western Provinces and the Punjab, modeled on a system in Madras Presidency. Among the observations made was the following:

[20] "Depositions," p. 41.   [21] "Depositions," p. 47.

It was formerly a great cause of complaint among the Magisterial Officers of the districts in the neighbourhood that military Sudder Bazars were a refuge for improper characters, who committed crime in their districts. This must not be allowed, and in the event of men of notoriously bad character lodging there, without the ostensible means of subsistence, they should be dealt with in accordance with the Regulations.[22]

Among the procedures recommended to deal with "bad characters" were the following:

The Jemadar [corporal, sergeant] of the Chowkee [post] must be held responsible for the protection of the whole of the space within his chokey [post], and he should take measures to prevent the harboring of people of notoriously bad character or without ostensible means of subsistence. The Duffadar [lieutenant] and Chowkeedars [guards] of the different Mohullas [neighborhoods] should report any one, who comes under that description. For that purpose the Jemadar [corporal] should examine daily all empty Bungalows and out houses.

... Off or on duty, Police Officers should notice all suspicious characters, and their companions, so that they may be prepared with a clue, when any offence has been committed in the neighbourhood, that steps may be taken for their apprehension.

... Suspicious places, Homes of ill fame, and other places, should be searched, in presence of respectable witnesses (Bunneah [grocer, merchant, or trader] if obtainable) but never without a perwanah [warrant] issued after deposition or on reasonable grounds of suspicion.[23]

The proposed regulations, which went into effect in 1854, also called upon the newly constituted "Cantonment Joint Magistrate" to provide to the provincial "Superintendent of Cantonment Police" the following information:

> *First* A census of the non military population in cantonments.
> *Second* A statement of the number of Houses taxed for Chowkeedaree Establishment specifying amount of taxation, realized monthly.
> *Third* A rough sketch of the plan of cantonments with the position of the different Bazars.[24]

While neither house tax enumerations nor cantonment bazaar maps were forthcoming in the archives, the extant military records did include censuses for some sadr bazaars. The following is the 1855 nonmilitary census for

---

[22] "Proposed Cantonment Rules," no. 310 of August 27, 1852, para. 120, Military Consultations, National Archives of India (hereafter MC, NAI).
[23] Ibid., paras. 32, 47, 48.   [24] Ibid., para. 1.

Meerut cantonment, showing the professions and population on the left and, where appropriate, transliterations and translations on the right.[25]

1st quarter report: 1 Nov 1854 – 31 Jan 1855

Public Establishment:
    1 Bazar Serjeant
    1 English Writer
    1 Kotwal   *kotwāl* = officer in charge, chief
    1 Chowdry   *chhaudharī* = chief (second in command)
    1 Mootsuddee   *mutasaddī* = clerk
    1 Jumadar Peon   *jamādār* = corporal, junior officer
    1 Naib Jemadar Peon   *nāyab* = deputy, lieutenant
    6 Peons
    3 Weighmen

People attached to the Sudder Bazar
    23 Antias   *āṇṭiyā* = wheat flour seller
    91 Bunneas or Otta Dallsellers   *baniyā* = grocer / *āṭā* = wheat flour / *dāl* = lentils
    91 Bajazs   *bajāj* = clothier
    50 Bessatees   *besātī* = petty trader
    6 Bookbinders
    7 Bakers
    33 Bamboo or charcoal sellers
    5 Ban or Moong sellers   *mūṅg* = green lentil; *ban/bān* = ?
    5 Bhungaras   *bhaṅg* = cannabis / *bhaṅgaṛā* = seller of *bhaṅg* [?]
    31 Butchers
    15 Bildars and Looneeahs   *beldār* = earth mover, digger / *lūniā* ?
    11 Bhoosahwallas   *bhūsā* = fodder, straw
    1 Bawd or dye   *dāī* = midwife, wetnurse
    7 Birdcatchers
    14 Bheesties   *bhistī* = water carrier
    236 Beggars and Paupers
    14 Bungalows
    1 Butter seller
    35 Barbers
    27 Carpenters

---

[25] "Reports on Sudder Bazars," nos. 111–114 of July 13, 1855, Military Proceedings (hereafter MP), NAI, pp. 16–17. This file contained reports from the following cantonments: Benares, Agra, Meean Meer, Meerut (shown here), Peshawar, Umballah, Dinapore, Delhi, Jullundur, Barrackpore, Chunar, Mooltan, Subathoo, Cawnpore, Berhampore, Rawul Pindee, Sealkote, Dughsai, Dum Dum, and Ferozepore. In the case of Meerut, figures were given for both the first quarter and second quarter (dated April 12, 1855), pp. 12–13. The categories and figures in the two tables are nearly identical, though the handwriting in the earlier table (from November 1, 1854 to January 31, 1855) is clearer; shown here are the first-quarter spellings. The few instances where the meaning of the term is unclear are indicated by a question mark.

The Sadr Bazaar: Uncommon Ground 23

12 Choorawallas   *chhurā* = knife / *chhurāwālā* = knife seller?
1 Chickwalla   *chik* = curtain, screen
1 Chippee or Chintzedier   *chippī* = patch / *chhīṁṭ* = chintz / chintz seller
2 Chickundozes   *chikan* = embroidered muslin / chikan seller
8 Dhoonas   *dhūnā* = gum, resin / dealers in gums and resins?
2 Dier or Ruffooguns   *rafū* = darn / *rafūgaṇ* = darner as well as dyer?
1 Distiller
3 Disturbund or Turband binders   *dastār-band* = turban maker
3 Dubber or Coopee makers   *kūpī* = small well or pit / *dabbar* = well digger?
3 Dubgun or silver sheet makers   *dabgan* = ? NB: *varaq* = fine silver foil for sweets
5 Executioners
28 Earthen pot sellers
1 English Sweetmeat seller
28 Flour or Soojee sellers   *sūjī* = semolina
2 Fishmongers
22 Firewood sellers
85 Grasscutters
38 Ghasees and Goalas   *ghās* = grass, straw / *gvālā* = cowherder, milkman
26 Goldsmiths
47 Green sellers
6 Gardens
5 Gardeners
23 Halways   *halwāi* = *agriculturalist or sweet seller*
2 Halwasohun wallas   *halwāsohaṅ* = halwa popular in Delhi/Haryana
40 Hide and Sheepskin tanners
214 Houses of Buneas   *baniyā* = grocer, merchant
629 Houses and Huts empty
2 Hermaphrodites or Hijras   *hījrā* = eunuch
21 Ironsmiths
2 Jewellers
78 Khangees or Mussulman Prostitutes   *khāngī* = kept woman, clandestine prostitute
117 Kusbees or Dancing Girls   *kasbī* = prostitute (lit., one who earns or gains)
16 Kusbees or Hindoo Prostitutes   *kasbī* = prostitute
4 Knife Grinders
3 Khoonchawallas   *khūṅchā* = streetfood hawker
9 Kussanas   *kasānā* = assayer, prover?
109 Koorees or Coolees   *kūlī* = laborer, carrier
12 Kunjurs   *kaṅjar* = string and rope maker/seller
9 Lacemakers and Patooas   *paṭuā* = stringer of beads; maker of braids, fringe
8 Milksellers
10 Masons

11 Naunbies   *naumbi* = ? [see Delhi list: *bhaṭiyārā*, innkeeper]
6 Naichabunds   *naichā* = hookah pipe / *naichāband* = hookah fixer?
3 Native Doctors
12 Oilsellers
14 Oilmen
13 Painters
29 Pansarees   *pansārī* = herbalist, druggist, spice seller
20 Parchers
8 Perfumers or Gundhees   *gandhī* = maker/seller of perfumes
2 Paper sellers
1 Poulterer
24 Pigkeepers & Khutticks   *khaṭik* = bird/animal keeper; vegetable, fruit seller
152 Pulladars or Baparees   *pallādār* = load carrier, esp. of grains
5 Places of Worship
13 Polishers
45 Shoesellers Hindoostanee
119 Shoemakers Hindoostanee and English
111 Shahookars   *sāhūkār* = merchant, shopkeeper, banker
29 Suroffs   *sarrāf* = bullion, money changer
2 Seal engravers
2 Sealing wax sellers & mooneehars   *mūnīhār* = ?
5 Saddlers
4 Soapboilers
38 Sweepers
421 Servants etc.
6 Tutteras   ? *tatahara* = kettle for warming water
1 Tuddeewalla   ? *tārīvālā* = seller of *tārī*, toddy or "native liquor"
24 Tumolees   *tamolī* = betel seller
31 Tape or mevan makers[26]   ? *mevam* = nuts; *mevam* = dried fruit
4 Tallow and candle makers
35 Tobacconists
64 Tailors
17 Thatehers   *ṭhaṭherā* = tinker, coppersmith, brazier, plumber
3 Tirmars [Turriers?]   ? *tīrmār* = arrow
3 Turners
1 Takenwalla who joins broken glasses
2 Woodsplitters
1 Watchmaker
37 Washermen

Cattle
201 Buffaloes
166 Bullocks
140 Cows and Calves

---

[26] The censuses for Umballah and Jullundur sadr bazaars list "Tape and cane sellers."

45 Tattoos   *taṭṭu* = pony
59 Boheelees and Rats   ?
19 Chuckras   ?

Several points are immediately apparent from this enumeration. First and most obviously, the bazaar was a lively and bustling center of commerce – for Indians and Britons alike.[27] An immense array of goods and services was to be had within its confines. This included luxury items such as jewelry, gold, fine embroidered muslins, and perfumes; everyday household objects such as shoes (both "Hindoostanee" and English), rope, soap, charcoal, candles, and kitchen knives; specialty comestibles such as *halwāsohaṅ*, betel nut (for *pān*), tobacco, *bhaṅg*, sweets (including English sweets), silver foil (for decorating delicacies, esp. sweets), and spices; and, of course, staples such as flour, *dāl*, oil, milk, and vegetables.[28]

Artisans and craftspeople also offered their wares and services in the bazaar. This included those in the building trades, such as masons, painters, carpenters, tinkers, and well-diggers. But also noteworthy are the specialized crafts such as iron-smithing, hookah pipe repair, book-binding, screen- and drapery-making, wood-turning, earthen pot-making, glass-repair, shoemaking, turban-tying, tailoring, and darning and patching. Household work such as polishing, sweeping, clothes-washing, and gardening were also for hire. Financial services were available too – including moneylending, banking, and money-changing.

Then there were those specialists who tended to the needs of the body. These included barbers (hair-cutting, shaves, and massage), wet-nurses and midwives, "native doctors," and three types of "prostitutes." Prostitution was, in fact, one of the largest professions, with a total of over 200 women thus employed in the Meerut sadr bazaar. In terms of numbers, this was exceeded only by load carriers (*pullādār*s and *kūlī*s) at 261 (152 and 109 respectively), "servants etc." at 421, and beggars and paupers at 236. The importance of prostitution to the economy of the bazaar, and the provisioning of the soldiery, was suggested as well in the

---

[27] For detailed illustrations of the various professions encountered in north Indian bazaars, dating from the early nineteenth century, see "Kitāb-i tashrīḥ al-aqvām, an account of origins and occupations of some of the sects, castes and tribes of India," 1825, Hansi Cantonment, Add. 27255, British Library; and "An album containing fifty-three drawings depicting occupations," ca. 1815–1820, Lucknow, AL.7970, Victoria & Albert Museum, London.

[28] Rice is not explicitly mentioned; however, other cantonment bazaars (including Barrackpore, Rawul Pindi, and Multan) indicate that rice was sold by the *dāl* merchants (only Cawnpore listed "rice sellers" as a separate category), so it is likely that rice was sold by the *baniyā* and perhaps also *besātī* shopkeepers in Meerut.

proposed rules for the policing of cantonments in the North-West Provinces of the Bengal Presidency, noted earlier. *Chaukīdārs* were warned, on pain of punishment, "not to molest Females, nor to exact any fee from Prostitutes."[29]

Given the range of goods and services available in the sadr bazaar, it is not difficult to understand why it would have exerted a gravitational pull – and not simply among the "bad characters" of official discourse and the hapless lover-cum-looter satirized in the song of "the Gûjar women of Sahâranpur." Further, by the mid-1850s the sadr bazaar at Meerut was becoming an especially attractive destination: The committee that supervised the census noted in January 1855 that the bazaar "appeared to be in a prosperous and flourishing condition" and "well supplied with provisions and water." Moreover, "[t]he roads have been leveled and widened and are kept remarkably clean, to which cleanliness great attention appears to be paid as also to the sanatory [*sic*] state of the Bazar. ... Several new bridges have been built and water courses (pukka) made through the principal streets." The only complaint was noted a few months later, namely, that the ongoing repairs made the roads "nearly impassable."[30] In short, the cantonment sadr bazaar was a pleasant place to spend time, shop, and relax. Given this fact, it is surprising how few images exist of cantonment bazaars (leaving aside the numerous collections of Company paintings that portray various occupations). Key exceptions may be found in the work of watercolorist William Carpenter, who visited India between 1850 and 1856 and early on painted numerous works depicting life in the sadr bazaar of Pune's cantonment in western India – two images of which are reproduced here (see Figures 1.2 and 1.3); see also the amateur watercolor painting by Alfred Frederick Pollock Harcourt (Figure 1.4) – the only roughly contemporaneous image of Meerut's bazaar of which I'm aware.[31]

The Gūjar women of Saharanpur were not alone in remarking upon the range and quality of goods available in the sadr bazaar. Rudyard

---

[29] "Proposed Cantonment Rules," para. no. 56. As we shall see in Chapter 3, the authorities made a point of aggressively prosecuting crimes against prostitutes.

[30] "Reports on Sudder Bazars," pp. 13, 17.

[31] On Carpenter, whose paintings from India were purchased by the Victoria and Albert Museum, see Mildred Archer and Ronald Lightbown, *India Observed: India as Viewed by British Artists 1760–1860* (London: Victoria and Albert Museum, 1982), pp. 108, 138. On Harcourt, see Mildred Archer, *British Drawings in the India Office Library*, vol. 1, *Amateur Artists* (London: Her Majesty's Stationery Office, 1969), pp. 206–207. Harcourt's image is, sadly, undated, but it was almost certainly completed after 1857. A postcard from 1918 (Figure 1.5), by Moorli Dhur & Sons in nearby Ambala, suggests that little had changed between 1857 and World War I.

The Sadr Bazaar: Uncommon Ground

Figure 1.2 "Shops for colours and flowers used at festivals, Sadr bazaar, Pune," by William Carpenter, probably July 1850
Source: Accession no. IS.84-1881. Victoria & Albert Museum.

Kipling played upon this theme in his 1884 poem, "Sudder Bazaar."[32] The goods on display in Kipling's poem include sweets, horses, quails, stamps, and fluffed wool. Equally if not more compelling were the sounds and sights of the bazaar, and, especially, the variety of people on display there. "The Mission bell's tinkling insistence," the muezzin's "call of the faithful to prayer," the "booming" guns of the fort, and the "tom-tomming" drums of the marriage procession, all provided the aural backdrop for the "mosaic of race-tints" that included Kabuli horse-dealers, Deccani quail-baggers, sturdy Jat farmers, fierce bearded Sikhs, cattle-tending "gowalas," *fakir*s, and the occasional British soldier (the archetypal "Tommy Atkins"). Despite these aural and visual stimulants, Kipling's imagined *flâneur* in this poem longed, incongruously (from the poet's tone), for a "tramp with my sweetheart" through the "wet walks of London."

---

[32] Rudyard Kipling, "The Sudder Bazaar," in *Echoes: By two writers* (with sister, Beatrice Kipling) (Lahore: Civil and Military Gazette Press, 1884). See the Kipling Society page for publication history, background, and glossary: www.kiplingsociety.co.uk/readers-guide/rg_sudder1.htm.

Figure 1.3 "Painting [of shops selling liquor and paan, with moneylender between]," by William Carpenter, probably July 1850
Source: Accession no. IS.85-1881. Victoria & Albert Museum.

The sadr bazaar is best thought of as a type of hybrid space necessitated by the rapid expansion of standing armies in the nineteenth century. Positioned strategically between the cantonment, the "civil lines," and the older Indian urban settlement, the sadr bazaar was where the military arm of the Raj gained access to Indian (and some European) goods and interacted with Indians – and, to some degree, vice versa. In the case of Meerut, the cantonment was (and still is) situated to the north of the city (see the accompanying map, Figure 1.1). Before and after 1857, the British regiments in Meerut were all located on the northernmost edge of the cantonment, with the Queens artillery and infantry regiments billeted to the east and cavalry to the west. The native infantry and cavalry were located to the south of the British cavalry lines, on the western edge of the cantonment. The sadr bazaar was directly east of the native infantry lines and directly south of the British infantry and artillery. Further to the east of the sadr bazaar were the "Civil Lines," housing the nonmilitary authority – the magistrate's court, the collector's office, the police lines, the jail, etc. To the south of all this lay the old city of Meerut. As such, the sadr bazaar was a hybrid Indian–European

The Sadr Bazaar: Uncommon Ground

Figure 1.4 "Bazaar in Cantonment, Meerut (U.P.)," by Alfred Frederick Pollock Harcourt, between 1857 and 1869
Source: WD2612, British Library, London.

market space that protruded north from old Meerut and was tucked in amid official authority on the east side and military power on the west. Here is where Indians and Britons who served the Raj could circulate beyond the confines of the "official order and ideology." Connected to but distinct from the military and official arms of the Raj, this "extraterritorial" or "liminal" quality rendered the sadr bazaar both unpredictable and dangerous.[33] Hence the need for the authorities to infiltrate and police it.

Surprisingly, given their importance to the revolt at Meerut, and to the life of north Indian cantonments more generally, sadr bazaars have received little notice in the secondary literature. This is especially

---

[33] On the marketplace, esp. during the periodic fair, as "extraterritorial" space beyond the "official order and ideology," see Mikhail Bakhtin, *Rabelais and His World*, trans. Helene Iswolsky (Bloomington: Indiana University Press, 1984), p. 154, and Peter Stallybrass and Allon White, *The Politics and Poetics of Transgression* (Ithaca, NY: Cornell University Press, 1986), pp. 28ff., cited in Anand A. Yang, *Bazaar India: Markets, Society, and the Colonial State in Bihar* (Berkeley: University of California Press, 1999), pp. 163–164. One can also think of this space, looking to Victor Turner (*The Ritual Process* [Chicago: Aldine, 1969]), as liminal and thus productive of anti-structural forces.

Figure 1.5 "Sudder Bazaar, Meerut," by Moorli Dhur & Sons, Ambala, 1918
Source: pepandtim/flickr.

noteworthy considering the attention historians have devoted to markets and commerce in the rise and consolidation of British rule in India.[34] By contrast, we have excellent analyses of the place of rumor in peasant and subaltern rebellion.[35] Even the 1966 study of the uprising at Meerut by J. A. B. Palmer failed to examine the sadr bazaar in any detail, though – like Williams – he noted that the revolt began in the bazaar and devoted a short chapter to a narrative of the violence and killings by the "bazar mob." His description of the sadr bazaar itself is limited to a brief paragraph in a chapter on the cantonment and focuses on its geographic dimensions:

---

[34] In addition to C. A. Bayly, *Rulers, Townsmen and Bazaars: North Indian Society in the Age of British Expansion 1770–1870* (Cambridge: Cambridge University Press, 1983), see Yang, *Bazaar India*. Neither examines the sadr bazaar, though Bayly does make occasional mention of cantonment bazaars generally. But see Bayly's earlier essay, "Town Building in North India, 1790–1830," *Modern Asian Studies* 9, 4 (1975): 483–504, which discusses military bazaars and grain supplies under the greater demands of the Company's standing army.

[35] Anand A. Yang, "A Conversation of Rumors: The Language of Popular 'Mentalités' in Late Nineteenth-Century Colonial India," *Journal of Social History* 20, 3 (Spring 1987): 485–505; Ranajit Guha, *Elementary Aspects of Peasant Insurgency in Colonial India* (Delhi: Oxford University Press, 1983), esp. the chapter on "transmission."

There was a small Cavalry Bazar behind (south of) the native cavalry lines and one very large bazar, known as the Sudder Bazar, or Chief Bazar, serving the native lines as a whole.[36] The Sudder Bazar lay in the angle between the Sudder Street and Abu Lane, and extended nearly to the Delhi road on the east. It gave the name to Sudder Street which bordered it on its western edge. Its dimensions were a half to three quarters of a mile, both north–south and east–west, but its outline was naturally irregular. Its northern portion was nearer to the nullah [drain, canal] and the Dragoon Bridge than was the northern end of the main native lines and it extended southwards about half-way down those lines. It was from the Sudder Bazar and parts of the city that the mobs or gangs emerged which committed many of the murders and most of the arson and looting on 10 May.[37]

The bulk of Palmer's cantonment chapter is given over to describing the locations of the British and Indian regiments, the roads and bridges (and the canal), and various public buildings such as the jail, the telegraph office, the barracks – in other words, information that can be gleaned by examining a detailed map of the cantonment. In later chapters he provides a narrative of the outbreak as it was racing through the various parts of the cantonment, beginning with "(a) The Native Infantry Lines" (chapter 7), "(b) The Native Cavalry Lines" (chapter 8), "(c) The Bazar Mobs" (chapter 9), and "(d) The European Troop Movements and the European Lines" (chapter 10). Insofar as he is concerned with the sadr bazaar, it is with respect to ascertaining the origin of the rumor related by the "supposed" cook boy to the musician Darean.[38]

The term *sadr* is usually translated as "chief," "main," or "central." Historians of late eighteenth-century and early nineteenth-century law and legal discourses will be familiar with the term from the institution known as the "Sudder Dewanny Adawlut." This was the "chief or central revenue court," established in the early 1770s by Warren Hastings, which dealt with matters impinging on civil and tax law. (So, for example, in Chapter 4, when Pension Paymaster Tombs sought clarification on the legal status of *sagāī* marriages, the question was forwarded to resident legal scholars at the Sudder Dewanny Adawlut in Bengal.) The term *sadr* originally comes from the Arabic and has the sense of an action, meaning "to proceed, to come forth, to become public, to be revealed." When transformed into a noun, it takes on the meaning of "the breast," "the foremost part or forecourt," or "the main gate." It is in this sense that the

---

[36] Technically this is misleading, as many Europeans made recourse to the sadr bazaar as well, which is why so many were killed there or fleeing from there on the evening of May 10.
[37] Palmer, *Mutiny Outbreak at Meerut*, p. 52.
[38] Ibid., 74 (73 for "supposed"; on 129 he calls the cook boy story "unsubstantiated"). See the following discussion, for more on the "cook boy."

term is used in the phrase "sadr bazaar", that is, as the "main" or "central" bazaar. It also possessed a more "public" profile: Whereas the regimental bazaars were for Europeans only and were located to the north of the "Abu Nullah" over which four bridges provided policeable access, the sadr bazaar was "in front of" or in the "forecourt of" the cantonment, with fairly easy access from the old city of Meerut, and thus accessible to all. Similarly, the sadr bazaar in older Mughal capitals were located under and adjacent to the fort.[39]

The sadr bazaar was, then, a key arena in Meerut – and in all cantonment towns – where Britons and Indians rubbed shoulders on a routine basis in a more or less nonofficial capacity. Also, because it was located on the edge of the cantonment and accessible to the residents of the old city, it was unclear whether it should fall within the jurisdiction of the civil authorities or the military authorities. Indeed, it was due to the very fact of its layered "more-or-less-ness," its legally ambiguous status – as "betwixt and between" civil, military, and public – that the policing and administration of the sadr bazaar became something of a headache in the mid nineteenth century.

The "Wretched" Cook Boy

According to both G. W. Williams (1858) and J. A. B. Palmer (1967), Havildar Sheikh Moula Bux witnessed the spark that set off the explosion of violence on the late afternoon of May 10, 1857. This spark was in the form of a rumor spread by an unnamed "cook boy" and "the musician," Darean. Williams places them at the center of the "evidence against the supposition of a pre-existing conspiracy" as well as his subsequent narrative or "outline of the events that occurred at Meerut."[40] Indeed, in the latter, he credited the cook boy with actually having "originated the report" that the British artillery and rifle regiments had been ordered to disarm the native regiments – and thus, setting off the chain of events that led to the military revolt. He arrived at this conclusion as follows:

As far as could be ascertained, the report was raised by a cook boy attached to the Rifles,[41] and confirmed by a Sowar [cavalryman] coming from the direction of the Brigade Major's house. As regards the former [the cook boy], it must be borne in mind, that the Rifles were present at the scene [of the ironing parade] on Saturday morning, and would doubtless amongst themselves discuss the

---

[39] See Bayly, "Town Building in North India, 1790–1830," 498, on the Mughal sadr bazaar of Agra.
[40] Williams, "Memorandum on the Outbreak at Meerut in May 1857," pp. 3, 6–7.
[41] A Queen's regiment, hence composed entirely of British troops.

probability of having eventually to disarm all the Native troops; that cook boys have a smattering of English, and may have caught up some expressions used by the soldiers, and hence originated the report; that when the Regiment was drawn up to proceed to Church, they [the cook boys] may have concluded that their destination was the Native lines, and in consequence gave the alarm. Thus a *wretched* cook boy lit the first spark, that so speedily set the Station in a blaze.[42]

Williams' use of the term "wretched" is curious. At first, it seems crafted to evoke a sense of irony: Even a momentous event such as 1857, Williams is suggesting, could be started by so lowly a figure as a cook boy.[43] But Williams' phrasing may also have alluded to the pecking order of servants in the British regiments. Palmer, in his examination of the evidence generated by Williams over a century later, noted that "[c]ook boys were menials employed to cook for, and wait on, European troops," adding that "they were no doubt mainly a poor type of Indian (Portuguese) Christian or other Eurasians, or very low caste Hindus."[44] Palmer does not reveal his grounds for his Eurasian speculation. It is possible that he was influenced on this point by the information chain in Bux's deposition, which described a musician named Darean as the source of the cook boy rumor. In the first half of the nineteenth century, regimental drummers, musicians, and bandsmen were frequently drawn from the ranks of Eurasian children of British soldiers and noncommissioned officers, as they were prohibited from enlisting as soldiers.[45]

Palmer's assertion notwithstanding, it is likely that the "cook boy" was drawn from the local countryside. Judicial records from the early nineteenth century suggest that workers from the "lower agrarian castes and service communities," including "Chamar leather workers, Kahar carriers, Teli oil-men and Kalwar liquor distillers all found jobs with

---

[42] Ibid., 6–7 (emphasis added). Cf. Wagner, *Great Fear*, pp. 134, 277n19.
[43] In this Williams would not have been unlike Cracroft Wilson, who would look to the "frail ones of the bazaar" to achieve much the same dramatic effect, or like later commentators such as George MacMunn, who made recourse to the figure of "Mees Dolly," a British woman who had "gone sour" and turned against her own kind; or like P. J. O. Taylor, who deployed Wilson, MacMunn, and Flora Steele (without crediting the latter two), to craft a moral tale of an Empire Ironically Saved by a Fallen Woman Wronged. See Chapter 2 for discussion.
[44] Palmer, *The Mutiny Outbreak at Meerut in 1857*, p. 155n11. Indeed, so marginal for Palmer is the figure of the cook boy that he doubts his very existence; he refers to him as the "supposed cook boy" and disregards the evidence about him as hearsay. Of course, Palmer does this to strengthen his argument that the revolt at Meerut was locally premeditated in the two weeks prior to May 10, even if it was not the product of a long-planned, multi-cantonment uprising. See pp. 73, 129–137.
[45] Christopher J. Hawes, *Poor Relations: The Making of a Eurasian Community in British India, 1773–1833* (London and New York: Routledge, 1996), pp. 40–41. Hawes does not mention cook boys in his study.

Europeans as cooks, stableboys, bearers and domestic servants" in Meerut, Ambala, Kanpur, and other cantonments in what was then "Upper India."[46] Whether or not they were low caste or mixed race, and notwithstanding the infantilizing nomenclature used to describe them, "cook boys" were not to be trifled with. As servants in the British regimental barracks, they were subject to – and hardened by – almost daily doses of physical violence. Fitz-William Thomas Pollok, recollecting his early service in Secundarabad (Hyderabad) in the late 1840s, described how British rank-and-file soldiers, or "Tommy Atkinses" as they were often called, were "hard pushed for amusement in those days..., [and] used not only to pit these cook-boys against each other, but would take a turn with them themselves." In the cases described by Pollok, the "amusement" sometimes boomeranged:

[V]ery many of these low-caste Madrassies are very powerfully built, and only require tuition and training to become nasty customers in a row. ... [They] learned not only to use their fists, but to stand a good deal of punishment; and as they were kept constantly in training they got as hard as nails and as strong as brewers' carmen, and became no mean proficients [*sic*] in the art of self-defence and attack.

In one case, a cook boy, clubbed on the head by an arrogant officer named Nightingale for requesting that his brother be relieved from service due to the constant abuse, decided to strip off his shirt and confront his assailant: "The man's muscles stood out like balls of whipcord, and the way he held up his maulies [fists] proclaimed that he was no novice at the game of fisticuffs." Nightingale barely ended up winning the brawl, mainly due to his longer reach (according to Pollok), but he described it as "the hardest fight he had ever had in his life." Moreover, his attempt to have the man punished for having "been most insolent" was met with an official shrug. The commanding officer felt, examining the cook boy's wounds, that he had been punished enough.

In a different case of "natives sticking up to Europeans" described by Pollok, a "matey boy" filed "a summons against his master," one "H.", for having "struck [him] in the presence of witnesses." "H." was subsequently fined by the cantonment magistrate. "Such a thing as a native hauling up his master for a blow was unheard of in those days,[47] and H. bided his time; he said nothing, and kept the boy on as if nothing had happened." Then suddenly, one day when the servant brought him his

---

[46] See Bayly, *Rulers, Townsmen and Bazaars*, pp. 215–216.
[47] Pollock was writing in the 1890s in the wake of much legal transformation, including the controversial Ilbert Bill of 1883–1884, which centered on the question of whether Europeans could be tried in courts presided over by Indians.

morning tea, "H." saw his chance. Exulting that there were no witnesses, he announced his intention to give the servant a "good thrashing." The "matey boy," taking advantage of the lack of witnesses, proceeded to give his "master" a thorough beating: "H. had not a chance; his boy was far stronger and a far better bruiser, and knocked his master into a cocked hat." "H." ultimately saved himself by landing his boot in the "very tender part" of the "boy's" groin, doubling him up and causing him to retreat. Pollok continued:

As for H., his mother would not have known him, and we could scarcely distinguish one feature from another. He had to go on the sick-list. His boy, who, we learned afterwards, had been a cook-boy in a battery of artillery, disappeared; and in after-life, if we wanted to get a rise out of H., we only had to stoop with our hands low down and whimper, "Master not fight fair," to drive him nearly mad.[48]

Pollok's phrasing suggests that while cook boys and their ilk may have been abused, they were not helpless; in fact, depending on the regiment in which they served, they could be expected to be skilled fighters. Of course, this may have been Pollok's way of dealing with his own mixed feelings about British mistreatment of Indian servants in his youth, now that he had arrived at the very end of his life amid the rising tide of Indian nationalism.[49] In any case, he occasionally inserts the word "man" in his narrative when the Indian servants gain the physical edge over their British masters.

The Madras Army possessed, it should be noted, a markedly different – arguably more meritocratic and less caste-bound – military culture than what was to be found in Bombay or, especially, Bengal.[50] Still, records from Bengal suggest that "cook boys" found ways to be resourceful there as well, and ironically this too may have further shaped Williams' estimation of them as "wretched." In 1855, when he was still cantonment joint magistrate in Agra, Williams noted in his summary Cantonment Police Report, under the heading "Abkaree cases," that "[a] certain class such as cook boys and coolies [had] long [been] employed in the illicit sale of

---

[48] Fitz-William Thomas Pollok, *Fifty Years' Reminiscences of India: A Retrospect of Travel, Adventure and Shikar* (London: Edward Arnold, 1896), pp. 46–49.
[49] On everyday violence by Britons against Indians in the late nineteenth and early twentieth centuries, see Elizabeth Kolsky, *Colonial Justice in British India: White Violence and the Rule of Law* (Cambridge: Cambridge University Press, 2009).
[50] See Randolf G. S. Cooper, "Culture, Combat, and Colonialism in Eighteenth- and Nineteenth-Century India," *The International History Review* 27, 3 (Sep 2005): 534–549. Especially important here, with respect to the professionalism of the Madras Army, is the work of D. F. Harding, esp. *Smallarms of the East India Company, 1600–1856*, vol. 4, *The Users and Their Smallarms* (London: Foresight Books, 1999), and the review by Cooper in *Modern Asian Studies* 36, 3 (July 2002): 758–764.

Liquor" to European troops.⁵¹ (*Ābkārī* referred to liquor licensing and excise.) Williams also noted that "cook boys" were the main culprits in cases of petty theft of rations from the regiments. A law had been drafted in 1852 and passed in 1853 to deal specifically with the smuggling of liquor into the barracks, though Williams reported that the problem persisted through other means.⁵² Meanwhile at Jullundur in the Punjab, Cantonment Joint Magistrate T. T. Hamilton insisted that he made "it a rule never to grant any pass for Liquor to any of the servants of the European Soldiers such as Cook Boys, Sickleghurs [polishers, cleaners], Barbers, Maiteys, or any of the servants attached to the Barracks." (All European troops were housed in barracks; Indian troops lived in clay-mud and straw hutments, referred to as "lines.") Rather, "the greater portion of passes granted are to the people of the Sudder Bazar," usually for "a marriage or Punchaitt among the Natives in the Station." Government evidently saw this as the weak link in the chain and subsequently banned sales of "chit" passes and required that "all liquor must be consumed on the premises of the Abkaree."⁵³ Contributing to the government's ruling, no doubt, was the fact that, according to the summary police report for Meerut in 1852, another method by which European soldiers had been gaining access to illicit liquor was via bazaar prostitutes, who would "send for liquor to their Houses for the soldiers, by which they derive considerable profit."⁵⁴ Technically, all liquor was to be accompanied by a *chaprāsī* who would remain until all the liquor was

---

⁵¹ G. W. Williams to J. Steel, Superintendent Cantonment Police, no. 11 of April 2, 1856, NWPCJP. On the illicit liquor trade and the Company military response, particularly in the context of a widening medical imperialism, see Erica Wald, "Health, Discipline, and Appropriate Behavior: The Body of the Soldier and the Space of the Cantonment," *Modern Asian Studies* 46, 4 (2012): 815–856.

⁵² "Draft Legislation on illegal selling of spirits to Europeans in Cantonments," nos. 51–54 of March 12, 1852, BMC, NAI. For the full text, see *The Law of India*, vol. 2, *Miscellaneous Laws*, comp. and ed. Andrew Lyon (Calcutta: Thacker & Spink, 1873), pp. 44–46 (Act 18 of 1853). Williams complained in his Agra Cantonment report of 1855 that though Act 18 of 1853 had checked the smuggling by cook boys and coolies, European shopkeepers had stepped into the breach and were increasingly "guilty of this crime." See also nos. 302–304 of July 8, 1859, MP, NAI, which contain an exchange of letters concerning a notorious pensioner named David Hunter who, with his wife and daughter, had developed a thieving [*sic*: thriving] business in selling poisonous liquor for 32 times it's [*sic*] value, to European Soldiers stationed in the Chinsurah Barracks."

⁵³ T. T. Hamilton, Suptd. Cantt. Abkaree, to Capt. C. F. M. Mundy, Major of Brigade, Jullundur, dated August 16, 1853, encl. no. 2 in 93 of October 14, 1853, MP, NAI. See no. 94 of same date for the ruling.

⁵⁴ Ibid. The proximity of prostitution and liquor consumption prevailed in the Maratha armies of the early nineteenth century as well. Thomas Broughton described how many soldiers in camp would "retire, at the approach of evening, to the arrack shop, or the tent of the prostitute; and revel through the night in a state of low debauchery." Thomas D. Broughton, *Letters from a Mahratta Camp during the year 1809, descriptive of the*

consumed, "but this system though affording some check, is easily evaded and the smallest bribe is readily pocketed and the liquor left at the disposal of the Purchaser."[55]

Thus, despite their "wretchedness," to say nothing of their rhetorical infantilization, "cook boys" were an established conduit of goods between the barracks and the bazaar. Whereas sepoys were expected to look after their own food arrangements, British troops were provisioned by the state from deductions previously withheld from their salaries. Any other goods had to be paid for from their own pocket.[56] It often fell to "cook boys" and other servants to purchase extra provisions, licit and illicit, from the sadr bazaar. And just as goods could be trafficked, so could information. On May 10, 1857, the news circulating in the sadr bazaar – that the Queen's artillery and rifle regiments were assembling to disarm the Indian regiments – was erroneous. But the fact that the news was said to have been provided by a "cook boy" would, without question, have served to lend it weight. False information does not invalidate the network through which the information travels. Quite to the contrary: As C. A. Bayly noted three decades ago, "information panics" invariably occur, but they rely on strong webs of transmission.[57]

Endings and Beginnings

We earlier recounted a song about the looting of the sadr bazaar in the wake of the military revolt at Meerut. Another of the songs that Chaube sent to Crooke, published as the fourth in the collection, invoked Meerut. Crooke called the song "The Mutiny – 1857" and added that it was "sung during the Mutiny and repeated by Râmeswar Dayâl Misrâ of Kotârâ, District Itâwâ[,] [and] recorded by Raghunandas, a teacher in

---

character, manners, domestic habits, and religious ceremonies of the Mahrattas. (Westminster: Archibald Constable and Co., 1813), p. 21.

[55] See G. R. Cookson, Cantonment Joint Magistrate, Meerut, to Steel, Sup. Cantt. Police, NWP, no. 309 of April 22, 1853, NWPCJP. As with European shopkeepers noted earlier, this problem persisted too, and well beyond the North-Western Provinces. See nos. 271–275 of October 28, 1859, MP, for a letter from Revd. A. H. Norman, Chaplain of Dum Dum Cantonment, to the Bishop of Calcutta complaining about "a piece of ground known as the Nya Bazaar and thickly populated with natives of the lowest class [in which] liquor of the vilest description is prepared and sold in large quantities to the European Soldiers while prostitutes in large numbers assemble under the eye of the Military Authorities who have no power to interfere."

[56] See the discussion in Douglas Peers, *Between Mars and Mammon: Colonial Armies and the Garrison State in Early Nineteenth-Century India* (London: I. B. Tauris, 1995), p. 132.

[57] Bayly, *Empire and Information*.

the Kotârâ School."[58] Unlike the song about the sadr bazaar, this song left no doubt that it was about the 1857 war:

> The war of year fourteen began at Meerut.
>> Bombay, Madras and Bengal are great markets.
>
> At the time of destruction, the British lost their heads
>> (as if) Kali is drowning England.
>
> Those very cartridges of kine and swine.
>> (When) the sepoys heard (of this) they tore off their uniforms.
>
> Dhawal Ram says,
>> Long ago, in the year fourteen, the English abandoned Calcutta.[59]

> *Chaudah kī sāl jaṅg Meraṭ se śurū huā.*
>> *Badal karāpat baṅgal baṛā haṭṭā hai.*
>
> *Bināś kāl āyeṁ matī bhaṅg bhaī faraṅgīṁ kī.*
>> *Kālī vilāyat dubāyā chattā hai.*
>
> *Gāī aur sūar vāhī ke kārtus.*
>> *Sunnat sipāhīṁ bikher dage lattā hai.*
>
> *Kahaiṁ Dhawal Rām,*
>> *Ikkabhī chaudah sāl bich bhāgaiṁ aṅgrez log chhoṛī kalkattā haiṁ.*

> चौदह की साल जंग मेरट से शुरू हुआ।
>> बदल करापत बंगाल बड़ा हट्टा है।।
>
> बिनाश काल आयें मती भंग भई फ़रंगी की।
>> काली विलायत दुबाया चत्ता है।।
>
> गाई और सूअर वाही के कार्तुस।
>> सुन्नत सिपाही बिखेड़ दगे लत्ता है।।
>
> कहैं धवल राम,
>> इक्कभी चौदह के साल बिच भागैं अंग्रेज़ लोग छोड़ी कलकत्ता है।।

As noted earlier, given the obvious anti-British tenor of these verses, especially in light of the overall nature of the songs that were featured in the 1911 article, it is baffling that Crooke (and Chaube?) claimed they were composed to "honour the British victories." Clearly the purported author of the song, Dhawal Ram (identified in the last line), was far from being "impressed by the overwhelming power of the British." If anything, the reverse was true. Not only were the British depicted as having "[lost] their heads," Dhawal Ram has them flee the main British seat of authority at Calcutta. Crooke's only comment on all this was his supposition that the "song was sung during the Mutiny." How else to explain the otherwise counterfactual celebration of the sepoys as victorious?

There is yet more here than meets the eye. Crooke's (and Chaube's?) mischaracterization is coupled with mistranslation. A close reading

---

[58] I have rendered into Devanagari Crooke's Romanized Hindi.
[59] Crooke, "Songs of the Mutiny," part II, p. 165. My translation, which, as we shall see differs from Crooke's on one or two key points.

reveals that the song was even more anti-British than Crooke was willing to allow, at least openly. He signaled this in a cryptic footnote at the end of the first verse: "The terms in the text are extremely interesting." He does not specify which terms, but the placement of this footnote occurs after the phrase "*badal karāpat baṅgal baṛā haṭṭā hai*" (बदल करापत बंगाल बड़ा हट्टा है). Crooke translated this as "Bombay, Madras, and Bengal are great *Presidencies*."[60] Crooke (and some of his readers) would certainly have known that the actual meaning of *baṛā haṭṭā* (बड़ा हट्टा) was not "great *Presidencies*," but "great *markets*."[61] By translating *haṭṭā* as "presidencies," Crooke rendered *nearly* invisible Dhawal Ram's rhetorical demotion of the British centers of colonial power to the status of commercial emporia and, by implication, the British to the status of shopkeepers. Crooke seemed to signal that he understood the slight even as he concealed it.

Dhawal Ram's song is noteworthy for other reasons. He asserts in the first verse that the "war of year fourteen *began at Meerut*" (emphasis added). By way of explanation, Crooke added a footnote to his translation of this line: "Samvat 1914 [=] A.D. 1857."[62] Crooke would have given little or no thought to Dhawal Ram's use of a Samvat date, though it likely inspired the peculiar wording of his title for the song, namely, "The Mutiny – 1857." For Dhawal Ram, Meerut was significant because it was where the war commenced. By contrast, most histories treat Meerut like a relative backwater in 1857, notable certainly for sparking off the revolt, but preferring to focus attention on the more dramatic theaters of combat, such as Delhi, Kanpur, and Lucknow, or the more personal dramas – such as, most famously, those of Mangal Pandey, Kuar Singh, and Rani Lakshmibai of Jhansi. As we shall see later, Dhawal Ram was not alone in ascribing outsize historical importance to the eruption of violence at Meerut.

In the second verse Dhawal Ram moves from calendar time to time itself. He does this by invoking *bināś kāl* (बिनाश काल), the "time of destruction." The full line reads, *bināś kāl āyem matī bhaṅg bhaī faraṅgīṁ kī / Kālī vilāyat dubāyā chattā hai* (बिनाश काल आये मती भंग भई फ़रंगी की / काली विलायत दुबाया चत्ता है), or, "at the time of destruction, the British lost their heads, (as if) Kali is drowning England." For Hindi speakers, the term *bināś kāl* brings to mind the adage, "*vināśkāle viprīt buddhi*" (विनाशकाले विपरीत बुद्धि), or "in the

---

[60] Crooke, "Songs of the Mutiny," part II, p. 165 (emphasis added). According to Crooke (or Chaube), बदल and करापत referred to Bombay and Madras, respectively.
[61] बड़ा = big, हट्टा (var. of हाट) = market.
[62] *Samvat* refers to what is commonly today called the "Vikram Samvat" dating system, which was (and is) routinely employed in the Hindi literary and scholarly milieu.

time of destruction, wisdom is negated." More literally: "destruction-time inverts wisdom." In other words, once a wrong decision is taken there is no turning back: Each subsequent decision builds on the previous one, ultimately giving rise to the annihilation of the previous order. In the case of Dhawal Ram's song, poor decision-making by the British (who "lost their heads")[63] was both symptom and cause of destruction-time. This is then underscored by the subsequent reference to Kali, the goddess of time (or काल, *kāl*), death, and destruction.[64]

What was the nature of this poor British decision-making? This is revealed in the following verse: *gāī aur sūar vāhī ke kārtus* (गाई और सूअर वाही के कार्तुस), "those very cartridges of kine and swine." When the sepoys heard of this, Dhawal Ram adds, they "tore off their uniforms" (*sunnat sipāhīṁ bikher dage lattā hai*, सुन्नत सिपाहीं बिखेड़ दगे लत्ता है). A more literal translation might be, "they tore off their rags." Dhawal Ram also engages in a bit of compression and inversion here, which probably slipped by Crooke, Chaube, and their readers. It is true that the sepoys removed their uniforms, and that sequentially this occurred after they refused to touch the notorious cartridges. But the latter occurred on April 24; the former on May 9. Over two weeks intervened between these two events, sixteen days that included a court of inquiry, a prolonged confinement, a court-martial, and a final "ironing parade" – after which the soldiers were shackled and marched off to the local municipal prison. It was at the last of these events, the "ironing parade," occurring on May 9, that the sepoys stripped off their uniforms – or rather, *were stripped of their uniforms* – in the presence of all the regiments in the cantonment. This was so humiliating an act that it led to the military revolt of the three "native" regiments on the following afternoon, May 10.

Dhawal Ram was not alone in laying emphasis on Meerut in the "War of Year Fourteen." Another argument for the significance of Meerut, also composed soon after the onset of hostilities, was written by Colonel George Carmichael-Smyth. Like Dhawal Ram, Smyth also highlighted the cartridge issue. But whereas Dhawal Ram connected the cartridges to the end of British rule in India, Carmichael-Smyth maintained the opposite, namely, that the cartridge controversy, coming to a head in Meerut when it did – due to *his* decisions – actually served to "save India" for the British.

---

[63] Lit., "became stupefied by *bhang*."
[64] I am grateful to Kailash C. Jha for his assistance in clarifying the layered meanings embedded in this verse, and especially for alerting me to the adage, *vināśkāle viprīt buddhi* / विनाशकाले विप्रीत बुद्धि.

Carmichael-Smyth was the commanding officer of the Bengal 3rd Light Cavalry and had given the order to conduct the firing drill on April 24, and he did so knowing full well that the cartridge matter was an explosive one among the soldiery. Not surprisingly, Carmichael-Smyth's wisdom in having issued the "firing drill" order was questioned at the time, including by the officer in command of the Meerut Division, Major-General William Hewitt. In a brief narrative that Carmichael-Smyth composed soon after the revolt, he stated that he had immediately informed Hewitt of what had transpired, namely, that the men under his command had refused a direct order to load their weapons. Hewitt's despairing response was, "Oh why did you have this parade [the firing drill]? my division has kept quiet all this time, and in a few weeks this cartridge affair would have blown over!"[65] Carmichael-Smyth would maintain, by contrast, that his insistence that his men perform the drill in late April – which led to their refusal, the court of inquiry and court-martial, the ironing parade, imprisonment, and the actual revolt on May 10 – while temporarily disastrous for Meerut was ultimately good for India (British India, that is). Carmichael-Smyth maintained that a preconcerted and simultaneous rising of the native soldiery in all cantonments across north India had been planned for late June. By forcing the cartridge issue, Carmichael-Smyth held that he sparked a premature eruption in one station that allowed the dozens of other cantonments to take precautionary measures. The quickly circulating news of the premature revolt in Meerut on May 10 and the capture of Delhi by the Meerut insurgents on the following day, he reasoned, allowed other cantonments and civil stations to prepare for the disaffection of their own native regiments.

Hewitt was not alone in questioning the wisdom of Carmichael-Smyth's decision to hold the firing drill. Late in the evening of April 23, before the firing drill, one of Smyth's subordinates, Captain H. C. Craigie, urgently requested (in a letter to the regimental adjutant) that the firing drill parade be put off, citing the agitation over the cartridges among the soldiers. Carmichael-Smyth did not, of course, comply with this request, and Craigie later received a reprimand from no less than the commander in chief both for suggesting the postponement and for addressing it to the adjutant rather than to Carmichael-Smyth himself. Given the momentous events that followed, and in light of Hewitt's and Craigie's remarks, it is not unreasonable to suppose that Carmichael-Smyth came in for criticism

---

[65] Major-General G. Carmichael-Smyth, *Papers regarding "the Indian Mutiny"* (British Library, Asia, Pacific & Africa Collection, shelfmark V 8828 (b)), p. 10. On Carmichael-Smyth's decision to hold the firing parade and its unfolding, discussed in the remainder of this chapter, cf. Wagner, *Great Fear*, pp. 111–116.

in the weeks and months after May 10.[66] This may have informed his decision to draft and print fifty copies of a narrative account soon afterwards (in which he identified himself as Colonel G. C. Smyth), which included his insistence that his actions, far from being ill-judged, caused a premature eruption of a revolt that would otherwise have exploded in unison across all north Indian cantonments to the great detriment of British rule in India, and to append to this narrative testimonials from friends and acquaintances that supported his claim.[67] Among these was a letter from Henry Vansittart of the Bengal Civil Service, then at Agra, who wrote, "It strikes me that India is not a little indebted to you; your firmness probably hurried on a catastrophe, which, had it been delayed for a few weeks, would have begun with the siezure [sic] of Delhi, Agra, Allahabad, and Phillour." Another supporting missive was from an unnamed "person in England, of great Indian experience," who wrote, "It is evident to every body [sic] that the mutiny shewing itself when it did, saved India, and saved many lives. The object of the rebels was evidently to begin the murdering at every station, on the same day."[68]

Central to both Dhawal Ram's and Carmichael-Smyth's accounts are the response of the sepoys to the cartridges.[69] As noted, the compressed

---

[66] As we shall see later, in the discussion of Kaye's monumental history of the rebellion, published between 1864 and 1876, there was an undercurrent of support for Craigie's behavior.

[67] Colonel G. C. Smyth, "Mutiny of the Third Light Cavalry at Meerut" (1858?). I am not aware of any surviving copies of the original printed document, but it was eventually published in *Annals of the Indian Rebellion, containing Narratives of the Outbreaks and Eventful Occurrences, and Stories of Personal Adventures, during the Mutiny of 1857–58*, comp. by N. A. Chick (Calcutta: Sanders, Cones & Co., 1859), pp. 92–97. Chick failed to provide any bibliographic information about the materials reproduced in the volume, including this document. In 1871 Smyth (who now went by the more aristocratic-sounding Major-General G. Carmichael-Smyth) printed "for private circulation" a much-expanded version, twenty-six pages long, entitled *Papers regarding "the Indian Mutiny."* A copy of this is held in the British Library. This 1871 pamphlet was prompted by new criticisms of Carmichael-Smyth's behavior and temperament in John Kaye's celebrated multivolume work, *A History of the Sepoy War in India* (London: W. Allen & Co., 1864–76). It is here, in this later pamphlet, that Carmichael-Smyth points out, on p. 7, that he had never (*contra* a remark in Kaye) published his original account (the version in the Chick volume) but rather "printed few loose sheets at the request of some friends." He repeats this statement on p. 8 and adds that "I could not, however, have circulated more than fifty of them as I only had fifty printed."

[68] Smyth, "Mutiny of the Third Light Cavalry at Meerut" (1858?), p. 92.

[69] Technically, the men of the 3rd Light Cavalry were "sowars," or mounted troops. However, the eighty-five "skirmishers" were "mounted infantry" and thus a kind of sowar–sepoy hybrid. In any case, the term "sepoy" has become the generic term for all troopers, foot and horse, and I use that here. The original meaning of the Persian term *sipāhī*, whence sepoy derives, is soldier. It made its way into Turkish in the sixteenth and seventeenth centuries as cavalryman. By the time it became current in Hindi-Urdu it referred to an infantryman.

action in Dhawal Ram's song joins the refusal of the cartridges and the tearing off of uniforms as a seamless act of rebellion, whereas, in fact, over two weeks passed between that initial refusal – which constituted the formal mutiny – and the actual military revolt of May 10. While Dhawal Ram's song compresses the action and describes the sepoys all acting in unison, Carmicheal-Smyth's account both elongates the sequence of events and suggests that there were a variety of opinions among the sepoys on both decisions – the mutinous refusal of the cartridges and the later military revolt. Few modern historians have probed the variety of sepoy responses to these points, preferring instead to simply assume that the army refused en masse to touch the cartridges, and then turned en masse against their officers.[70] This is not entirely surprising: As imperial historiography gave way to postcolonial critique, the idea that any Indian would actually choose to support imperial institutions in a time of crisis – especially an institution so profoundly based on racial hierarchy as the Bengal Army – became increasingly difficult to imagine.

But the fact bears repeating: There was disagreement in the ranks about the composition of the cartridges and there were Indian soldiers (including noncommissioned and commissioned officers) who were willing to perform the firing drill, many of whom ultimately sided with the British against the revolt of their countrymen. Unfortunately, there is no easy access to conversations that took place away from official ears, so in many cases it is hard to know precisely what was said. But what records that do exist reveal some noteworthy inflection points and a key moment of crisis.

First, with respect to the cartridges: Carmichael-Smyth's decision to order the firing drill, he tells his readers, was initially prompted by a journey he made in mid-March to the Haridwar fair to purchase "remounts" (fresh horses) for his regiment. While at the fair he heard the news of the refusal to conduct the new drill by the 19th Native Infantry at Behrampore in late February. After the fair he spent a few days in the nearby hill station of Mussoorie where his friend, the brewer John Mackinnon, told him of having encountered a party of sepoys in the foothills who not only spoke favorably of the refusal of the 19th Native Infantry but added that they themselves "also would *join in a mutiny*, and that they knew *the whole army would mutiny*."[71] Carmichael-Smyth

---

[70] Notable exceptions include Saul David and J. A. B. Palmer, who both focus on the transition from mutiny to revolt in order to probe the question of whether there was a pre-concerted conspiracy.
[71] Smyth, "Mutiny of the Third Light Cavalry at Meerut," pp. 90–91 (emphasis in original). This portion of Smyth's 1859 account is identical to that found in his later version, Carmichael-Smyth, "A Brief Account of the Mutiny of the 3rd Light Cavalry,"

immediately wrote to R. M. Curzon, the military secretary to the commander in chief, to convey this news. He learned soon after that an order had been issued to alter the controversial firing drill: "the men were now to load without biting their cartridges." Instead, they would simply tear the cartridges with their hands. Thinking that his regiment "would be much pleased to hear of it," Carmichael-Smyth returned to Meerut on April 23 and scheduled a "firing parade" for the 24th to demonstrate the new drill to his men. To prepare for the parade, Carmicheal-Smyth had the havildar and his orderly, later identified as Brij Mohan Singh,[72] go through the motions of the new muzzle-loading technique on the evening of the 23rd. The orderly loaded and fired the weapon twice in his presence. Later that evening Craigie sent his aforementioned note to the regimental adjutant, urging that he intervene with Carmichael-Smyth to defer the drill, and in the night the orderly's house was burned down, along with a "horse hospital" close to the magazine. Nevertheless, on the following day, the 24th, Carmichael-Smyth tells his readers, the regiment appeared on parade at the appointed time, though "not a single man *had come on parade with his cartridges*" (emphasis in original).

Unreported by Carmichael-Smyth, and perhaps unbeknownst to him, many and perhaps most of the men of his regiment had on the previous night sworn an oath – the Hindus on the Ganga, the Muslims on the Quran – to refuse the cartridges until the entire army had consented to them.[73] This information came to light in depositions later gathered in 1858 by Williams. The men who gave the relevant depositions – Kooman Singh (Havildar), Rundheer Singh (Trooper), and Zalim Singh (Trooper) – had been members of the 3rd Light Cavalry but had not joined in the May 10 uprising, and had been subsequently assigned (after the revolt) to the Meerut Mounted Police. Two of them also reported that on the evening of April 24, Brij Mohan Singh had reported to his fellow cavalrymen that he had learned how to load and fire according to

---

in *Papers regarding the Indian Mutiny* (1871), p. 9; in the 1871 pamphlet more detail is forthcoming, including (on p. 20) the name of his Mussoorie friend, the "Mountain Whitbread" or brewer, John Mackinnon; the location of Mackinnon's encounter with the sepoys, "at Boneittee just north of Nahun" (very close to Kasauli, in the hills north of Chandigarh); and the regiment to which the sepoys belonged, the 66th Native Infantry, a Gurkha regiment known popularly as the "Nusseeree Battalion."

[72] Though Brij Mohan Singh is not identified in Smyth's 1859 or 1871 narrative, he is specifically named later in Carmichael-Smyth's 1871 pamphlet, pp. 17–18, introducing a certificate issued by J. Cracroft Wilson attesting to his "fidelity."

[73] See Williams, "Memorandum," p. 5; and "Depositions Taken at Meerut by Major G. W. Williams," pp. 6–9 (depositions 12–14). How many of the men in the regiment swore the oath is unclear, but a close reading of the depositions suggests that the oath was administered in a small-group setting whose participants were encouraged to then administer it to others in turn.

the new drill. In response to being called "a mean fellow" by some of the men, he assured his critics that "they would all have to do the same [and] it would be seen, who would dare to refuse."⁷⁴ The men who took the lead in criticizing Brij Mohan Singh, denouncing the cartridges, and organizing the swearing of the oath were two naiks (captains), Peer Ali and Kudrut Ali. Zalim Singh said they vowed to "refuse ... the cartridges, and bid them tell all the men to do likewise, [and] also to report to their captains, that till every regiment had agreed to use the cartridges, they would not take them."

The fact that not a single man brought his cartridges to the parade ground on the following morning, April 24, indicates that, whether or not all of them had sworn the oath, they were united in their distrust of the cartridges – and of their officers' intentions. Undeterred, Carmichael-Smyth explained to the regiment why he had ordered the parade and "directed the Havildar Major to show them how they were to load without biting the cartridge, which he did, and fired one off."⁷⁵ Carmichael-Smyth then ordered the distribution of the cartridges and commanded a portion of the regiment, known as "skirmishers," numbering ninety men, to load and fire.⁷⁶ Significantly, the first two men to whom the cartridges were handed were Pir Ali and Kudrat Ali.⁷⁷ Save for five noncommissioned officers, the group refused to take the cartridges, saying they would get a "bad name" – most likely, the term they used was *badnām* (बदनाम), signifying that their reputations would be tarnished. They added, however, that "if all the men would use them they would do so." After repeating the order and being met with continued resistance, Carmichael-Smyth dismissed the regiment and reported the proceedings in writing to the officer commanding the station and in person to the general in command of the division, Major-General

---

[74] Deposition of Kooman Singh, in "Depositions Taken at Meerut by Major G. W. Williams," p. 6. Zalim Singh (pp. 8–9) gives a similar account. By "mean fellow," Brij Mohan's detractors meant "low" or "vile," no doubt for having polluted himself by accepting the cartridges.

[75] Carmichael-Smyth, "A Brief Account of the Mutiny of the 3rd Light Cavalry," in *Papers regarding the Indian Mutiny* (1871), p. 9. According to Carmichael-Smyth's testimony at the court-martial, this was Shaikh Baksh Ali or "Shaik Bucksh Ally." See *Indian Mutiny Papers*, vol. 1, ed. George W. Forrest (Calcutta: Military Department Press, 1893), p. 231.

[76] Palmer, *Mutiny Outbreak at Meerut in 1857*, p. 10, citing Hugh Gough, *Old Memories* (Edinburgh and London: William Blackwood and Sons, 1897), p. 10, explains that the skirmishers were "ninety in number and drawn fifteen from each troop." (Each cavalry regiment consisted of six troops.)

[77] Smyth's testimony from the court-martial, *Indian Mutiny Papers*, p. 231. It may be, then, that Smyth knew they were the leaders of the refusal.

Hewitt.[78] A court of inquiry was held the next day and the eighty-five men who refused the command to load their rifles remained in their lines until orders were received that they should be placed under guard pending a court-martial, which was held on May 6–8.[79] The tribunal, presided over "by Native Officers, some of their own regiment," found the men guilty of mutiny and "sentenced [most of them] to ten years' imprisonment with hard labor." An "ironing parade" was scheduled for following day, May 9, which took place on the European Parade Ground "in the presence of all the troops at the station, both European and Native." It was at this ironing parade that the eighty-five men were stripped of their uniforms, clapped in irons, and marched off to an ordinary prison under the jurisdiction of the "civil authorities."

~ ~ ~

Those Very Cartridges of Kine and Swine

Gāī aur sūar vāhī ke kārtus / गाई और सूअर वाही के कार्तुस)

Dhawal Ram and Carmichael-Smyth agreed, then, on more than just Meerut as the beginning of the end. They concurred, as have all accounts of 1857, that the spark that "lit the fuse" of the mutiny was the questionable cartridges, presumably slathered (as it was widely held) with cow and pig fat. Hence Carmichael-Smyth's excitement about the order to alter the drill: No longer would the men be asked to put the cartridges in their mouths. Henceforth they would simply tear the cartridge with their fingers. It seems to not have occurred to Carmichael-Smyth, or any of the officer corps,[80] that changing the drill in this way might have had the *opposite* of the intended effect – that, rather than mollify the men under their command, it could confirm their suspicion that something was amiss with the cartridges.

It is worth examining the firing parade more closely. Happily, there are two revealing accounts from the skirmishers' point of view: First, during the court-martial on May 6–8, Havildar Mattadin Singh submitted a statement on behalf of his fellow accused. It is worth including in full:

---

[78] This section of Smyth's 1871 account, ibid., pp. 9–10, is slightly more detailed than the 1859 version.
[79] Smyth does not provide the dates in his two privately printed accounts, but they are given in *Indian Mutiny Papers*, appendix E.
[80] Indeed, it seems to not have occurred to historians either. In any case, I have not come across anyone forwarding this line or argument in the literature.

On the evening of the 23rd ultimo, at about half-past 7 o'clock, about five or six men of the 3rd troop were standing in the lines; they were saying to each other that Brijmohun Sing [sic] had just said that he had that day fired off two of the new greased cartridges; there will be a parade to-morrow morning; the colonel and the adjutant will be present, and the new cartridges are to be used; we shall then see whether any one, Hindu or Mussulman, will refuse to use them. After this a number of us said to each other: If we use the greased cartridges we shall lose our caste, and shall never again be able to return to our homes. We then consulted as to what was to be done, and came to the conclusion that we ought to report the circumstances to the captains of our troops, so that something might be done to save our caste. The native officers of troops reported the circumstances to the captains commanding troops. We all went to our respective huts. Early in the morning, as we were ordered to turn out for parade, we all went there without knowing what had been done or said the night before by captains of troops. The adjutant came down to parade shortly afterwards, and then the colonel stood in front of the skirmishers and said: "I have invented something; listen to what I am about to say. If you will fire off these cartridges, the Commander-in-Chief will be much pleased, and you will have a great name, and I shall likewise get great praise, and I will have the whole affair published in the papers." The colonel called the havildar-major to the front, and said to him: "Take a carbine, load and fire it off in the way I showed you yesterday," and then he said to us that we should have to load and fire in the same manner. The havildar-major brought his carbine to his side, and having handled his cartridges, was about to bite off the end, when the colonel stopped him, saying: "Tear it with your hands." He loaded and fired. The colonel then said: "Where are the cartridges; bring them here." Kot-dafadars brought the cartridges tied up in cloth. The colonel went to the right and said: "Will you take those cartridges?" All said – "No, we won't take them." We would not take them as we had great doubts about them; so the colonel had to induce us to take them, a thing he had never done before. When the colonel had put us "threes about" to dismiss us from the parade, we begged to make a statement to him. He fronted us, and we said – "If the other regiments will fire one cartridge, we will fire ten." The colonel said – "There are no other cartridges for other men." We said – "There are pistols." The colonel then again put us "threes about" and dismissed us.

There are some key differences between Mattadin's account of the firing parade and Carmichael-Smyth's. First, Mattadin Singh says that on the evening before the parade Brijmohan had fired off two of the "*new greased* cartridges" (emphasis added). Second, Mattadin Singh's wording suggests that Carmichael-Smyth claimed credit for the alteration of the drill, employing the phrase "I have invented something." The Hindustani is not given in the court-martial proceedings, but it is likely that the verb he used was *ījād karnā* (ईजाद करना), to devise, contrive, invent. Third, Mattadin points to Carmichael-Smyth's expectation that the successful performance of the drill would please the commander in chief and therefore not only enhance the reputation of the regiment but, perhaps more importantly, garner praise for himself. It may seem odd for a commanding officer to have behaved in so self-aggrandizing a manner, but what matters here is how Carmichael-Smyth was perceived by his men – and a crucial point here is that from the skirmishers' point of view, Carmichael-Smyth seemed to not only be taking credit for having contrived a new drill but also was eager that he and his regiment bask in the consequent official acclaim.[81] Fourth, and most importantly, Singh describes the demonstration of the firing drill by the havildar-major. Recall that Carmichael-Smyth's account of this moment in his pamphlet was fairly perfunctory: "I directed the Havildar Major to show them how they were to load without biting the cartridge, which he did, and fired one off."[82] Mattadin gives more detail:

> The colonel called the havildar-major to the front, and said to him: "Take a carbine, load and fire it off in the way I showed you yesterday," and then he said to us that we should have to load and fire in the same manner. The havildar-major brought his carbine to his side, and having handled his cartridges, was about to bite off the end, when the colonel stopped him, saying: "Tear it with your hands." He loaded and fired.

With Mattadin Singh's account it becomes easier to imagine the scene. The entire regiment is apprehensive about the nature of the cartridges, so much so that the men refuse to bring any ammunition with them to the parade ground – despite the fact that they had been ordered to perform a firing drill. After some initial remonstrances, Carmichael-Smyth announces that he has come up with, or "invented," a new method and he orders the senior-most Indian officer to demonstrate the loading and firing of the weapon. As the havildar-major grasps the cartridge and moves it toward his mouth, Carmichael-Smyth stops him and says, "tear it with your hands." He obeyed, loaded, and then fired.[83] This must have struck the men as odd. If the cartridges were clean, why suddenly stop the havildar-major from putting one in his mouth? Doubtless they would

---

[81] In the court-martial proceedings, Carmichael-Smyth seems to confirm this point. Under cross-examination by the court, he stated that "[w]hen I came on parade, the adjutant informed me that the men had not taken their cartridges, and it was on that account I ordered the havildar-major to take a cartridge and load and fire before them; and it was then also that I said, when the whole army heard of this way of loading, that they would be all much pleased, and exclaim 'Wah, Wah!'" *Indian Mutiny Papers*, vol. 1, appendix E, p. cxliii.

[82] Carmichael-Smyth, "A Brief Account of the Mutiny of the 3rd Light Cavalry," in *Papers regarding the Indian Mutiny* (1871), p. 9. According to Carmichael-Smyth's testimony at the court-martial, this was Shaikh Baksh Ali or "Shaik Bucksh Ally." See *Indian Mutiny Papers*, vol. 1, p. 231.

[83] Under cross-examination by the court, Smyth elaborated slightly: "Previous to ordering the men to take their cartridges, I made the havildar-major load and fire off his carbine, to show them how it could be loaded without putting the cartridge to the mouth; this the havildar-major did before them." *Indian Mutiny Papers*, vol. 1, appendix E, p. cxliii.

have conjured an image of Brijmohan loading and firing the new greased cartridges the day before. Then Carmichael-Smyth ordered the *kot dafādār*, or magazine sergeant-major, to bring some cartridges, which were tied in cloth bundles. Not surprisingly, they refused to take them.

The second account from the point of view of the mutineers was by one of the "ring-leaders," Naick Meer Kudrut Ally (*Nāyak* or Corporal Mīr Qudrat 'Alī). He was allowed to cross-examine Carmichael-Smyth on the cartridges being distributed by the kot dafādār.[84]

QUESTION – Did you show us the cartridges that we might see whether they were old ones or new ones?
ANSWER – The kot-dafadars had them in their hands; you might have examined them in any way, but you refused to touch them.
QUESTION – Were the cartridges, which we refused, put aside and confined with us?
ANSWER – No, all the cartridges of the regiment are precisely the same; there are not two kinds.

Qudrat Ali's questions are revealing. Recall that the skirmishers had declined to bring their ammunition to the parade ground. According to the instructions issued the day before, "each man was ordered to receive three cartridges." Qudrat Ali's first question suggests that the men suspected that the new bundles of cartridges brought by the kot dafādār were tainted with the offending grease. This would have only heightened the apprehensions due to Carmichael-Smyth suddenly ordering the havildar-major to *not* put the demonstration cartridge in his mouth.

The significance of Qudrat Ali's second question, whether the cartridges that they had refused on the parade ground were put aside and confined with them, is less clear. It is inconceivable that men under confinement would be allowed any ammunition, tainted or otherwise. So Qudrat Ali might have been insinuating that the cloth-bundled cartridges were spirited away after the regiment was dismissed, and that the cartridges being displayed as evidence during the court-martial could not constitute proof that the cartridges being distributed on April 24 were untainted.

What seems clear, by contrast, is that the decision to alter the firing drill, to have the men tear the cartridge paper with their fingers rather than their teeth, was perceived by the men of the regiment – and the Indian soldiery more generally – as a tacit admission on the part of the British officer corps that the proposed new cartridges were, in fact, greased with objectionable substances.

---

[84] *Indian Mutiny Papers*, vol. 1, appendix E, p. cxliii.

2 Humiliation

Let's recap: At 5 pm in Meerut, on May 10, 1857, the 3rd Light Cavalry and the 20th Native Infantry, plus most of the 11th Native Infantry, rose up, killed several of their officers, burned their regimental "lines" (or huts, arranged in lines), and marched off to Delhi to wage war against the British. Much additional killing and mayhem occurred in Meerut on the night of May 10, mainly at the hands of a mob that emanated from the "*sadr* bazaar," or the main bazaar serving the cantonment. Meerut represented a major origin point for the events that would come to be remembered variously as "the Sepoy Mutiny", the Great Rebellion of 1857, and India's First War of Independence. The folksinger Dhawal Ram, quoted in Chapter 1, understood the significance of Meerut in this way, as did Lieutenant Colonel George Munro Carmichael-Smyth, the commanding officer of the Bengal 3rd Light Cavalry.

But why did the Meerut *sipāhī*s – or, actually, the *sipāhī*s (infantrymen, or sepoys) and *sawār*s (cavalrymen) – suddenly decide to cross the proverbial Rubicon on May 10, 1857? Was it, as Dhawal Ram insisted, because of "those cartridges of kine and swine" that the men "tore off their uniforms"? Not exactly. It is true that two weeks earlier eighty-five "skirmishers" of the 3rd Bengal Light Cavalry had refused to touch the suspicious cartridges during a "firing drill" that had been ordered by their commanding officer, Colonel Carmichael-Smyth, and this constituted a formal mutiny in his eyes and, ultimately, the eyes of fourteen of the fifteen native officers that later presided over the eventual court-martial. Similar mutinies had taken place in the Bengal Army in the previous months. The eighty-five skirmishers were duly convicted and then subjected to a humiliating "ironing parade" on May 9, during which they were stripped of their uniforms, placed in irons, and marched off to prison like common criminals. But despite their emotional distress, they had departed the parade ground in a more or less orderly fashion, even saluting some of their officers. Meanwhile their brothers in arms, the men who had *not* been court-martialed and paraded in irons, but who had been forced to watch the humiliation of their eighty-five comrades, decided sometime during the night of May 9 to take matters into their own hands. They rose up on the late afternoon of the 10th – thus starting "The Mutiny," "The War of Year Fourteen," and "India's First War of Independence."

G. W. Williams, superintendent of police for the North-Western Provinces, argued soon afterwards that the revolt was a spontaneous uprising, a product of a baseless rumor ricocheting across the Meerut cantonment and sadr bazaar that the British artillery and rifle regiments had been ordered to attack the native regiments. Based on extensive interviews and witness depositions, Williams identified a "wretched cook boy" as the originator of the rumor. But, as noted in Chapter 1, Williams also reported that in the course of his investigations he had been told that on Saturday afternoon or evening – that is, on May 9, the day before the revolt – "the men were taunted by the disreputable inhabitants of the Sudder Bazar for allowing their brethren to suffer on account of their religion."[1] He did not provide a source for this claim and he did not indicate who those disreputable inhabitants might be. In the event, he discounted this report in favor of competing testimony that the spark for the uprising was not lit till the following day, Sunday, May 10.

It is almost certain that the source for Williams' report about the taunting by the "disreputable inhabitants of the Sudder Bazar" was one J. Cracroft Wilson. Prior to the revolt, Wilson had been the judge in Moradabad District, about seventy miles east of Meerut. After the revolt at Meerut and the civil rebellion that followed, he was appointed special commissioner in Moradabad District and spent many months in command of an irregular cavalry unit pursuing insurgents across the region – including parts of Meerut District. He drafted a report based on these operations in 1858, while Williams was compiling his depositions and narrative. Like Carmichael-Smyth, Wilson was convinced that a province-wide uprising was planned for May 31, three weeks after the Meerut revolt – also a Sunday – during which "all European functionaries" were to be murdered and the reins of government seized by the rebels, all in one fell swoop. However, according to Wilson's theory, further elaborating on Carmichael-Smyth's account, the rush of events in Meerut conspired to force the premature eruption of violence. For Wilson, the key factor in sparking this premature eruption was the merciless taunting of the soldiers by the women of the bazaar on the night of May 9. As a result, the British were able to prepare for

---

[1] Williams, "Memorandum," p. 5.

52 Humiliation

subsequent mutinies in the other cantonments and, over time, send reinforcements and relief columns into Hindustan. Thus, for Wilson – and, as we shall see, many others – the women of the bazaar inadvertently helped to doom the rebellion to failure.

Wilson did not indicate in his report what his sources were. He simply stated that his convictions were based on his "[c]arefully collating oral information with facts as they occurred."[2] Regardless, Wilson's version became the *Ur*-text for almost all subsequent British historical narratives concerning the role of bazaar women in Meerut in 1857. Consequently, it is worth repeating here in full:

> From this combined and simultaneous massacre on the 31st May, 1857, we were, humanly speaking, saved by Lieutenant-Colonel Smyth, commanding the 3rd Regiment of Bengal Light Cavalry, *and the frail ones of the Meerut bazaar*. Colonel Smyth had been engaged at the Hurdwar fair as president of a committee for passing remounts into the public service. On his return to the head-quarters of his regiment, he found that some dissatisfaction had been expressed by some of the troopers as to taking the same pistol cartridges which had been served out to the regiment for the two previous years. He insisted upon their being served out to, and taken by, the men. His order was obeyed. The men refused. A court martial was convened. Eighty-five men of the 3rd Light Cavalry were sentenced to various terms of imprisonment, and, having been put in fetters, were escorted to the Meerut jail, which is situated on the road to Delhi. *And now the frail ones' taunts were heard far and wide, and the rest of the regiment was assailed with words like these: –* "*Your brethren have been ornamented with these anklets and incarcerated; and for what? Because they would not swerve from their creed; and you, cowards as you are, sit still indifferent to their fate. If you had an atom of manhood in you, go and release them.*" The mine had been prepared and the train had been laid, but it was not intended to light the slow-match for another three weeks. *The spark which fell from female lips ignited it at once.* Meerut was in a blaze, and the night of the 10th May, 1857, saw the commencement of a tragedy, never before witnessed since India passed under British sway.[3]

Wilson's account possesses several interesting features. Most striking, of course, is the sense of irony that permeates it: British rule in India was preserved by the premature eruption of the violence at Meerut, a premature eruption occasioned by taunts that "fell from female lips." Wilson

---

[2] I discuss the possible sources for Wilson in the Entr'acte and Conclusions, Reflections.
[3] J. C. Wilson, Commissioner on Special Duty, to G. F. Edmonstone, Secretary to Government, Allahabad, dated Camp Calcutta, December 24, 1858, reproduced in *Freedom Struggle in Uttar Pradesh*, ed. S. A. A. Rizvi and Moti Lal Bhargava, vol. 1 (Lucknow: Information Department, 1957–1961), p. 404. Wilson's report, originally printed from Allahabad in 1858 and Calcutta in 1859, was later republished privately by Wilson as *Narrative of Events attending the Outbreak of Disturbances and the Restoration of Authority in the District of Moradabad, in 1857–58* (London: Anglo-American Times Press, 1871); the passage appears on p. 2 (emphasis added).

did not make the sexual metaphor explicit, but given his phrasing and the fact that he is referencing prostitutes, it is hard to resist the notion that he understood the violence on May 10, 1857 as a premature eruption by undisciplined lovers. Another noteworthy feature of the account is that Wilson described the women as "the frail ones of the Meerut bazaar." An archaic meaning of the noun "frail" is "woman," most likely deriving from the associated adjectival connotations of mentally fragile, unchaste, and liable to fall from virtue. The terms "frail" and "frail ones" were common euphemisms for prostitutes in the nineteenth and early twentieth centuries, along with "public women."[4]

Inscription

For generations of historians, the bazaar women of Meerut became a staple of the 1857 narrative.[5] And since Wilson was the principal source for most writers, the women are almost invariably described as courtesans or prostitutes. Here, for example, is how the scene was recently described for popular audiences in New Delhi:

> The 85 sepoys were taken into custody and confined to a hospital during their court martial. For punishment, on May 9 they were taken to the Parade Ground, where they were stripped of their uniforms and fitted with leg irons. Then they were marched 3 km to the new jail, which is known as Victoria Park today. ... The alleys of the crowded Sadar Bazaar area also tell their own tales. The prostitutes of this market taunted the Indian soldiers for failing to save their 85 comrades from humiliation. That added strength to a rumor that the British forces were going to disarm the "native troops", and that sparked an uproar. Indian soldiers started attacking Englishmen.

This description is from a panel display called *"Kranti se Gandhi"*, or "From Revolution to Gandhi," at the Gandhi Memorial Museum in

---

[4] For example, the *Nashville Dispatch* contained a news item titled "The Frail Ones" on August 13, 1863, which gave notice that "all the public women of this city to report at the Provost Marshall's office on or before the 15th day of August, and that on presentation of a Surgeon's certificate and payment of five dollars, they will receive licenses." See http://tn.gov/tsla/cwsb/1863-08-Article-113-Page143.pdf. See also Robyn Anderson, "'The Hardened Frail Ones': Women and Crime in Auckland, 1845–1870" (MA thesis, University of Auckland, 1981). For similar usages in the early twentieth century, including by Raymond Chandler in 1939, see https://en.wiktionary.org/wiki/frail.

[5] Though there were important exceptions. G. W. Forrest, *A History of the Indian Mutiny* (Edinburgh and London: William Blackwood and Sons, 1914), pp. 33–35, does not mention the women of Meerut. Nor does S. N. Sen, *Eighteen Fifty-Seven* (Calcutta: Government of India, 1957), 59–65, who also dismisses Wilson's conspiracy theory (p. 402). More surprising is the lack of mention of the Meerut women in Palmer's detailed account of Meerut, *The Mutiny Outbreak at Meerut in 1857*, esp. pp. 68–73. Like Sen, Palmer discusses (and dismisses), Wilson's premature eruption theory (p. 133).

54 Humiliation

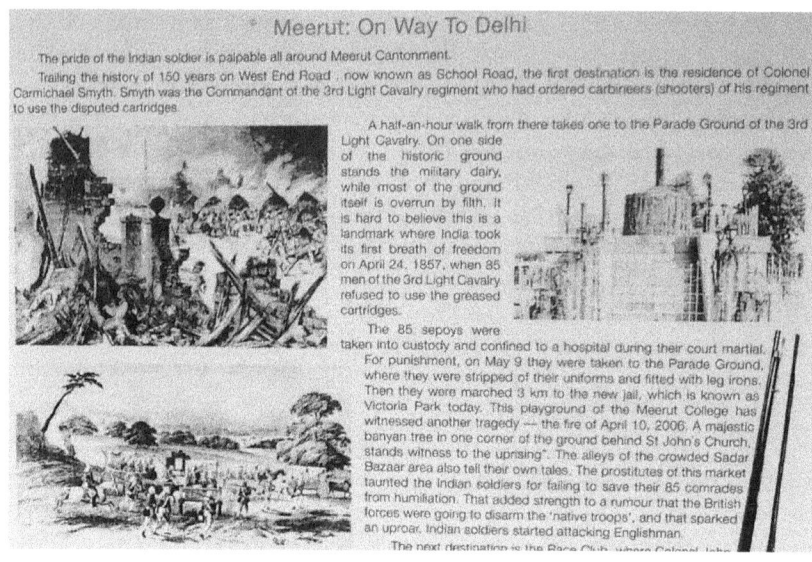

Figure 2.1 Placard on display in the garden at the Gandhi Memorial Museum, Birla House, Tees January Marg, New Delhi, 2013
Source: Photograph by the author, 2013.

New Delhi (see Figures 2.1 and 2.2).[6] The display, which consists of a series of twenty or so large, laminated poster boards that combine narrative with images, stands along one side of the garden in which Mohandas K. Gandhi was gunned down on January 30, 1948.[7]

It did not take long for the women of Meerut to enter the secondary historical record. The first published narrative history to feature them was John Kaye's four-volume *History of the Sepoy War in India, 1857–1858*.[8] In volume 2 of this work, published in 1864, Kaye described the scene as follows:

---

[6] Visited twice to examine the display, on January 5, 2013 and March 16, 2014.

[7] Though it may at first appear incongruous that a shrine to mark the murder of India's "apostle of nonviolence" would celebrate such a bloody chapter in South Asian history as 1857, it so happens that anxieties about gender and masculinity were bubbling just below the surface for Gandhi's assassin as well. See Ashis Nandy, "Final Encounter: The Politics of the Assassination of Gandhi," in Ashis Nandy, *At the Edge of Psychology: Essays in Politics and Culture* (Delhi: Oxford University Press, 1980), pp. 70–98.

[8] John Kaye, *A History of the Sepoy War in India, 1857–1858*, 4 vols. (London, 1864–1876) (emphasis added). This was later revised and continued by Colonel G. B. Malleson and published in six volumes in 1888–1889. The bazaar women episode is not mentioned in two summary narratives that appeared soon after the uprising, namely, Charles Ball, *The History of the Indian Mutiny*, 2 vols. (London: London Printing and Publishing Company, 1858), see vol. 1, pp. 55–56; and Rev. J. Cave-Brown, *The Punjab and Delhi in 1857, being*

Inscription 55

Figure 2.2 The shrine marking the site of Gandhi's assassination in the garden of the Birla House, Tees January Marg, New Delhi, 2013; the series of history placards is to the left of the garden, beneath the row of trees
Source: Photograph by the author, 2013.

The 3rd Cavalry were naturally the most excited of all. Eighty-five of their fellow-soldiers were groaning in prison. Sorrow, shame, and indignation were strong within them for their comrades' sake, and terror for their own. *They had been taunted by the courtesans of the Bazaar, who asked if they were men to suffer their comrades to wear such anklets of iron;*★ and they believed that what they had seen on the day before was but a foreshadowing of a greater cruelty to come.⁹

Kaye's source for this passage, which he identifies in footnote 41 (where I have placed a star), was the official report by Wilson. The wording of Kaye's reference to Wilson suggests that he was conscious of the possibility that assigning such a key role in the rebellion to courtesans of the bazaar might occasion some eye-rolling skepticism on the part of his readers. Thus he was careful to point out in the note that "[t]his is stated

---

a narrative of the measures by which the Punjab was saved and Delhi recovered during the Indian mutiny, 2 vols. (London: Blackwood, 1861), see vol. 1, pp. 52–53.
⁹ Kaye, *A History of the Sepoy War in India*, vol. 2, p. 42 (emphasis in original).

very distinctly by Mr. J. C. Wilson (an excellent authority) in his interesting Muradabad Report." Kaye then proceeded to quote from the relevant section of that report in the remainder of the footnote – though he avoided the question of a wider conspiracy and whether the Meerut uprising constituted a premature eruption that thwarted it.

G. B. Malleson, who issued an expanded version of Kaye's work in 1888–1889 (retaining Kaye's original language regarding Meerut), would himself decide to leave out of his own extremely successful if controversial one-volume history (1891) any reference to the role of the bazaar women.[10] Possibly he felt their inclusion would undercut his larger argument – and the basis of the controversy that surrounded the book – that the uprising was not spontaneous but the result of a carefully hatched conspiracy, in which the Maulvi of Faizabad, the Rani of Jhansi, and the Nana Saheb of Bithur took leading roles. If so, this was an ironic choice, given that Wilson had understood the agency of the bazaar women of Meerut as a key factor in explaining the very failure of that conspiracy.

Within five years of Malleson's account a new work would appear that would do more than any other to cement the image of the women of Meerut in the British historical understanding of 1857. Significantly, this took the form of historical fiction: Flora Annie Steel's *On the Face of the Waters* (1896). Steel's book was the most popular of the "Mutiny novels" to appear in the late nineteenth century and probably was the most popular of all time prior to John Masters' *Nightrunners of Bengal* (1952). The chapter in which Steel recounts the scene in the Meerut bazaar is entitled, with an Old Testament flourish, "The Word Went Forth". Her description of the Meerut bazaar after the ironing parade on May 9 begins in "the lane of lust," where a sepoy was visiting a bazaar prostitute – or rather, "harlot". But the woman tartly rebuffs the sepoy's advances saying, "We of the bazaar kiss no cowards." She then twists the knife, slyly asking, in reference to the eighty-five imprisoned skirmishers, "Where are your comrades?" The following scene is worth quoting in full:

The man to whom she said it, a young dissolute-faced trooper, dressed in the loose rakish muslins beloved of his class – the very man, perchance, who had gone city-ward that morning, and dropped an alms into the yellow fakir's bowl – stood for a second in the stifling, maddening atmosphere of musk and rose and orange-blossom; stood before all those insolent allurements, balked in his passion, checked in his desires. Then, with an oath, he dashed from her insulting charms; dashed into the street with a cry:

---

[10] See G. B. Malleson, *The Indian Mutiny of 1857* (London: Seeley and Col., Ltd., 1891), pp. 62–69.

"To horse! To horse, brothers! To the jail! To our comrades!"
The word had been spoken. The speech which brings more than speech, had come from the painted lips of a harlot.
The first clang of the church bell – which the chaplain had forgotten to postpone – came faintly audible across the dusty plain, making other men pause and look at each other. Why not? It was the hour of prayer the appointed time. Their comrades could be easily rescued – there was but a native guard at the jail. And hark! from another pair of painted derisive lips came the same retort, flung from a balcony.
"Trra! We of the bazaar kiss no cowards!"
"To horse! To horse! Let the comrades be rescued first; and then – "[11]

Steel spent many years in India, mostly in the Punjab where her husband was posted, and was able to do extensive research in the official records. As a result, her novel was widely praised for its historical accuracy and verisimilitude. For example, Sir George MacMunn (about whom I have more to say later), writing in the 1920s, felt that "Mrs. Steele [sic] alone has gripped the whole story, of glory, or tragedy, the pathetic feelings of the soldiery who rued their folly, the relentless grip of the cholera-stricken and fever-gripped avengers, and this touch of the courtesans who put a torch to the fuel."[12] For her own part, Steel made it clear in her preface that she intended her book "to be at once a story and a history." Whether it succeeded in either was "for the reader to say", but

[a]s the writer, I have only to point out where my history ends, my story begins, and clear the way for criticism. Briefly, then, I have not allowed fiction to interfere with fact in the slightest degree. The reader may rest assured that every incident bearing in the remotest degree on the Indian Mutiny, or on the part which real men took in it, is scrupulously exact, even to the date, the hour, the scene, the very weather. *Nor have I allowed the actual actors in the great tragedy to say a word regarding it which is not to be found in the accounts of eye-witnesses, or in their own writings.*[13]

In the case of the words of the women of Meerut, Steel's debt to Wilson is clear. His "spark which fell from female lips" had become the basis for

---

[11] Flora Annie Steel, *On the Face of the Waters* (New York: Macmillan, 1897), pp. 190–191.
[12] Sir George MacMunn, "Mees Dolly (An Untold Tragedy of '57)," *Cornhill Magazine*, (Sep 1927), p. 330. Note, however, that Steel refers to the women not as courtesans but "harlots."
[13] Steel, *On the Face of the Waters*, p. v. Emphasis added. As we shall see later, precisely what Steel meant by "actual actors" seems to have been aggressively misinterpreted. For a provocative reflection on history and the novel, and fact and fiction, see Jill Lepore, "Just the Facts, Ma'am: Fake Memoirs, Factual Fictions, and the History of History," *The New Yorker* (March 24, 2008), pp. 79–83.

her artful phrases, such as, "The speech which brings more than speech, had come from the painted lips of a harlot," or, "And hark! From another pair of painted derisive lips came the same retort, flung from a balcony."

Wilson would soon be yoked to another immensely popular and, in its own way, romantic account of 1857 – told not as a mere mutiny and civil rebellion but as a patriotic war of independence. V. D. Savarkar first wrote his *First War of Indian Independence* in Marathi in London in 1908 and then translated it into English in the following year. Savarkar's principal debt was, ironically, to Malleson: The latter's anti-British conspiracy became the former's nationalist revolution; and the nefarious conspirators became noble freedom fighters. But whereas Malleson had studiously avoided discussion of Wilson's bazaar women, Savarkar returned them to the narrative. Rather than referring to them as courtesans, prostitutes, harlots, or "frail ones of the bazaar", he described them simply as the "womenfolk of the town." Thus:

> This [the humiliation of the ironing parade] was in the morning. The Sepoys could not possibly control themselves any longer. They returned to their barracks, smarting inwardly under the insult and shame of seeing their brethren being imprisoned by foreigners for what was nothing more than an act of self-respect in defence of their religion. *When they strolled out in the bazaars, the women folk of the town said to them scornfully, "Your brothers are in prison, and you are lounging about here killing flies! Fie upon your life!"*★ How could they, already chafing under injury, hear women taunting them so in the open street, and still remain doing nothing? All over the lines that night there was a number of secret meetings of the Sepoys. Were they to wait now till the 31st of May?[14]

In footnote 3, the location of which I have marked with a star, Savarkar cites "J. C. Wilson."

Did Savarkar resist the urge to refer to the bazaar women as courtesans or prostitutes so as to remain scrupulously consistent with Wilson's language? Or was he unaware of the implications of the term "frail ones"? Either is possible, though it is more likely that he was aware of the use of the term "courtesan" in Kaye and "harlot" in Steel, but felt conflicted about the prospect of India's sacred War of Independence having any connection whatever to women whom he considered morally tainted. Another instance of a similar prudishness occurs later in the text, when he discusses the conspirator-patriots meeting on the banks of the Ganga near Kanpur. Afterwards one of them, Shams ud-Din, visited the house of one "Azizan", a well-known courtesan of Kanpur and supporter of the rebellion there, and reveals to her the secret plan. As Savarkar described it:

---

[14] V. D. Savarkar, *First War of Indian Independence* (first published 1909; 4th underground edition, n.d., pub. Mayuresh), p. 93 (emphasis added).

Their secrets were known to the sacred Ganges alone and in her hands they were safe! But this much is well known that, on the following day, Sham-su-ddin came to the house of his beloved Azizan and told her that within two days the Feringhis would be destroyed and India would be free! Shams ud-Din did not give this news of freedom to her as empty bravado; for, the heart of this beauty yearned as much for India's freedom as that of her brave lover. Azizan was a dancing girl very much loved by the Sepoys; she was not one, however, who sold her love for money in the ordinary market, but in the field of freedom it was given as a reward for the love of country. We will soon show further on how a delightful smile from her beautiful face encouraged fighting heroes and how a slight frown from her dark eyebrows hastily sent back to the field cowards who had come away.[15]

Thus far historical discussion of the role of bazaar women at Meerut stemmed from Wilson's 1858 reference to the "frail ones." In 1927 some new information emerged that raised troubling questions (for the British) about the identity of one of those women.[16] Mutiny historiography was winding down by this time – though new scholarship was appearing, in part influenced by the rising nationalist critique of imperialism on moral grounds, that called into question the behavior of the British in 1857.[17] The new information that emerged in 1927, about a mysterious woman named "Mees Dolly," may in retrospect be seen to have reflected and perhaps even fed into the doubts about empire that were gaining momentum in this period, even if its author, Sir George MacMunn, himself seemed to possess no qualms about the blessings of British rule. MacMunn had served many years in the British Indian military, had written numerous essays and books on matters military and historical, and perhaps was best known as the author of the martial race theory in Indian army circles. Thus he was well versed in the nineteenth-century primary source material. What had drawn MacMunn's attention and would eventually lead to his discovery of "Mees Dolly" was a stray reference in a letter of June 8, 1857, from W. Henry Norman, who had served as adjutant general of the force that besieged Delhi, to his wife in

---

[15] Savarkar, *First War*, pp. 186–87; for the follow-up reference to Azizan, see p. 197. Azizan, or "Azeezun" as she was often called, is well attested in the historical record, though whether she traded sex in exchange for patriotic service is not known. As we shall see later, she was a more complicated figure than Savarkar allows.

[16] MacMunn, "Mees Dolly," pp. 327–331. This and the following two paragraphs are drawn from this source. I am grateful to Clare Anderson for first alerting me, many years ago, to the "Mees Dolly" story as told by the journalist and popular historian P. J. O. Taylor (see later in the chapter).

[17] The best known of these by English writers were Edward Thompson, *The Other Side of the Medal* (London: Hogarth Press, 1925), and F. W. Buckler's 1922 essay, "The Political Theory of the Indian Mutiny," republished in M. N. Pearson, ed., *Legitimacy and Symbols: The South Asian Writings of F. W. Buckler* (Ann Arbor: University of Michigan Press, 1985).

Simla. "By the way," Norman wrote, "I must mention that a European woman was hung [sic] at Meerut, being implicated in the arrangements for the first outbreak."[18] According to MacMunn, Norman possessed a spotless reputation as a man of supreme judgment, as someone unlikely to write anything that was not an unimpeachable fact, especially "to that anxious gathering of women and wounded in the hills, already agog with every piece of ill-considered gossip." Yet, MacMunn observed, "never in any story or in any history has any hint of such a supreme tragedy" – namely, the hanging of a European woman for involvement in the Mutiny – "ever been given." The mystery had, he wrote, "always intrigued me greatly", not least because no one else seemed to have noticed the passage. Even two of Norman's sons, whom MacMunn knew well, knew nothing about it – though they, like MacMunn, insisted that Norman "would never have mentioned it if it had not been true." MacMunn "hunted high and low, in highways and byways, for any record or dispatch or memoir or anything in the summaries of events in the Meerut district or what was then the North-West Provinces." To no avail: "the history [was] silent, completely silent."

MacMunn originally had noticed the Norman reference in 1912 or 1913. In 1920 he became the grand master of the Freemasons in the Punjab, a position that afforded him frequent opportunity to travel to various "stations" and interact with "many of what are known as the domiciled community of India" – some "pure European, whether born in India or in the United Kingdom, others are of mixed descent."[19] For someone upon whom "the romance of the Great Sepoy Mutiny has always had the deepest hold," this new position afforded him an exciting new avenue of research. At one such Masonic meeting, MacMunn was directed to "a Mutiny man" – as veterans of the conflict were known. Engaging the ancient veteran, whom he referred to as "old Tom Maginnis,"[20] in conversation, he soon learned that not only had he been

---

[18] This passage occurs in *The Memoirs of Field Marshall Sir Henry Wylie Norman*, ed. and arr. Sir William Lee-Warner (London: Smith, Elder, & Co., 1908), p. 68, in the context of an extended engagement on June 8 during which "the 75th are said to have killed a European, formerly in the artillery, who had directed the fire on us."

[19] See the biographical note included in the "Guide to the Papers of Lieutenant-General Sir George MacMunn [MSS 021]," Special Collections, University of New South Wales, for a concise summary of MacMunn's career. He served in India in 1892–1897 (Burma), 1904–1914, and 1920–1924.

[20] MacMunn indicated in a footnote ("Mees Dolly," p. 329n1) that this was not his real name; presumably he changed it for the essay, to protect the veteran's privacy. "Maginnis" allegedly told MacMunn that when the uprising occurred, he had been a "Trumpeter in the Bengal Horse Artillery Depot at Meerut." A few days after May 10, he "was sent to the Khaki Risallah as a trumpeter." According to appendix I of G. W. Williams, "Narrative of Events Connected with the Outbreak in 1857," there were a total

at Meerut, he had served as a trumpeter in the storied volunteer force known as the "Khakee Risallah." MacMunn's pulse quickened: the Khakee Risallah had fought far and wide in the Meerut district, putting down the rebellion and restoring order. He asked the old man whether he had ever heard of "any European woman joining the mutineers, or having anything to do with them." After stroking his long beard and sipping some whisky, the aged one hesitantly recalled that a couple of Eurasian women had been carried off, though he did not remember that they had actually joined the rebel cause. Then a glimmer of recollection lit his eye: "Wait now, sir, while I think ... I wonder if you are speaking of Miss Dolly – 'Mees' Dolly, as I've heard them natives call her."

MacMunn eventually concluded that the details that emerged from his interview with the aged "Maginnis" were "probably the foundation of Captain Norman's letter."[21] He began with the context: "In most Bazaars attached to large cantonments now and again some unfortunate European or Eurasian women have at one time or another established themselves. In these days no English woman would be allowed to remain in such a position, though to this day at times some of mixed parentage may be found." MacMunn then referred the reader to that "wonderful book of the Indian Mutiny" in which "Mrs. Steele [sic] has told the story, well known at the time, of how the courtesans in the Bazaar had started the outbreak at Meerut, by jeering at the men of the Light Cavalry." As noted earlier, MacMunn preferred Steel's to all the other Mutiny novels – and histories – that had appeared in the previous half century. "But," he noted, "even Mrs. Steele [sic] has not told of 'Mees' Dolly." MacMunn continued:

---

of six trumpeters in the Risallah who had been attached to two Bengal horse regiments at Meerut (the 3rd Light Cavalry and the 4th Lancers). Of these, five were Europeans, and of these five, two were named McKinlay – one from each regiment.

[21] For a skeptical reading, see Kim Wagner, *The Great Fear of 1857* (London: Peter Lang, 2010), pp. 133, 276–277n16, who writes that "[a]ppealing as the story may be, it is completely unsubstantiated." While it is true that no other sources on Mees Dolly have appeared, and that it is hard to know what to make of MacMunn's tale, I take a more agnostic position. There were numerous cases of British "regimental women," that is, officially sanctioned wives of men in the Queen's regiments, who fell afoul of regulations for dabbling in the illicit sale of native liquor; some of these drifted to the bazaar to set up houses of refreshment-cum-brothels. See, e.g., the case of Sarah Duff of Dinapore, in 22–23 of May 16, 1851, Military Consultations, National Archives of India (hereafter MC, NAI), New Delhi. Duff, the wife of a private in Her Majesty's 80th Foot, "had established herself in the Bazar where she became such a nuisance that the Cant. Magistrate on application removed her from its limits. She has however fixed her residence in one of the many Bazars in the vicinity of this Regt and her house is the resort of all the worthless characters in it." The remainder of the consultation file makes clear that this was not an isolated problem.

It seemed that a European woman lived in the Saddar Bazaar at Meerut, and Maginnis thought that she was pure white, "but country-born,[22] like myself, sir." Rumour had it that she was the widow of a sergeant, and had been in trouble for theft, and had eventually drifted to the Bazaar. A fortnight after the outbreak at Meerut, just after the troops had marched against Delhi under Brigadier Wilson, the Khaki Risallah scouring the country had found a European woman about to drive away from a small bungalow, apparently derelict, in the Stud Farm at Hapur.[23] She was, he remembered, brought in under escort, and he had heard, he thought, that she was wanted for egging on the mutineers and helping at the murder of two Eurasian girls who also lived in the Bazaar. " ... I soon went on to Delhi, sir, and I think I remember hearing she was popped [executed]."

MacMunn acknowledged that by the end of their interview, "Maginnis was really pretty hazy, and I found after a bit that he was prepared to agree to any suggestion that I made to help the story out." Still, MacMunn was convinced of the truth of the tale and was certain it substantiated Norman's letter to his wife. Piecing together bits and pieces of "stories that I had heard elsewhere," MacMunn surmised that Mees Dolly had "drifted to the Bazaar after some lawless life of adventure, following possibly on a conviction for theft ... , and kept a house of refreshment of sorts." Eventually, "no doubt enraged by the cold shoulder shown to her on all sides," she "had turned sour, and was found on the side of the mutineers" – like so many others "[r]ight through history" who "go sour against their own folk." His final lines summed up, for him, the moral of the story: "surely no tragedy of a waste product was ever greater. *Sunt lacrymae rerum.*"[24]

Possibly one reason MacMunn was drawn toward a tragic rendering of the "Mees Dolly" story is that, by the time he was writing, "no English woman would be allowed to remain in such a position." Whether or not this was true (and the work of Ashwini Tambe and Harald Fischer-Tiné suggests otherwise[25]), there is no question but that matters of race loomed large for MacMunn. It is easier to explain why he avoided telling the story of Mees Dolly as a tale of imperial irony: He did not subscribe to the theory (*pace* Wilson) that the uprising was the result of a

---

[22] That is, born in India.
[23] It should be noted that there is no mention of "Mees Dolly" or anyone remotely resembling her being captured at the stud farm at Hapur in either Williams' narrative or in Dunlop, *Service and Adventure with the Khakee Ressalah.*
[24] There are tears for misfortune.
[25] Ashwini Tambe, *Codes of Misconduct: Regulating Prostitution in Late Colonial Bombay* (Minneapolis: University of Minnesota Press, 2009); Harald Fischer-Tiné, "'White Women Degrading Themselves to the Lowest Depths': European Networks of Prostitution and Colonial Anxieties in British India and Ceylon ca. 1880–1914," *Indian Economic and Social History Review* 40 (2003): 163–190.

premeditated conspiracy that had run off the rails due to a premature eruption of violence. Indeed, he did not mention Wilson at all in his 1927 essay. In a later work he would write that "[t]he less responsible accounts of the Mutiny have talked of plots and plans, but the careful enquiries made afterwards quite failed to produce any evidence of such."[26] If no simultaneous strike had been planned, there would be no reason to think that a premature eruption at Meerut somehow doomed the prospects for success. Irony was therefore, for MacMunn, an inappropriate register for narrating the tale of Mees Dolly. He preferred tragedy.

The task of harnessing "Mees Dolly" to irony would fall to the journalist and amateur Mutiny historian P. J. O. Taylor, writing in the late 1980s and 1990s (see later in this chapter). Meanwhile the women of the Meerut bazaar continued to make appearances in the historical literature, albeit in a more cursory and uneven manner. In his centenary account, *The Sepoy Mutiny and Revolt of 1857*, R. C. Majumdar referred to how "the people at large, and even some courtesans, taunted the sepoys for their pusillanimity" after the humiliation of the ironing parade.[27] By contrast, the official centenary volume by S. N. Sen, *Eighteen Fifty-Seven*, ignored altogether Wilson's account of the humiliations leveled by the women of the bazaar, but did mention that "[a] maid servant heard from a Kashmiri girl or her mother that the sepoys were contemplating an armed rising, and the sepoys heard that two thousand pairs of iron had been made ready and it was intended to disarm all the Indian troops." But, Sen added, "the city people took no notice of these rumours, the shops opened as usual and business went on as smoothly as ever and the normal crowds thronged the city roads and thoroughfares." This passage in Sen is clearly based on the depositions collected in 1858 by G. W. Williams, the superintendent of police – though, as we shall see in the following section, Sen took some liberties with this source.[28]

---

[26] Sir George MacMunn, *The Indian Mutiny in Perspective* (London: G. Bell & Sons, 1931), p. 39. He adds here: "The story that some men of the 3rd Cavalry had been taunted by the courtezans [sic] of the bazaar is true." Curiously, in the same volume he later writes (p. 185) that "[t]here is a strange allusion in Norman's letters from Delhi to one of the Directors of the East India Company, of a European woman 'hung at Meerut for her share in the Mutiny there' to which no clue is available." Perhaps he'd come to distrust Maginnis' story of "Mees Dolly"?

[27] R. C. Majumdar, *The Sepoy Mutiny and Revolt of 1857* (Calcutta: Firma K. L. Mukhopadhyay 1957), p. 50.

[28] Sen, *Eighteen Fifty-Seven*, p. 59. Sen dismissed out of hand Wilson's conspiracy theory, p. 402. Majumdar, for his part, was open to the possibility of a pre-existing conspiracy, and cites Wilson among others in support; see Majumdar, *The Sepoy Mutiny and Revolt of 1857*, pp. 204–207.

The women of the Meerut bazaar reappear in what is often regarded as the most popular British treatment of 1857 written in the twentieth century, namely, Christopher Hibbert's 1978 classic, *The Great Mutiny: India 1857*. Hibbert took a novel approach to the bazaar women, however: Instead of following the script laid down by Wilson, Kaye, Steel, and Savarkar, he described the women's taunts in such a way as to *undercut* their agency in sparking the uprising:

> Several officers of this regiment [the 20th] had been sitting quietly talking in their Commanding Officer's bungalow when they had been called down to the men's lines where about seventy badmashes from the bazaar were clamouring outside the regimental magazine. Some sepoys, it was said, had assured the prostitutes in the bazaar – who were taunting them with their failure to rescue their imprisoned comrades – that they need not worry, for the native troops were going to mutiny that very evening; and a rumor had since got about that the European soldiers had been ordered to disarm all the native regiments. By the time the officers arrived in the lines both the sepoys and the rabble of the bazaar appeared dangerously close to violence.[29]

Hibbert's account departs considerably from Wilson's, so much so that it would appear to be based on a possible third source. Unfortunately, a scouring of the possible sources fails to satisfy. The three sources that Hibbert relied upon for this section of text are a memoir by Sir Hugh Gough entitled *Old Memories*, a section of N. A. Chick's *Annals of the Indian Rebellion*, and letters of Roland Richardson of Kirkland held in the National Library of Scotland. None of these provide support for the claim that the sepoys of the 20th had reassured the prostitutes of the bazaar that they were in fact going to rise up on that very afternoon/evening, on May 10.[30] In fact, they don't mention the women of the bazaar at all.

The phenomenal success of Hibbert's volume reflected a renewed interest in the history of the British Raj in India, particularly during moments of empire *in extremis* – a postimperial nostalgia that some critics

---

[29] Christopher Hibbert, *The Great Mutiny: India 1857* (New York: Penguin, 1978), p. 82.

[30] Hibbert wrote for a popular audience and unfortunately adopted a loose citation style. Though the passage occurs on p. 82, the only possible note that conceivably refers to it is note 27 on p. 83; the brief endnote text is on p. 405. Chick's *Annals* is a compilation of sources; the text in Chick cited by Hibbert is from W. H. Carey, *The Mahomedan Rebellion; its Preminitory Symptoms, Outbreak and Suppression; with an Appendix* (Roorkee: Directory Press, 1857), pp. 41–43. It is also included in *Freedom Struggle in Uttar Pradesh*, vol. 6, Rizvi (ed.), pp. 26–28. The Gough reference is Sir Hugh Gough, *Old Memories*. I am grateful to Dr. Maria Castrillo, curator of manuscripts and archives at the National Library of Scotland, for her assistance with the Richardson of Kirkland letters.

derided as "the rage for the Raj."[31] Richard Attenborough's *Gandhi* would appear in cinemas in 1982; David Lean's filmic interpretation of E. M. Forster's *Passage to India* soon followed; Paul Scott's *Jewel in the Crown* likewise attracted large British and American audiences. The "rage for the Raj" was not restricted to Western audiences however: P. J. O. Taylor began a popular column for the *Statesman* newspaper (simultaneously published in Delhi and Calcutta) in the late 1980s offering nuggets from the British Indian past; and one of his first (and easily the most popular of his) contributions on the subject of 1857 was about "Mees Dolly".

Whereas MacMunn was gripped by the tragic quality of the Mees Dolly story, Taylor presented it as a supremely ironic misadventure, so much so that it teetered on the edge of a Monty Pythonesque imperial farce. Taylor did this by making recourse to Wilson's theory of premature eruption brought on by "the spark which fell from female lips," the lips of the "frail ones of the Meerut bazaar". Thus in Taylor's reading "Mees Dolly" – a "fallen" British woman scorned by her own race – condemned the British Empire but saved it in the process, all in the same breath. He concluded his piece thus:

She was well-known in the bazar: I cannot prove it – and nobody will ever be able to do so now – but it might well have been her house that the troopers frequented: it is fascinating to think that it might have been from her lips that the fateful taunts came! ... What if the "female lips" were those of Mees Dolly? Then she may be said to have saved, quite inadvertently, the British Raj in India: with hindsight perhaps the authorities might not have hanged her![32]

There is more to Taylor than meets the eye. MacMunn is obviously the source for Taylor's piece, even to the point of adopting his phrasing – e.g., his reference to Mees Dolly having "turned sour." Yet Taylor fails to credit him as the source or mention him at all. And it turns out that MacMunn was not the only author that Taylor drew upon in his essay. He also appropriated large chunks of Steel's chapter on Meerut (cited earlier), likewise without mentioning her, and passed it off as dialogue

---

[31] Anita Desai, "The Rage for the Raj: How the Festival of India Lost India," *The New Republic* 193, 22 (November 25, 1985): 26. Desai's essay focuses on Paul Scott's multivolume novel *The Raj Quartet* (New York: Morrow, 1976).

[32] P. J. O. Taylor, "Mees Dolly," in *A Companion to the "Indian Mutiny" of 1857* (Delhi: Oxford University Press, 1996), pp. 217–218. Similar versions appear in P. J. O. Taylor, *A Star Shall Fall: India 1857* (New Delhi: Indus, 1993), pp. 234–237; *Chronicles of the Mutiny and Other Historical Sketches* (New Delhi: Indus, 1992), pp. 21–24; and, before that, in Taylor's column for *The Statesman* (New Delhi), October 6, 1989. The only reference to any sources on Mees Dolly in Taylor's account is a cryptic aside that "if I ever get to visit a certain Regimental Museum, who knows, I might find her real name." There is no mention of MacMunn who is clearly Taylor's main source.

from the historical record. This included Steel's wording for the taunts flung at the soldiers, the soldiers' own frenzied exclamations in response, and even Steel's wry comment on Mutiny historiography. Here is Taylor:

> "We have no kisses for cowards!" was the cry. Were they really men, they were asked, to allow their comrades to be fitted with anklets of iron and led off to prison? And for what? Because they would not swerve from their creed! Go and rescue them, they were told, before coming to us for kisses. Who was the first to break under the jeers? We shall never know his name. But suddenly the cry went up: "To horse! To horse, brothers! To the gaol, to our comrades!" And the Great "Mutiny" had begun. No consideration of caste, or religion or patriotism. ... just a taunt from a pair of painted lips!

It will be recalled that Steel had introduced her novel by noting that she had tried to write both a story and a history, but that it was up to her readers to decide whether she had succeeded in either. Apparently, at least if Taylor is any judge, she had succeeded only too well. Taylor had turned her invented dialogue into the stuff of history. Purists may object that Taylor was merely a journalist and Mutiny buff, an amateur historian at best. Be that as it may, two recent histories of 1857 have deployed Taylor's ventriloquism of Steel (and, of course, MacMunn) in their own reconstruction of events at Meerut. Indeed, Jane Robinson (*Angels of Albion: Women of the Indian Mutiny*) and Saul David (*The Indian Mutiny: 1857*) not only adopt Taylor's close paraphrasing of Steel as historically factual, they unequivocally identify Mees Dolly as the main prostitute of the bazaar who ("with her sisters", in Robinson's case) rebuffs the advances of the disconsolate men of the 3rd Light Cavalry with the retort, "we have no kisses for cowards!"[33]

★★★

Was "Mees Dolly" too good – or, to paraphrase Mae West, too bad – to be true? More generally, did the courtesans or prostitutes of the Meerut bazaar really spark off the single greatest armed challenge to the British Empire in the nineteenth century? More generally still, what was the nature of the relationship between these women and the "native" soldiery?

---

[33] Jane Robinson, *Angels of Albion: Women of the Indian Mutiny* (London: Viking, 1996), pp. 30, 32; and Saul David, *The Indian Mutiny: 1857* (London: Viking, 2002), p. 84. To her credit, Robinson also cites MacMunn; but given the way she attributes Steel's script to Mees Dolly, it is clear that her main source is Taylor (the version she cites is *Chronicles of the Mutiny and other Sketches*, 24). David simply cites Robinson, *Angels of Albion*, 30, 32.

I return to these questions momentarily, and in the chapters that follow. What the foregoing suggests, however, is that the image of the anti-imperial bazaar prostitute captured the imagination of numerous writers during the course of the nineteenth and twentieth centuries. And not just writers. It is difficult to imagine a more colorful confirmation of the image of the spirited 1857 prostitute than the character "Heera" portrayed by Rani Mukherjee in Aamir Khan's 2007 film, *The Rising: The Ballad of Mangal Pandey*.[34] True to Bollywood form, there is much in the way of historical invention: While "Heera" clearly feels nothing but contempt for her British clients, she and her fellow "nautch girls" are not portrayed in the role of revolutionary spine stiffeners. Though Heera and her colleagues do prompt some patriotic soul-searching on the part of Aamir Khan's Mangal Pandey early in the plot (this occurs while they are being inspected for "venereal diseases" when the injured hero is brought to the cantonment clinic after being viciously beaten by some British officers), Heera ultimately ends up serving as one of two dewy-eyed supporting actors who are torn by their transgressive love for Aamir Khan's nobly savage Mangal Pandey – the other being Captain Gordon, played by Toby Stephens.[35]

What to make of all this? The English-language *reading* public – in India and Britain – seems to have long been captivated by the prospect of the British Empire brought to its knees and inadvertently saved by "fallen women," even (or especially) when it was revealed that one of those fallen women may have been British. Whether the register was irony, romance, tragedy, or farce, there seems to have been something deeply satisfying about locating causative agency with lowly bazaar women involved in the sex trade. For some, the tale seems to have functioned at a mythic level as a kind of providential redemption of the imperial project, as though woman had stood forth to test British resolve in a trial by fire and, in preordaining Britain's triumph, thereby served to forgive Britons of their myriad sins. But for Bollywood audiences, it would appear that a drama in which women are agents is largely out of bounds, especially when it comes to such a sensitive historical topic as 1857.

---

[34] *The Rising: The Ballad of Mangal Pandey*, dir. Ketan Mehta (Yash Raj Films, 2005), 2h 30m.

[35] Gordon's "bromantic" attentions are eventually distracted by the appearance of a soon-to-be immolated widow (or *sati*), thus completing the gender stereotypes. Mangal Pandey was stationed at Barrackpore and his single-handed mutiny and subsequent execution on April 8, while indisputably real, did not open the floodgates of rebellion across northern India – Amitabh Bachhan's concluding narration notwithstanding. For a wide-ranging and insightful discussion of the historiographical implications of "The Rising," see Dipesh Chakrabarty and Rochona Majumdar, "Mangal Pandey: Film and History," *Economic and Political Weekly* 42, 19 (May 12–18, 2007): esp. p. 1774.

Deposition

In the wake of the uprising, indeed even as its dying embers were being extinguished, the superintendent of police for the North-Western Provinces, G. W. Williams, was deputed to investigate the violence at Meerut and Kanpur (Cawnpore). The principal object of his investigations at Meerut was to confirm or refute reports that the recently established police constabulary had taken a lead in the killing spree that followed the military revolt by the 3rd Light Cavalry and the 20th Native Infantry (along with large portions of the 11th Native Infantry). Williams also sought to determine whether and to what degree the uprising there was the result of a premeditated conspiracy. As regards the former question, there could be no doubt: Not only were most of the police clearly guilty of "culpable negligence, and willful disregard of their first duty as policemen, i.e. to afford every assistance in quelling the disturbance, and saving life and property," but Williams also noted that "Europeans were murdered in the Sudder Bazar, in many instances, in close proximity to Police Stations," and that "others were assaulted by men in the police uniform." Even the officiating kotwal, who "on one occasion ... succeeded in dispersing a band of plunderers", himself "subsequently prevented any seizures being made, either of persons or property, fearing the personal revenge of the mob." He also apparently went out of his way to protect "his own fraternity, the Goojurs."[36]

As to the question of premeditation and conspiracy, Williams expressed guarded skepticism. He acknowledged that there was plenty of evidence regarding a growing sense of ill-feeling among the soldiery concerning their religion, that the cantonment and bazaar were rife with rumor, and that there was even some early information circulating on the day of the outbreak that an uprising was afoot. Nonetheless, he noted that statements about the prior existence of ominous signs and later allegations of conspiracy all "vanished ghostlike into thin air" when investigated. At the end of his memorandum, Williams threw down a gauntlet: "Those therefore who have received any information regarding such a conspiracy should undoubtedly come forward and have the same attested, both for the punishment of the guilty, and for the security of the public hereafter." For good measure, he added:

If any such plot throughout the Native Army existed, the Meerut troops were indeed rash and insane to mar the whole, simply that they might hasten the release of their companions, which a short time subsequently could have been

---

[36] Williams, "Memorandum," pp. 1, 4.

effected with far greater chances of success, less risk to themselves, and with infinitely grander results to the cause they had at heart. Granting the existence of such a conspiracy, how can we account for such mad rashness on the part of these conspirators?[37]

Williams submitted his report from Allahabad on November 15, 1858. Wilson would submit his report nearly six weeks later, on December 24, from Calcutta. Significantly, Wilson would introduce his report with his theory of premeditated conspiracy, the taunts of the frail ones, and the premature eruption at Meerut.

Were Williams and Wilson engaged in a kind of proxy debate on the question of conspiracy and premature eruption? This seems certain in retrospect, though neither mentions the other's name in their respective reports. "How can we account for such mad rashness on the part of these [hypothetical] conspirators?" Williams asked. Wilson's response, of course, was that the manly pride of the men of the 3rd Light Cavalry and 20th Native Infantry had been called into question by the only group that could have done so with any serious effect, who truly understood the ins and outs of manhood, namely, the "frail ones of the Meerut bazaar." Indeed, as noted at the beginning of this chapter, Williams seems to have tried to anticipate this argument, suggesting that he may have had some prior intimation of Wilson's theories: Recall that in his summary narrative of the outbreak at Meerut, Williams noted that he had "also been informed that the men were taunted by the disreputable inhabitants of the Sudder Bazar for allowing their brethren to suffer on account of their religion, and the cry of 'Deen, deen,' was even thus early raised." But in the very next sentence Williams made clear that he had doubts about the truth of the story (see the italicized portion of the following quoted passage). That he did not refer specifically to bazaar *women* is noteworthy. The reason for this may have been that he possessed markedly different evidence regarding the women of the bazaar, in the form of a young woman named Sophie. He alluded to it in that same next sentence:

However, *whether the foregoing be true or not*, the decision of an appeal to arms, most probably was arrived at on Saturday or Sunday; as the depositions prove that the Cashmerian Girl, Sophie, received an intimation of the coming outbreak from a sepoy, at about 2 p.m. on the day of the revolt, which passed on to the mother of Mussumat Golab Jaun; it, through the latter, reached the ears of the late Dr. Smith; but he, as many others would have done, treated it merely as an idle bazar report, such as prevailed even before sentence was passed on the Sowars.[38]

[37] Williams, "Memorandum," p. 12.
[38] Williams, "Memorandum," pp. 5–6 (emphasis added).

70 Humiliation

Not unlike debates over the legal status of sati in the early nineteenth century, Williams and Wilson seemed to be relying on women to score points in a debate over whether 1857 was a premeditated conspiracy gone awry.[39] No doubt this seemed like a matter of great import at the time. By the late twentieth century, by contrast, the issue had taken on the quality of spectacle. For historians in the early twenty-first century, the outcome of this debate matters not at all. However, the details of the evidence adduced on both sides should concern us: Not only do those details bring us closer to historical actors who have for too long been neglected, but bazaar women and the way cantonment men interacted with them offer clues to understanding the way that gender and sexuality and emotion and manliness structured the hybrid space of the cantonment and sustained military power and British rule in India.[40] We have received some glimpses of this, albeit through a glass darkly, with respect to the bazaar women originally invoked in the narrative of Wilson – and in the literarily inflected derivations thereof by Wilson's many successors. Now it is time to let Sophie and her fellow "Cashmerians" have their say.

Williams recorded seventy-one depositions at Meerut. He was deputed to the task "at the close of 1857" and he submitted his report in mid-November 1858. We may presume his first order of business was identifying his witnesses and taking their statements, and that this occurred in the first four or five months of 1858. He would have then spent the summer months, possibly in one of the hill stations, studying the testimonies, cross-checking facts, and communicating with subordinates in Meerut to gather additional evidence to clarify unresolved issues. October would have been set aside for drafting his introductory memorandum and organizing his evidence. Witnesses included sepoys, residents of the bazaar and town, merchants, clerks, servants, laborers, policemen, and civilian employees.

The depositions of the "Cashmerian" women begin with that of "Mussumut Golab Jaun," no. 32. This is followed by no. 33, the deposition of "Mussumat Zeenut," and no. 34, "Mussumut Sophie." Deposition no. 35 was a brief follow-up report by the officiating kotwal who checked on statements made by Sophie. They are given here in their entirety:

---

[39] And as noted earlier, this "debate" continued in the centenary histories of Sen and Majumdar in 1957.
[40] Cf. Durba Mitra, *Indian Sex Life: Sexuality and the Colonial Origins of Modern Social Thought* (Princeton: Princeton University Press, 2020), and the way prostitution structured social scientific and medical discourses on women and India in the late nineteenth and twentieth centuries.

Deposition

No. 32. – *Deposition of Mussumat Golab Jaun, Cashmerian, residing in the Sudder Bazar.* – At the time of the out-break, I was residing with the late Dr. Smith; was on that day in his house, and informed him of the intended out-break, of which, I heard from my mother; she learnt it from a Cashmerian girl, named Sophie, who was told by a sepoy, at about 2 p.m. on that day, that the troops would mutiny and massacre the Europeans. Dr. Smith replied, I always brought him bazar reports void of foundation, and took no notice of it.

I therefore quietly sat down, at about 5 or 6 p.m., sound of musketry was heard from the infantry lines, and all at once, I saw hundreds of men running towards the parade, after a while people began to rush into the bungalow. I begged my master to fly, but he refused, asking where we could go to; and we then stood by the garden hedge; meanwhile, my mother sent a dooly [*ḍolī*, covered sedan chair] for me from the sudder bazar, in which I left, my master remaining behind, the mob had not then entered the compound though crowds surrounded it. As I passed, they wished to kill me, but hearing I was a woman, allowed me to pass. The girl Sophie was turned out of the bazar, and her house knocked down.

No. 33. – *Deposition of Mussumat Zeenut, Cashmerian, residing in the Sudder Bazar.* – On the day of the out-break, I was residing in the sudder bazar. About 2 p.m. on that day, I heard from Mussumat Mehonee, mother of Sophie, that there was to be a disturbance that day, and that she had heard it from the sepoys, I did not believe it, still mentioned it to my daughter Golab Jaun. At 6 p.m., when I heard firing, I sent a dooly for her, I can give no information of the disturbance in the sudder bazar, I do not know where the Cashmerian girl Sophie is.

No. 34. – *Deposition of Mussumat Sophie, Cashmerian, residing in the City of Meerut.* – At the time of the out-break, the date of which I do not remember, I was residing in the sudder bazar, on the day it occurred no one was in my house, but Goolam Hossain, my servant. At 4 o'clock, Pundit Dhurm Narain, who was formerly in the office of the Meerut cantonment joint magistrate, came to my house, but left, when the out-break commenced, to return home, I then closed the doors; my mother is named Mehree, she left for Loodhiana, some two months before the out-break. I reported her departure at the cotwalie, I never heard of the out-break before it commenced. The sowars and sepoys did not frequent my house.

No. 35. – *Report of Bukhtawur Singh, officiating Cotwal of the Sudder Bazar, Meerut.* – Agreeably to orders received, I made enquiries of the neighbours of Mussumat Sophie, and learned that sowars were in the habit of visiting the house, and that her mother had left previous to the out-break; her house, with others in that neighbourhood, was razed to the ground.[41]

---

[41] "Depositions Taken at Meerut, by Major G. W. Williams, Superintendent of Police, N.W.P.," pp. 23–24. Though far less prominent in literary fiction than Wilson's "frail ones," Williams' "Cashmerians" also make an appearance in the Mutiny novel in the form of the composite character "Sophie" who is alluded to in a brief dialogue in J. F.

There is much of interest in these statements. For instance: The relationship between bazaar women and the civil authorities, the military, and the medical profession (Dr. Smith was, Williams informs us elsewhere, a surgeon on the "veteran's establishment");[42] the role of "bazaar women" and the circulation of information; the relationship between the bazaar and the cantonment as hybrid space; "bazaar women" and respectability ("Mussumat" is equivalent to "Miss" and suggests that these women were not simply "common" prostitutes, a term with its own particular logic; Sophie had a servant, and Zeenut had the wherewithal to send a dooly for her daughter); daughters and their mothers; and, of course, the significance of the term "Cashmerian."

Let us first begin with Williams and how he read these depositions. The first and most basic conclusion that he drew from the statements by Golab Jaun and her mother Zeenut was that Sophie had been told by a sepoy at 2 pm that an outbreak of violence was imminent. Sophie, interestingly, denied this – and she also denied that her mother had passed on such information to Zeenut: Her mother, she claimed (correctly, according to the follow-up report by Bukhtawur Singh), had long since left for Ludhiana (and, she added – to further impeach Zeenut's report – "my mother is named Mehree"). For Williams, the fact that Sophie only learned of the impending violence at two in the afternoon constituted evidence that there was no premeditated conspiracy; rather, a sepoy or sowar close to Sophie had merely shared the information with her – perhaps so she could pass it along, to warn others (including especially the British), or perhaps he told her to impress her.[43]

More broadly, there is no mention in the depositions gathered by Williams of any taunting of the soldiery by the women of the bazaar.

F. (J. F. Fanthome), *Mariam: A Story of the Indian Mutiny* (Benares: The Chandraprabha Press, 1896), pp. 135–136. The story was based on the experiences of one Mrs. Lavater and her daughter Mariam during the Shahjahanpur rebellion. The author addresses the relation of history to fiction in his preface (pp. i–vi) and notes that he heard the story "from 'Mariam's' own lips." According to Rajat Kanta Ray, *The Felt Community: Commonalty and Mentality before the Emergence of Indian Nationalism* (Delhi: Oxford University Press, 2003), p. 475n39, "J. F. F." was a survivor of the Shahjahanpur massacre, in which Mariam's father was killed; the story was later retold by Ruskin Bond as "Flight of the Pigeons" and subsequently made into a film, *Junoon* (1979), dir. Shyam Benegal.

[42] Dr. T. Smith, surgeon for the 58th Regiment Native Infantry, had applied for and received permission to retire to the Meerut cantonment in 1852, which was approved the following year. See nos. 101–102 of November 12, 1852 and 78–79 of June 10, 1853, MP, NAI. He complained of a "rheumatism of old standing," due to which he had been allowed to go on medical leave for a year prior to his retirement.

[43] A close reader might ask whether this is where Hibbert got the idea that the soldiers were reassuring the prostitutes on Sunday that a revolt was planned. Possibly Hibbert was trying to reconcile Wilson's "frail ones" with Williams' "Cashmerians."

Deposition 73

If anything, bazaar women – "Cashmerians" according to the depositions, whose line of work Williams left unstated – were warning each other and, in Golab Jaun's case, her "master" (Dr. Smith) that violence was coming. What, then, provoked the soldiers to suddenly rise up in Williams' view? As noted in Chapter 1, Williams pointed to a rumor that was circulating after the ironing parade on May 9, that the two regiments were about to be disarmed in their entirety "and that sets of irons [that is, iron shackles for wrists and ankles] sufficient to confine the whole force" were "in course of preparation."[44] Two separate depositions spoke directly to this issue.[45] The first was by Kooman Singh, who had been a havildar in the 3rd Light Cavalry, who stated that "[a] rumor spread to the effect that 2,000 sets of irons, were ordered to be prepared in two nights and a day, for the rest of the men." Rundheer Sing, trooper of the 3rd Light Cavalry, gives slightly more detail:

Q. – Do you know whether the mutiny was preconcerted?
A. – No, the men objected to the cartridges, two naiks, Koodrut Ali, and Peer Ali, persuaded the men to take an oath to refuse them, till every regiment had consented to use them. After the 85 were sent to jail, *a report circulated, that two thousand sets of irons were being prepared for those who might still persist in refusing them.*
Q. – Where did you first hear this report?
A. – I cannot tell; it was spread abroad every where [*sic*].
Q. – Was the mutiny planned for the 10th May?
A. – No, nothing of the kind.

The image, then, of a markedly different kind of bracelets and anklets for men, was in the air in the afternoon and evening of May 9. Given this fact, it is reasonable to presume some connection between this fact and the bracelet/anklet imagery employed in the gender inversion taunts recorded by Wilson. However, it would be a mistake to simply conclude that the rumor about 2,000 shackles somehow evolved over time into a story about the men being taunted by the women in terms that employed gender inversion and the bracelet imagery. It seems equally plausible to conclude that the shackling rumor prompted snide remarks and even taunts on the evening of May 9, and that the women of the bazaar may have taken a part or even the lead in this.[46] It is worth noting in this

---

[44] Williams, "Memorandum," 6.
[45] Williams, "Depositions Taken at Meerut" (No. 12. – *Deposition of Kooman Singh, late Havildar in the 3rd Irregular Cavalry, now Wordee Major in the Mounted Police*, and No. 13. – *Deposition of Rundheer Sing, Trooper, of the 3rd Light Cavalry, now with the Mounted Police, at Meerut*).
[46] This is reflected, in fact, in Wilson's phrasing: "Your brethren have been ornamented with these anklets and incarcerated; and for what?"

context that the bracelet imagery is fairly common as a form of gendered ridicule in Bhojpuri, a regional language of eastern Uttar Pradesh and western Bihar that would have been familiar to many of the *sipāhī*s. Thus a 1971 study of Bhojpuri folk literature includes a song by women who tease men in terms that are strikingly similar to the imagery employed in Wilson's account:

> If you feel shy then hide in the house,
> O husband, not like a man but like a woman.
> Wear a sari and bangles and hide your face,
> We women would save your honor.
>
> *Lāge śaram lāj ghar meṅ baiṭh jāhu,*
> *Mard se banī ke lagāiyā āe harī,*
> *Pahirke sāṛī chūṛī muṅhvā chhipāi lehu,*
> *Rākhī ebi tohri pagariyā āe harī.*
>
> लगे शरम लाज घर में बैठ जाहु
> मर्द से बनी के लगाइया आए हरी
> पहिरके साड़ी चूड़ी मुंहवा छिपाइ लेहु
> राखी एबि तोहि पगड़िया आए हरी[47]

Thus, while Williams and Wilson stood on opposite sides on the question of conspiracy, they actually were less far apart than they themselves might have thought on the question of the gendered ridicule suffered by the men of the regiments. For Wilson, the humiliation of the men occurred at the hands of the women of the bazaar; for Williams, a more general sense of humiliation was in the air, due to the pervasive power of rumor backed by a general apprehension that the impending prospect of being stripped of one's uniform and being shackled with iron bracelets and anklets was more than simple punishment – it was inherently demeaning on gendered grounds. This explains, more so than the extreme heat of the day or the length of time it took to perform the ritual,

---

[47] Shridhar Mishra (*Bhojpuri Lok Sahitya – Sanskritik Adhyayan* [Bhojpuri Folk Literature – A Cultural Examination] [Allahabad: Hindustani Academy, 1971] [?], p. 158), cited in Pankaj Rag, *1857: The Oral Tradition* (New Delhi: Rupa, 2010), 43. I have derived the Devanagari from the Romanized version provided by Rag. The word for "bangles" used here is *chūṛī*. The term for honor is *pagaṛī*. Bhojpur was, with Awadh, a major recruiting ground for *pūrbiyān*, or "easterners," and became a center of the rebellion, particularly under the leadership of Kuar Singh of Jagdishpur in what was then Shahabad District in southwest Bihar. Despite the 1857 overtures of Rag's work, he does not mention the Meerut episode or the bazaar women. The folk ditty is cited, rather, to contextualize the gender symbolism in many of the songs about 1857, according to which martial prowess and bravery are associated with masculinity. For another song, comparing the Raja of Baundi (who remained loyal to the British) to an "irresponsible young woman," or *lauṅḍī* (lit., servant girl, promiscuous woman), see Rag, *1857: The Oral Tradition*, p. 167.

why "the condemned men made much outcry, taunting their comrades or appealing for rescue."[48] It seems the stage was set for a long, painful, and emotional night, whether or not the women of the bazaar themselves felt inspired to taunt the remaining men of the regiments.[49]

This brings us back to Sophie and the "Cashmerians", since they are the women whose voices have actually survived – shaped, of course, by the seen and unseen pressures of the official police record. Williams does not actually make note of the fact, but there is nothing in their depositions that directly contradicts Wilson. Let us review the depositions. Williams and his men first questioned Golab Jaun and then Zeenut. Golab Jaun noted, probably in response to what had been a follow-up question by Williams, that Sophie had been "turned out of the bazar, and her house knocked down." Apparently Zeenut was also questioned about Sophie's whereabouts, because after she described sending the dooly for her daughter, she remarked, "I can give no information of the disturbance in the sudder bazar, I do not know where the Cashmerian girl Sophie is." When Williams and his men finally tracked Sophie down, she was "residing in the City of Meerut." Thus she had found a new place, presumably in the main bazaar of the city, a mile or so south-southwest of the cantonment and its bazaar. She provides no information about why she was turned out of the sadr bazaar and her house knocked down, but her answers to Williams' questions make it clear that she was in no mood to be thought of as a British informant. Contrary to Golab Jaun and Zeenut's deposition, Sophie claimed she was home alone for most of the day, save for her servant, and that no soldiers visited her. The only visitor she had was one Dhurm Narain, "formerly in the office of the Meerut cantonment joint magistrate" she noted pointedly, but he left for home when the outbreak started. In fact, she denied in general that

---

[48] Palmer, *Mutiny at Meerut*, 68. Note that according to this recounting, the prisoners themselves seemed to be taunting or appealing to their fellow soldiers. The exact source for Palmer is unclear, but was probably the Kaye papers in the British Library. Cf. the young J. C. E. Macnabb's letter reproduced in Patrick Caddell, "The Outbreak of the Indian Mutiny," *Journal of the Society for Army Historical Research* 33, 135 (1955): 118–122, where the men are described as being fairly well behaved during the ironing parade, save for some weeping by brothers, fathers, and sons of the condemned men.

[49] On the despair and humiliation of the soldiers and the rumors flying around the cantonment and bazaar, see Wagner, *The Great Fear of 1857*, esp. pp. 131–134; Wagner includes in his narrative the taunts of the prostitutes (p. 133) as well as the shackling rumor (p. 134), but does not connect them. More important for Wagner is the fact that May 10 was the fifteenth day of Ramadan. Thus the violence took on the quality of a "sectarian riot" (pp. 143–144) – though Wagner notes (p. 145) also that such clashes "were never just about religion. They were inevitably tied to broader issues concerning access to resources, or commercial and economic competition, or were brought about by the intervention of the colonial state."

sepoys and sowars visited her house. She denied knowing about the outbreak beforehand. She denied that her mother was even in Meerut, let alone passing information to Zeenut. Indeed, she even denied that her mother was named "Mehonee," which is the name Zeenut had used for her.

It would appear Sophie was nervous. We never learn why, according to Golab Jaun, she was turned out of the bazaar. Bukhtawur Singh reported that "her house, with others in that neighbourhood, was razed to the ground," suggesting that he did not believe (or did not want to give the impression) that she was being singled out by the bazaar mob. But neither did he explicitly state that the mob *did not* turn her out of the bazaar. He did note that, contrary to what Sophie had alleged, "sowars [cavalrymen] *were* in the habit of visiting the house" (emphasis added). On the other hand, Bukhtawur Singh confirmed a different part of Sophie's evidence, namely, that her mother had left Meerut long before May 10. For her part, Sophie seemed to avoid the issue of whether she had been turned out of the bazaar and her house knocked down – or if she did confirm these facts, they were not included in the written deposition.

Sophie's careful answers to Williams' questions, particularly in light of what appear to be the more forthcoming statements from Zeenut and Golab Jaun, suggest some dissembling on her part or, at the very least, a firm reluctance to talk. Possibly she felt exposed, and that she had suffered enough. If we allow that her house was torn down and that she was turned out of the bazaar (and there would seem to be no reason for skepticism), then it seems likely that these "facts" – particularly the latter – had something to do with the politics of the mob. Was Sophie being punished for having passed information about the uprising? Could word have gotten around so quickly to this effect? Or perhaps she already had a reputation for being a source of information for the authorities, and the mob decided to take the opportunity of the mayhem on May 10 to punish her for it. This would explain her reluctance to admit to anything during the deposition.[50]

Sophie may have been caught between two worlds in other ways. At first glance, the term "Cashmerian" suggests that Sophie and company were simply Kashmiris. Certainly this is possible. But often in the eighteenth and nineteenth centuries the term Kashmiri obscured more

---

[50] It is noteworthy that Azizun of Kanpur adopts a similar ambivalent stance and denies everything. In her case, her involvement in the rebellion is very clear. I am grateful to Prof. Saumya Gupta of JDM College, Delhi University, for raising this point in a seminar at the Nehru Memorial Museum and Library in April 2013.

than it revealed, particularly in reference to women known colloquially by the British as "dancing girls" or "nautch girls." For whatever reason, but possibly having to do in part with their lighter skin, Kashmiri women were highly sought after. There is some evidence that female performers styled themselves (or were styled) Kashmiris so as to widen their market appeal. Probably the most famous case of this is Begam Samru of Sardhana, about whom several stories circulated concerning her parentage and place of origin, one version of which was that she was a Kashmiri of Georgian antecedents.[51] That she was early in life being conveyed about the Lahore-Delhi-Agra region as a slave-concubine-nautch-girl seems fairly certain.

Another indication of the appropriation of Kashmiri identity by non-Kashmiris to increase their value comes from early nineteenth-century Calcutta. According to a letter to the *Calcutta Journal* from 1819, signed "AN ARMENIAN," a "dancing girl" named "Bonnoo Jaun," who performed to great acclaim during that year's Durga Puja celebrations and who was described in the local press as a "Cashmerian," was in fact the daughter of one "Rutton" and an "English Merchant of Calcutta," unnamed. As the writer put it, "the above-named Girl is no more a *Cashmerian* than I am." He surmised that she had "been found fair enough to be passed off for a *CASHMERIAN*!" "AN ARMENIAN" could not resist adding that "She was on Wednesday last, publicly married for *three months only*, to a rich Mogul Merchant, who paid One Thousand Rupees in cash, as a Marriage Settlement, besides Two Hundred Rupees to be paid Monthly."[52] The salacious tone of the letter

---

[51] Thomas Bacon, *First Impressions and Studies from Nature in Hindostan*, vol. 2 (London: Wm. H. Allen and Co., 1837), p. 35, who claimed to have witnessed her *darbār* at Sardhana, wrote that "she was by birth Cashmerian, but by family Georgian. While quite a child, she was the companion of *Nauchnies*, for which life she was herself educated." See Michael Fisher, "Becoming and Making 'Family' in Hindustan," in Indrani Chatterjee (ed.), *Unfamiliar Relations: Family and History in South Asia* (Delhi: Permanent Black, 2004), pp. 95–98, 116n4–5, for a concise treatment of the various versions. Also: Mahendra Narain Sharma, *The Life and Times of Begam Samru of Sardhana (A.D. 1750–1836)* (Sahibabad: Vibhu Prakashan, 1985), pp. 59, 65n3. Sharma cites Bacon as well as a letter from Bussy to De Castries, March 3, 1874, Pondicherry Records, on her Kashmiri origins. He also reproduces (pp. 192–193) an 1836 letter of intelligence from the lieutenant governor of the North-Western Provinces to the governor general (no. 66 of May 23, 1836, Foreign Dept Political Consultations, National Archives of India), according to which Begam Samru was "said to have been a dancing girl or prostitute, procured by Company commission and sent from Delhi as a concubine to Walter Reynard [Reinhardt], commonly called Sombre corrupted by the Natives into Sumroo."

[52] Reproduced in *Selections from Indian Journals*, vol. 1, *Calcutta Journal*, comp. Satyajit Das (Calcutta: K. L. Mukhopadhyay, 1963), pp. 356–357 (emphases and full caps in the original).

aside, one might likewise presume that Golab Jaun had arrived at a not dissimilar arrangement with Dr. Smith of the Meerut veteran's establishment.

There would seem good reason, therefore, to not take the term "Cashmerian" at face value but rather treat it as a marker of professional accomplishment or assumed status, that the woman styling herself as such sought to convey the impression that she was a cut above the ordinary run-of-the-mill "nautch girl" or bazaar prostitute, as it were. It is likely that Sophie and the other "Cashmerians" were included under the category "Khangees [from *khāngī*] or Mussulman Prostitutes" in the Meerut cantonment census report from 1855, cited in Chapter 1.[53] The Meerut cantonment census juxtaposed Khangees, of whom there were seventy-eight, to "Kusbees" (from *kasbī*), numbering 133.[54] The letter from the man signing himself as "ARMENIAN" is also significant for the claim that the woman claiming Kashmiri identity was allegedly a product of "mixed" European-Indian birth. By the mid nineteenth century, the terms being used for such persons included "Eurasian," "East Indian," and, slightly later "Indo-British." As David Arnold and C. J. Hawes have persuasively argued, by the 1820s there were alarming numbers of destitute Eurasians swarming the larger stations in Bengal as well as "up the country" in what would become the North-Western Provinces. Numbers are hard to come by, but Hawes estimated that between 2,000 and 3,000 children, "many of them Eurasian," were being cared for in charitable institutions in the three presidency towns and "elsewhere in British India." But he added that,

[f]or each Eurasian child who was accommodated there was another should [*sic*: who?] could not be and who faced an adult life without education or training. In this inadequate provision lies one of the central reasons for the development of a large under-class of Eurasians whose existence was to cause such concern to British authority.[55]

---

[53] "Reports on Sudder Bazars," nos. 111–114 of July 13, 1855, MP, NAI, pp. 16–17. According to John T. Platts, *A Dictionary of Urdu, Classical Hindi, and English* (London: W. H. Allen & Co., 1884), p. 486, *khāngī* was from the Persian and was either an adjective meaning private, domestic, and household, or a noun connoting a "kept woman" or "clandestine prostitute."

[54] A total of 117 of the Kusbees were listed as "Dancing Girls" and sixteen as "Hindoo Prostitutes." Platts (*Dictionary*, p. 833) defines *kasbī* as "prostitute, harlot, courtezan [*sic*]."

[55] Hawes, *Poor Relations*, pp. 21–22. See also David Arnold, "Poor Europeans in India, 1750–1947," *Current Anthropology* 20, 2 (1979): 454–455; Fischer-Tiné, "'White Women Degrading Themselves to the Lowest Depths'"; and Harald Fischer-Tiné, '*Low and Licentious Europeans*': *Race, Class and White Subalternity in Colonial India* (New Delhi: Orient Longman, 2009).

Deposition 79

It seems reasonable to conclude that there were, therefore, thousands of Eurasian children in the major towns and cities with little or no means of regular support. By the 1840s, and despite the creation of orphanages in the 1820s to care for and educate those thousands of Eurasian children who "would now have been wandering around the lanes of the metropolis, in the most wretched and forlorn condition" (Hawes), the problem of "Eurasian paupers" would get worse. Even women who were, in theory, provided for by the regiments were a source of concern. For example, the authorities complained frequently about the tendency on the part of both native and "half-caste" wives attached to British regiments to turn to "illicit means of support" to make ends meet.[56] Partly this referred to the sale of illicit "native liquor" in the cantonment, but it seems clear that much anxiety was also due to the possibility that "regimental women" were engaging in what might be termed opportunistic sex work, that is, prostitution.[57]

Regimental women engaging in "misconduct" returns us to the realm of "Mees Dolly." Recall the euphemism MacMunn employed to refer to her initial line of work, namely, running a "house of refreshment." As we have seen, this was a common pattern and did not preclude sex work. But there is another reason MacMunn's "Mees Dolly" tale resonates here, in light of Sophie's apparent anxieties. Mees Dolly was hanged not simply for "egging on the mutineers" but also for "helping at the murder of two

---

[56] Hawes, *Poor Relations*, pp. 33, 42, 69 (for the latter quote).

[57] In addition to the case of Sarah Duff, described in note 21, see (for the "stoppage" of subsistence allowances for wives of British soldiers due to "misconduct") nos. 118–120 of February 6, 1852, MP, NAI, deemed "a complex issue that seems to begin with Mrs. Barker of the Queen's 80th Foot." Barker was accused of selling a glass of spirits to a soldier. Regulations concerning the conduct of regimental wives originated in the 1820s. Paying passage for "women of bad character" became a much-debated issue, as the government was reluctant to create a system whereby a woman of "profligate and abandoned character" might be incentivized to seek, via "misconduct," free passage to Europe, unaccompanied by her husband – a benefit denied "to the most respectable Soldier's Wife." (See nos. 213–215 of November 8, 1850, MP, NAI, concerning a Mrs. Rafter. The policy of arranging for free transport was terminated upon consideration of her case.) On "Mrs. Ceane, alias Ryan," a "woman of bad character" who was "turned out of Cantonments," see nos. 65–66 of February 28, 1851, MP, NAI. Ceane/Ryan was "twice convicted of selling spirits to the soldiery, imprisoned for 4 months, and the second time fined Rs. 500 which she paid (so she must have made a good trade of it!)." In the end, the government confirmed its unwillingness to incur the cost of her travel, observing: "if all the naughty women were to have free passages to Europe, the expense would be considerable in the course of the year." On the question of whether and how to return to Ireland the wives of gunners Shannon and Stack of the 3rd Troop, 2nd Brigade, Horse Artillery, Jullunder, who were convicted of adultery and deemed "infamous characters," "abandoned women," "incorrigible," "ungovernable women," and "a perfect nuisance in the Barracks" in the official correspondence, see nos. 151–152 of February 21, 1851, MP, NAI.

Eurasian girls who also lived in the Bazaar."[58] If Mees Dolly was, in fact, real,[59] and if Sophie was, in fact, a Eurasian styling herself a "Cashmerian" and (through her mother) passing information to the British, then we can begin to perceive an additional logic whereby Sophie might have preferred to remain quiet during her interrogation by Williams and his men. Losing your house is one thing. Losing your life is another.

~~~

The war began, as noted at the outset, in Meerut. If Wilson is to be believed – and, as we shall see in the Entr'acte chapter, there is an additional reason to believe him – it began in Meerut because the men of the 3rd Light Cavalry and 20th Native Infantry (and a large portion of the 11th Native Infantry) found themselves unable to withstand the emotional force of the taunts being leveled at them by women. This is further evidence that emotions were central to 1857.[60] But while 1857 may be understood thus, via emotion, as a proto-nationalist expression of a "felt" patriotism couched, *pace* Wagner, in terms of *fear* – fear of the loss of caste and religion – the initial, decisive explosion of violence at Meerut had, ironically, little to do with patriotism, caste, and religion. Rather, it had everything to do with gender and humiliation, or rather a fear of humiliation in terms of gender inversion. For some observers, this particular humiliation possessed a sharp sting because of the identity of those who delivered the taunts. As Flora Anne Steel put it, offering a wry comment on the way historians had sought to explain 1857 over the previous decades:

The word had been spoken. Nothing so very soul-stirring after all. No consideration of caste or religion, patriotism or ambition. Only a taunt from a pair of painted lips.[61]

---

[58] MacMunn, "Mees Dolly," p. 331. Taylor ("Mees Dolly," p. 217) puts it thus: "She was wanted for helping in the murder of two Eurasian girls and, significantly, for 'egging on the mutineers'. She was hanged." Taylor left out the detail that the girls "lived in the Bazaar."

[59] It is worth noting here that in 1850 one of the several women of the 75th Foot (an Irish regiment stationed at Umballah) whose subsistence allowance was suspended due to "misconduct" was a "Mrs. Esther Donnelly." See nos. 50–51 of May 17, 1850, MP, NAI. Donnelly would easily abbreviate to "Dolly." Umballah (now Ambala), like Meerut a major cantonment, was 100 miles north/northwest of Meerut. There was frequent movement between the two stations.

[60] Ray, *The Felt Community*. See also his *Exploring Emotional History: Gender, Mentality and Literature in the Indian Awakening* (Delhi: Oxford University Press, 2001).

[61] Steel, *On the Face of the Waters*, p. 191.

Whether or not we agree with Steel that the military revolt was the result of "a taunt from a pair of painted lips," it seems reasonable to conclude that the uprising at Meerut, without which 1857 (the event) would have unfolded quite differently or perhaps not at all, was the result of the men of the 3rd Light Cavalry, 20th Native Infantry, and (most of the) 11th Native Infantry facing the prospect of deep humiliation, a deep humiliation predicated on the question of gender and honor.

That prostitutes played a key role in 1857 has long been recognized – or rather, taken for granted. As should be evident from the first part of this chapter, the brief appearance of prostitutes on the stage of history at Meerut became, over the course of the century that followed, a staple of the "Mutiny narrative." Meerut thus became a moral tale, a parable – employing irony (Wilson), romance (Steel, Savarkar), tragedy (MacMunn), or all three combined, as ironic farce (Taylor).

The records of and narratives about women and men at Meerut reveal the world that made the events of 1857 – the hybrid world of the cantonment and its environs, especially its "sadr" or main bazaar. It was a world of stark gender divisions and fraught emotions. And what is particularly striking about this world is that even as femininity was widely understood to epitomize utter weakness, cowardliness, and impotence – so much so that for a man to be perceived to be behaving like a woman constituted the most extreme degradation imaginable – the actual women of the cantonment bazaar were able (or were, at the very least, perceived to be able) to comment authoritatively on the masculinity of the soldiery. We take up this theme in greater detail in Chapter 3.

3 Frail Ones

Let us highlight some key points from Chapters 1 and 2: (1) The sadr bazaar was ground zero of the Meerut revolt; (2) one of the largest professions in the sadr bazaar was "prostitution";[1] (3) the taunting of the Indian soldiery at Meerut by bazaar women – "the frail ones of the Meerut bazaar," as they were described by Cracroft Wilson – was reportedly a key factor in driving the men to rise up in revolt; and (4) the catalytic role of the "frail ones of the Meerut bazaar" in the military revolt at Meerut quickly became a staple of 1857 historiography, evolved considerably over the decades (as did the historiography), and resonates still in popular representations of the revolt.

We might add a fifth point: A close examination of the depositions gathered by G. W. Williams in the wake of 1857 reveals that, in the hours just preceding the military revolt, a small group of women residing in and near the sadr bazaar at Meerut – "Cashmerians," according to the official record – passed along information about the impending violence to a senior British pensioner. As with the so-called frail ones of the Meerut bazaar, the precise occupation of these "Cashmerians" is opaque. It would not be unreasonable to conclude from their testimony that they served as temporary socio-sexual companions of men in the cantonment, both British and Indian – a point that is examined further in this chapter. The broad point, however, is that women who seemed to provide sexual labor and/or social companionship in and around the sadr

---

[1] The term is placed in quotation marks because, as noted in the Introduction and Chapter 1 and as is expanded upon in this chapter, it fails to capture the range of professional, literary, artistic, and erotic pursuits that characterized women engaged in "sex work" in north India in the mid nineteenth century. As has been noted in recent feminist social and cultural theory, both "prostitute" as well as the now more favored "sex worker" carry distinct moral implications. When I make recourse to the term "prostitute" here, it is either because that was the term used in the primary sources or, in some cases, for the sake of simplicity; in any case, scare quotes should be assumed throughout.

bazaar – whether "frail ones" or "Cashmerians" (and there are many other terms to which observers made recourse in the nineteenth century) – occupied a pivotal place in the overlapping emotional and informational grid of the cantonment.

The aim of this chapter is to better understand these "bazaar women" – as they were often described (see Figures 3.1 and 3.2) – in the social, cultural, and political world of northern India. We will begin with some facts and figures, then return to the question of language. But the bulk of this chapter focuses on the interactions of women engaged, in one form or another, in the performative sex and companionship trade with the police and judicial branches of the Company state in the 1850s, on the eve of the rebellion.

As noted in Chapter 2, prostitutes were said to account for 7.59 percent of the total Meerut sadr bazaar population (211 of 2,780) in 1855. They were the fourth largest group in the bazaar, after "Beggars and Paupers" (8.49 percent or 236 persons), load carriers ("Pulladars and Coolies", at 9.39 percent, numbering 261), and "Servants" (15.14 percent, numbering 421). As we shall see, the figures for these occupations varied considerably by cantonment, probably a result of the novelty of such census-taking, having only commenced in 1854–1855 and, consequently, the likelihood that there was a lack of methodological consistency in delimiting categories, systematizing terminology, and gathering data. Thus "servants" were sometimes listed as such, but as often as not separate figures were simply given for "sweepers", "khidmatgars" (manservants), "ayahs" (nursemaids), "bearers," etc. Similarly, sometimes "pulladars" were listed as a category, but often were not; in these cases, the population for the category I call "load carriers" (a term that does not appear in the censuses) was derived from the figures shown only for "coolies." Likewise, instead of the category "prostitute," which is used in the censuses, one sometimes encounters terms such as "kusbee" and "khangee." In Meerut, "khangee" (*khāngī*) was glossed as "Mussulman Prostitute" while "kusbee" (*kasbī*) was either glossed as "dancing girl" or "Hindoo Prostitute." (The term "nautch girl" was another frequently employed euphemism, particularly favored by the British, especially in north Indian Company Painting; see Figures 3.3–3.6) In Delhi's sadr bazaar, where the terms "khangee" and "kusbee" were not employed by the bazaar census enumerators, a distinction was made between "Hindoo" and "Moosulman" prostitutes. However, it seems likely that "khangee" and "kusbee" would have been familiar terms in Delhi, given the geographic proximity of the Meerut cantonment.

84 Frail Ones

Figure 3.1 "Wuzeerun. Bazar Woman. Mahomedan. Saharunpoor," 1868–1875
Note: Watson's caption for this image includes the following: "This photograph represents a Mahomedan bazar woman, or professional courtesan. Her dress is a yellow tunic, green silk trowsers, and red Cashmere shawl. There is little to be said for women of this class, who exist under many denominations all over India, and the nature of their profession debars description of them. Many are dancing women, Mahomedans as well as Hindoos. They can never contract real marriage, though some of them avail themselves of the form 'Nika,' under the Mahomedan law, the offspring of which is legitimate, though in a secondary degree. In such cases those married and secluded become honourable women." See Chapter 4 for more discussion of the points regarding "secondary" or "nika" marriages. The question of honor and respectability of "bazar women" looms large in the following chapters.
Source: J. Forbes Watson, *The People of India: A series of photographic illustrations, with descriptive letterpress, of the races and tribes of Hindustan* (London: The India Museum, 1868–1875), vol. 3, image no. 165. From the New York Public Library.

Frail Ones 85

Figure 3.2 "Diljan. Bazar Woman. Saharanpoor," 1868–1875
Source: J. Forbes Watson, *The People of India: A series of photographic illustrations, with descriptive letterpress, of the races and tribes of Hindustan* (London: The India Museum, 1868–1875), vol. 3, image no. 166. From the New York Public Library.

A breakdown of select "professions" for eight cantonments in 1855 is given in Table 3.1. These sites were chosen because they were, apart from Delhi, large cantonments and included figures for prostitutes (though sometimes, as noted, prostitutes were listed under different designations).[2]

---

[2] Additional cantonments included in the "Sadr Bazaar Reports," not used in the present table, were: Benares, Meean Meer, Peshawar, Dinapore, Jullundur, Barrackpore, Chunar, Mooltan, Subathoo, Berhampore, Sealkote, Dughsai, and Dum Dum.

Figure 3.3 "Beswā" (prostitute), Hansi Cantonment, 1825, artist unknown

Note: I am grateful to Aftab Ahmad for assistance with the term *Beswā*. It would appear to be related to the more conventional Hindi term *veśyā*. Curiously, the British Library version of this ms. has the inscription *paswā* (پسوا) for this image, which is translated for cataloguing purposes as "harlot." See Add. 27255, f.137v, digital available at https://imagesonline.bl.uk/asset/9019/ (last visited on January 17, 2025).

Source: *Kitāb-i tashrīḥ al-aqvām* (An account of origins and occupations of some of the sects, castes and tribes of India). Compiled for James Skinner, Hansi Cantonment, 1825. Image courtesy of the US Library of Congress.

Several points emerge from the enumeration in Table 3.1. First, as noted earlier, the percentages vary widely by cantonment, most likely a result of a lack of coordination between cantonment authorities over

Frail Ones 87

Figure 3.4 (Untitled) a "nautch" scene, Hansi Cantonment, 1825, artist unknown
Source: Kitāb-i tashrīḥ al-aqvām (An account of origins and occupations of some of the sects, castes and tribes of India). Compiled for James Skinner, Hansi Cantonment, 1825. Image courtesy of the US Library of Congress.

how to collect data and the classificatory delimitations.[3] Second, while "Bunneas" (grocers, merchants) and "Tailors" possessed a relatively small proportion of the population in the Meerut sadr bazaar, they

---

[3] For example, in Umballah "Beggars and Paupers" were not listed; the figure given in the table is for "Jogees and Sages," a category that was not included in Meerut. There was only one category of prostitute in Umballah, namely, "Prostitute." Figures for load carriers, as in Meerut, include both "pulladars" and "coolies." In Cawnpore "Beggars and Paupers" were not listed; the figure given in the table is for "Fucqueers." Prostitutes were listed as "prostitutes." There were no "pulladars," only "coolies." In Agra "servants" was not a census category; instead, separate figures were given for "khidmutgars," "sweepers," "ayahs," and "bearers." No "pulladars" were shown, only "coolies." Prostitutes were listed as such. In Delhi "prostitutes" were divided between "Hindoo" and "Moosulmen." "Servants" was not a listed category, but "sweepers" was. "Coolies" were listed; but no figures were given for "pulladars." In Ferozepore the category "prostitute" was replaced by "Public whore or kusbies." The only recognizable "servant" categories were "servants or kahars" and "sweepers or Mathors." The only "load carrier" profession was "coolie." In Jullundur "prostitutes" were listed as "kusbees or prostitutes." "Load carriers" were "coolies and laborers" and "palleydars." The category "Servants" was not included, though figures were given for "sweepers" and "khidmuttgars."

Figure 3.5 "Nách Girl. Aurat-e barqāz," Lucknow, 1815–1820, artist unknown
Source: A Lucknow album containing fifty-three drawings depicting occupations, 1815–1820. Accession no. AL.7970:16. Image courtesy of the Victoria & Albert Museum, London.

constituted a sizable presence in the remaining cantonment sadr bazaars. The discrepancy for "Bunneas" may be because in Meerut "Bunneas" referred to "Otta Dallsellers" (flour and lentil sellers), whereas elsewhere the term "Bunnea" (or variations thereof) referred to grain/flour and *dāl* sellers generally; sometimes, as in Agra, the term "Bunnea" was eschewed in favor of simply listing the profession as "Ottah and grain sellers." In Meerut, separate figures were given for "Antias" (flour dealers, numbering twenty-three), "Bessatis" (petty merchants, numbering fifty), and "Flour or Soojee sellers" (numbering twenty-eight). If these figures are added to the figures for "Bunneas" in Meerut, the number of "Bunneas" rises to 192 persons, or 6.91 percent of the sadr bazaar population, slightly higher than the percentage in Umballah's sadr bazaar. The meager figures for "Tailors" in Meerut, by contrast, is a mystery.

Frail Ones

Figure 3.6 "Aurat-e barqāz. A Nátch Girl. Zan-e Katarānīh. A Khutteranee woman," Lucknow, 1815–1820, artist unknown
Source: A Lucknow album containing fifty-three drawings depicting occupations, 1815–1820. Accession no. AL.7970:36. Image courtesy of the Victoria & Albert Museum, London.

A similar point emerges with respect to the category of "Beggars and Paupers." While this was the largest single group listed in the sadr bazaar of Meerut, the category did not even appear in any of the other sadr bazaar censuses. The figures given in Table 3.1 for Umballah reflects the number of "Jogees and Sages" recorded there; for Cawnpore, the figure is for "Fucqueers," a variation of *fakir*. I have included these figures under the category of "Beggars and Paupers" because this is how ascetics and holy men of one sort or another were generally regarded by the authorities. There is much more that may be said on this score, including the possibility that Meerut – for reasons yet undetermined – attracted itinerant ascetics. If so, it raises

Table 3.1 Percentages of select bazaar "professions" in eight cantonments, 1855

Occupation	Rawul Pindee	Ferozepur	Jullunder	Umballah	Meerut	Delhi	Agra	Cawnpore
Prostitutes	5.99	3.67	9.82	3.03	7.59	8.33	12.05	0.52
Load carriers	7.94	3.43	2.79	4.54	9.39	10.12	10.04	7.04
Servants	5.78	4.91	6.50	4.54	15.14	2.58	9.04	16.94
Beggars/paupers	0.00	0.00	0.00	2.02	8.49	0.00	0.00	0.57
Tailors	7.73	6.52	2.49	3.03	2.30	11.13	10.04	2.50
Bunneas	9.75	11.25	12.99	6.81	3.27	9.13	14.06	12.77
Bazaar population	1385	2915	1324	1982	2780	504	498	1918

Source: "Reports on Sudder Bazars," nos. 111–114 of July 13, 1855, Military Proceedings, NAI.

questions about the role that ascetics may have played in the run up to the military revolt.⁴

Like ascetics and grain/flour sellers, prostitutes were also a source of categorical confusion for officials in cantonment towns. Meerut was unique among the censuses in that the enumerator, probably joint magistrate Cookson, referred to prostitutes as either "kusbees" or "khangees." "Kusbee" was glossed as either "Dancing Girl" or "Hindoo Prostitute," and "khangee" as "Mussulman Prostitute." In most of the other sadr bazaar censuses, the term "prostitute" was employed with no supplementary clarification. The exceptions were Ferozepore, where the term used was "Kusbie or Public Whore"; and Delhi, where the term "Moosulmen Prostitute" was used. According to John Platts' late nineteenth-century *Dictionary of Urdu, Classical Hindi, and English*, the term "kusbee" (or rather *kasbī*) meant "artisan, artificer, trader," but also "prostitute, harlot, courtesan".⁵ The term had an identical meaning in Persian, whence it came into Hindi-Urdu, and is derived from *kasb*, which connotes "gain, acquisition, industry; art, trade, profession, [and] handicraft," in addition to "prostitution" and "harlotry."⁶ At the very least, these definitions suggest a degree of artistic and aesthetic accomplishment not present in the term "prostitute." Whereas *kasbī* connoted a more public, bazaar-oriented occupation, the term khangee (or *khāngī*, also from Persian), as an adjective, conveyed a sense of matters that were relegated to the "private, domestic, and household" space. Consequently, the noun derived from *khāngī* meant "kept woman" or "clandestine prostitute."⁷

Given the sizable numbers of kusbees and khangees in the Meerut sadr bazaar, it is striking that neither term appears in Williams' 1858 narrative memorandum on the revolt in Meerut or in the depositions that he collected. The depositions did include, as noted earlier, however, testimony by three bazaar women called "Cashmerians." A close reading of the depositions of the "Cashmerians" suggests that they may approximate the description of *khāngī*, that is, as "kept woman" or "clandestine prostitute," though this ultimately is speculation.⁸ To review: The three

---

⁴ Cf. William R. Pinch, *Warrior Ascetics and Indian Empires* (Cambridge: Cambridge University Press, 2006), chapter 4.
⁵ John T. Platts, *A Dictionary of Urdu, Classical Hindi, and English* (London: W. H. Allen & Co., 1884), p. 833.
⁶ Francis Joseph Steingass, *A Comprehensive Persian-English dictionary, including the Arabic words and phrases to be met with in Persian literature* (London: Routledge & K. Paul, 1892), p. 1029.
⁷ Platts, *A Dictionary of Urdu, Classical Hindi, and English*, p. 486.
⁸ There is also the possibility that "Cashmerian" was a euphemism for a woman wishing to present herself as a *tawā'if*, or highly cultured courtesan. See the discussion in Chapter 2.

women designated as "Cashmerian" in the depositions were named Golab Jaun, Zeenut, and Sophie. In addition to being identified as "Cashmerian," all three were given the prefix "*Mussumat*" (*musammāt*), a term derived from the Arabic that connoted a modicum of respectability, akin to Lady, Miss, or Ma'am.[9] What do we learn about the Cashmerians from their testimony? Golab Jaun reported that she "was residing with the late Dr. Smith at the time of the outbreak." The nature of their relationship was unclear, though she referred to Smith in her deposition as "my master."[10] She also noted that Smith had dismissed her initial warning, remarking that "I always brought him bazar reports void of foundation." (No doubt he later regretted his dismissive attitude.) Golab Jaun reported having received the information about the impending violence from her mother, Zeenut. For her part, Zeenut said that "on the day of the outbreak, I was residing in the sudder bazaar." It was Zeenut (again, according to Golab Jaun) who had sent a "dooly" (*ḍolī*) or covered sedan chair to Smith's bungalow, which Golab Jaun used to make her escape. (Smith subsequently was killed by the mob.) Both Golab Jaun and Zeenut claimed that the original information about the impending violence came from Sophie, who heard it from a sepoy or sepoys.[11] But Sophie, for her part, denied all this, insisting that "[t]he sowars and sepoys did not frequent my house." She acknowledged that at the time of the outbreak she "was residing in the sudder bazaar," but that "on the day it occurred no one was in my house, but Goolam Hossain, my servant." She then corrected herself slightly to say that "at 4 o'clock, Pundit Dhurm Narain, who was formerly in the office of the Meerut cantonment joint magistrate, came to my house, but left, when the out-break commenced, to return home." She then "closed the doors." Sophie's testimony was later contradicted by Bukhtawur Singh, officiating kotwal of the sadr bazaar, who was ordered to further investigate her claims. He interviewed Sophie's neighbors and learned that *sawār*s (cavalrymen) had, in fact, been in the habit of visiting her house. He added that her house, along with others in the neighborhood, had been razed to the ground.

Were Cashmerians counted as "khangees" in the 1855 sadr bazaar census? It seems possible, even likely, though of course it is impossible to be certain. Golab Jaun lived with Dr. Smith and referred to him as her

---

[9] Steingass, *A Comprehensive Persian-English dictionary*, p. 1239.
[10] See Conclusions, Reflections for more discussion of this point.
[11] Golab Jaun said that Sophie had passed the news directly to Zeenut, whereas Zeenut reported that Sophie had told her own mother, apparently misidentified by Zeenut as "Mehonee," who had then told her. See Chapter 2 for the full text of the depositions.

"master," and Sophie's answers suggest a desire for privacy if not outright secrecy – behaviors consistent with a *khāṅgī* as a "kept woman" and/or "clandestine prostitute." Sex was never mentioned, but this is typical of official discourse which tended to elide matters of sexual behavior and sexuality.[12] As for Sophie and secrecy: She not only denied foreknowledge of the attack, she denied any prior interaction with the mutinous cavalry regiment. She also implicitly denied trafficking in information: She pointed out that her mother, whom Zeenut had identified (but misnamed) as a key link in the information chain between herself and Sophie, had left Meerut for Ludhiana prior to the outbreak of violence. She did admit that Pundit Dhurm Narain (of the joint magistrate's office, no less!) visited her house on the afternoon of May 10, but she did not say for what purpose. If nothing else, Sophie's testimony suggests a desire to be discrete, if not downright secretive, about her doings.

To some degree, Sophie's manifold denials are understandable: She not only lost her house in the mayhem, but she may also have been at risk of losing her life. As noted in Chapter 2, it was privately reported in the late summer of 1857 that two Eurasian girls had been murdered during the revolt in Meerut and that a brothel keeper (later alleged to have been named "Mees Dolly," according to George MacMunn) was implicated in the killing – a brothel keeper who was "guilty of egging on the mutineers." Elsewhere in north India, "Cashmerian" was used a euphemism for Eurasian "half castes." Is it possible the Cashmerians were Eurasians seeking to bolster their social status and desirability in an era increasingly less tolerant of mixed-race children? And if so, were the two Eurasian girls murdered for passing information to the British?[13]

Cashmerians, frail ones, kasbees, khangees, public whores, clandestine prostitutes, kept women. The variety of terms used to describe women engaged in "sex work" in the mid nineteenth century stands in indirect proportion to what historians today would like to know about them. This is due largely to the nature of the historical record. Further, most work

---

[12] See Anjali Arondekar, "Without a Trace: Sexuality and the Colonial Archive," *Journal of the History of Sexuality* 14, 1/2 (2005): 10–27. On strategies for navigating the "colonial archive" and finding alternative sources on sex and sexuality, see Charu Gupta, "Writing Sex and Sexuality: Archives of Colonial North India," *Journal of Women's History* 23, 4 (2011): 12–35.

[13] Their vulnerable position and conflicted politics in 1857 may be perceived as well in the oppressions and opportunities that confronted "dancers" and "courtesans" in Delhi during the summer of 1857; see Dalrymple, *Last Mughal*, esp. pp. 12–13, 208, and 326–327.

that has been done on prostitutes in British India focuses on the period after about 1860, the bulk of which arises from documents detailing official anxieties over "Venereal Diseases" and the felt need for increased surveillance over and control of prostitutes' bodies, especially those that came into contact with the rank-and-file British and, to a lesser degree, Indian soldiery.[14] Much less work has been done on prostitution in the period prior to 1860, and that which has tends to focus more on concubinage, courtesanship, and family politics.[15] The impression that one may be left with, having immersed oneself in this literature, is that the late Mughal courtesan-cum-concubine somehow evolved during the course of the late eighteenth and early nineteenth centuries into the cantonment prostitute of the regimental *"lāl bāzār,"* or "red bazaar," as the prostitute quarters were often known in the early decades of the nineteenth century (especially in the Madras and Bombay Presidencies). There may well be some truth to this simplistic linear progression, even if we should bear in mind that a version of *lāl bāzārī* prostitution seemed to exist well prior to 1757, while the *gharānā*s or households of the cultured courtesan continued to exist (if not thrive) well into the late twentieth century.[16] While

[14] Kenneth Ballhatchet, *Race, Sex and Class under the Raj: Imperial Attitudes and Policies and their Critics, 1793–1905* (London: Weidenfeld and Nicolson, 1980); and Philippa Levine, *Prostitution, Race, and Politics: Policing Venereal Disease in the British Empire* (New York: Routledge, 2003); cf. Mitra, *Indian Sex Life*. For an examination of the early nineteenth-century evidence, see Douglas Peers, "Soldiers, Surgeons and the Campaigns to Combat Sexually Transmitted Diseases in Colonial India," *Medical History* 42, 2 (1998): 137–160; and "Privates off Parade: Regulating Sexuality in the Nineteenth-Century Indian Empire," *International History Review* 20, 4 (1998): 823–854, in which Peers complicates the general argument about increasing regulation of sexuality by British authorities in the nineteenth century.

[15] For example: Indrani Chatterjee and Sumit Guha, "Slave-Queen, Waif-Prince: Slavery and Social Capital in Eighteenth-Century India," *Indian Economic and Social History Review* 36, 2 (1999): 165–186; Indrani Chatterjee, *Gender, Slavery and Law in British India* (Delhi: Oxford University Press, 1999); Durba Ghosh, *Sex and the Family in Colonial India: The Making of Empire* (Cambridge: Cambridge University Press, 2006); Vijay Pinch, "*Gosain Tawaif*: Sex, Slaves, and Ascetics in Rasdhan, 1800–1857," *Modern Asian Studies* 38, 3 (July 2004): 559–597; and Ramya Sreenivasan, "Drudges, Dancing Girls, and Concubines: Female Slaves in the Rajput Polity, 1500–1850," in Indrani Chatterjee and Richard Eaton (eds.), *Slavery and Society in South Asian History* (Bloomington: University of Indiana Press, 2006), pp. 136–161.

[16] On the latter, see Veena Talwar Oldenburg, "Lifestyle as Resistance: The Case of the Courtesans of Lucknow," in V. Graff (ed.), *Lucknow: Memories of a City* (Delhi: Oxford University Press, 1997), pp. 136–154. On the former, the *lāl bāzārī* prostitutes, the late sixteenth-century Badauni offers the most famous passage: "the prostitutes of the imperial dominions, who had gathered together in the Capital in such swarms as to defy counting or numbering," Akbar "made to live outside the city, and called the place *Shaitanpura* [Devil-ville]. And he appointed a keeper, and a deputy, and a secretary for this quarter, so that any one who wished to associate with these people, or take them to his house, provided he first had his name and condition written down, might with the connivance of the imperial officers have connection with any of them that he pleased. But

this chapter cannot delve too deeply into this complex question, it is hoped that the discussion that follows will shed light on some key structural dynamics that allowed for the expanded recruitment of young women and girls for work in the sex trade in the increasingly fraught moral climate of mid nineteenth-century British India.

Sixteen Prostitutes of the North-Western Provinces

How to go about finding prostitutes in the archives? Philippa Levine, who has worked on prostitution, race, and disease in the later nineteenth century, observes that prostitutes only begin to appear in large numbers in the official records after legislation concerning sexually transmitted maladies and the emergence of a felt need for "lock hospitals" in which to enforce treatment; this point is reinforced in and indeed structures more recent work, most notably Durba Mitra's exploration of the discourse of sex and prostitution in modern India. So we are immediately faced with a temporal challenge. Then there is the wider problem of the language of respectability that tends to permeate certain nineteenth-century records (noted by Anjali Arondekar), what might be termed "the prose of counter-sexuality." The popular journalist-historian P. J. O. Taylor, for example, noted that while "comfort women" were a common enough feature of pre-Mutiny regiments, propriety required that they remained unmentioned in official dispatches. "Had it been known generally in England that such women existed," he writes, "there would have been an outcry, and Queen Victoria would certainly have been most displeased. As a result there is little reference to such persons, particularly in official correspondence." However, Taylor did find one private letter from the Punjab that "lets the cat out of the bag," describing how cartloads of "native women" were brought on long-march deployment in the field (see Figures 3.7 and 3.8 for an illustration from 1835 by a nostalgic officer).[17] Though the unnamed author of Taylor's letter did not make clear the precise nature of the role the women played in this regiment, referring to them simply as "dusky beauties" and "ladies," the tone is

---

he did not permit any man to take dancing-girls to his house at night, without conforming to these conditions, in order that he might keep the matter under proper control." 'Abd al-Qādir ibn Mulūk Shāh, known as al Badā'ūnī, *Muntakhabu-t-tawarikh*, vol. 2, translated by George S. A. Ranking (Calcutta: Asiatic Society of Bengal, 1898, reprint New Delhi: Atlantic, 1990), pp. 311–312.

[17] I am grateful to Dr. Sonal Singh for alerting me to this image and to Laura Callery and Anna Szapiro of the Yale Center for British Art for clarifying its provenance.

96   Frail Ones

Figure 3.7 "Bengal Troops on the Line of March," 1835 (?), by W. A. Ludlow
Source: Rare Books and Manuscripts, L 530 (Folio B), Yale Center for British Art, Paul Mellon Collection.

Figure 3.8 "Cart in which Native Females ride," detail of "Bengal Troops on the Line of March," 1835 (?), by W. A. Ludlow
Source: Rare Books and Manuscripts, L 530 (Folio B), Yale Center for British Art, Paul Mellon Collection.

such that makes it quite clear that their position in the regiment was not only secure but of considerable importance to the men.[18]

Taylor's archival reflections notwithstanding, prostitutes do appear in official records connected to the Company Army – just not in the official records Taylor consulted.[19] Kenneth Ballhatchet encountered occasional references to prostitutes prior to 1860 in the Military Proceedings, mostly consumed, however, with the question of disease and varying methods of maintaining health among the British soldiers and focused on the utility of "lock hospitals." These have been explored in greater detail by Douglas Peers.[20] Unfortunately, despite this pioneering work, while we learn much about official military attitudes toward sex and soldiering, we learn little about the women themselves. However, if one trolls through the Criminal Judicial Proceedings, prostitutes crop up – not in droves, but with sufficient regularity and occasionally in strikingly sharp detail.[21] This is all the more remarkable when we consider that prostitution did not come under any formal legal restriction in India until the passage of the Contagious Diseases Act of 1868 which

---

[18] Taylor does not provide the source for the passage, which is on p. 188 of his *Companion to the Mutiny of 1857*: "On July 26th (1857) we had to cross the Beas River. Engineers reported the bridge of boats fairly safe ... Just then there appeared the conveyances bearing the native ladies attached to the regiment. Tommy Atkins was much agitated: would they or would they not get over? Ladies seated in ekkas, carts, had tops and curtains descended hiding the dusky beauties ... just as the line of ekkhas [sic] had passed the centre of the bridge a cry was heard. It is gone! Too true the boats which had held together during the passage of HM's soldiers, the camels and the baggage, gave way under the immense responsibility now entrusted to them, and amid despairing cries boats and ekkhas [sic] were borne away by the current of the swollen river ... which way would they be taken? ... watched by anxious eyes the boats bearing their precious burdens gradually but surely neared the shore, and as they touched, many willing hands caught and secured the wandering boats, the ekkhas [sic] were brought safely to land, and the ladies restored to their position with the regiment."

[19] The probable reason Taylor did not encounter such records is, first, that official correspondence dealing with political and military events after May 10, 1857 tended to focus on deployment of troops, combatants, and punishment of soldiers who rebelled, deserted, or simply failed to report for duty promptly in the summer of 1857 (which charge, until September of 1858, was usually treated as desertion and punished by death); and second, that the official records that Taylor consulted tended to be concentrated in the Foreign Political, Foreign Secret, and Military Department Proceedings, or in the various "Mutiny Papers" held in the National Archives in India and Allahabad Archives. By contrast, as is made clear, the Judicial Department proceedings for the 1850s do include reference to prostitutes, and they are far less likely to employ polite or ironic euphemisms.

[20] See Peers, "Soldiers, Surgeons and the Campaigns to Combat Sexually Transmitted Diseases in Colonial India," and "Privates off Parade."

[21] See, for example, Indrani Chatterjee, "Colouring Subalternity: Slaves, Concubines and Social Orphans in Early Colonial India," in Gautam Bhadra, Gyan Prakash, and Susie Tharu (eds.), *Subaltern Studies X: Writings on South Asian History and Society* (Delhi: Oxford University Press, 1999), esp. pp. 62–68.

sought, as noted earlier, to control the spread of venereal diseases by controlling prostitutes' bodies.[22] The attention of the judicial and police authorities was not due to a proclivity on the part of prostitutes for crime: Indeed, more often than not, based on the available records, prostitutes tended to not be the ones engaging in criminal activity; rather, they were usually the ones being preyed upon by criminals. In other words, based on a survey of the Criminal Judicial Proceedings from the North-Western Provinces held in the India Office Records of the British Library, prostitutes usually appeared because they were *victims* in cases of murder, wounding, and theft. On occasion they are seen to be the ones doing the thieving and (very rarely) murdering, but this was the exception rather than the rule.

Some important caveats are in order here regarding the nature of the evidence afforded by the Criminal Judicial Proceedings. Not all crimes were described in sufficient detail in these records to enable the reader to discern the identities of those involved. Usually the only crimes that merited sustained prose descriptions were those of a "heinous" nature. Sometimes these crimes were included in an annual police report, which was a summary of the crimes that occurred during the previous calendar year; sometimes a particular crime, due to its unusual features, was deemed important or interesting enough to merit its own dedicated correspondence between a district magistrate and divisional commissioner. Petty crimes, though they were included in final tabulations, did not merit mention in the official proceedings unless they erupted into serious violence. The salient point, then, is that what follows should not be taken as an exhaustive analysis of *all* crimes and disputes involving prostitutes in the North-Western Provinces; rather it is a reflection on crimes that both involved prostitutes and rose to a level of significance to merit inclusion in the official record being sent to the lieutenant governor of the province sitting in Agra, and thence to Calcutta and London.

---

[22] As noted earlier, there were abortive attempts to institute lock hospitals in the early nineteenth century, but these were abandoned by the 1830s when it appeared that they served, inadvertently, to increase the rate of contagion. See Ballhatchet, *Race, Sex and Class under the Raj*, chapter 1. Post-1868 legislation, such as the various provincial "Prevention of Prostitution Acts" and the wider "Suppression of Immoral Traffic Act," began describing prostitution as a species of deplorable behavior, verging on the criminal; these eventually evolved into the "Immoral Trafficking Prevention Act" of 1956. Significantly, drafters of legislation were careful not to criminalize the actual women engaged in prostitution, who were seen to be the main victims of the practice. The goal was to punish the sin, not the sinner, but the effect was usually the same in that it marginalized prostitutes and made their profession increasingly dangerous.

That said, the numbers are still suggestive.[23] For example, if we take the nineteen-month period beginning on January 1, 1855 and ending on July 31, 1856, there were sixteen discrete cases involving women identified as "prostitutes" in the North-Western Provinces that were serious enough to warrant mention in the Criminal Judicial correspondence sent to the lieutenant governor at Agra.[24] One or two of these cases involved more than one woman, though most involved only one. The regional breakdown is as follows: five cases in the Meerut Division; four in the Agra Division; two in the Benares Division; two in the Saugor Division; two in the Delhi Division; and one in the Allahabad Division. Of these sixteen cases, only two involved prostitutes as criminals; and in one of these, a woman (in Delhi) was implicated in a crime simply because stolen property was found in her house. In the remaining fourteen cases, prostitutes were the victims of crime. In half of these, the woman in question was murdered. There was an additional case of attempted murder of a prostitute by a spurned sepoy named Madaree, in which the intended victim, named Bilaso, appeared, in the words of W. G. Probyn the officiating magistrate, "to have had a most wonderful escape" – though her mother and sister were severely wounded and a man asleep in her doorway killed.[25] In only one case was a prostitute implicated in a murder: a Rajput brought a "mistress" from Oudh to his house in Jaunpur District; she was accompanied by a man named Bhani Singh who called himself her brother. In the night Bhani Singh murdered the Rajput and decamped with the woman.[26] Four of the cases resulted

---

[23] See the Appendix for a tabular statement of these cases and the records from which they are drawn.

[24] I have not included cases involving women identified as "concubines," of which there were three instances; nor have I included cases involving women said to be entertaining multiple lovers. All the women in the cases I have included here were identified explicitly as "prostitutes" – save for one case, in Russulgunge Cotwalee, Allyghur, in the Meerut Division, where the woman was identified as "Tuwaif" (*ṭawā'if*, courtesan) There were several additional cases where women were engaged in extramarital relationships of longstanding that may have had a contractual nature, but because the term 'prostitute' was not used to describe these women, their cases were not included in the tabulations. An additional case was recorded for Mirzapoor in the Benares Division (see no. 118 of July 8, 1856, North Western Provinces Criminal Judicial Proceedings, India Office Records, British Library [hereafter NWP-CJP]), but it dated from 1837 and was included due to the release of the prisoner over uncertainty as to his actual identity; hence it is also not included in the tabulation.

[25] No. 363 of August 22, 1856, NWP-CJP: W. G. Probyn, Offtg. Mag. Furruckabad, to G. F. Harvey, Commr. Agra Dv., dated July 11, 1856.

[26] No. 98 of July 8, 1856, NWP-CJP: H. C. Tucker, Commr. of Benares Dv., to Secy. Govt. NWP, dated March 15, 1856. This case may have been an incidence of a slightly different species of crime that appeared to be fairly widespread across northern and central India, in which gangs of "Beriahs" used their women as sexual bait to lure men whom the Beriahs would then rob and kill. See e.g. No. 18 of March 1, 1856, NWP-CJP:

100   Frail Ones

in the wounding of a prostitute, two of which involved either theft or attempted theft. In only two cases were prostitutes the victims of theft where they did not also suffer some form of bodily harm.

To put these numbers and crimes in perspective, consider that the annual police report in 1855 for the *district* of Meerut (not to be confused with the entire Meerut Division, comprising several districts) stated that there were a total of 2,640 crimes reported.[27] Most of these cases appeared to stem from various kinds of agrarian conflicts, such as boundary disputes, grass-cutting rights, and cattle theft, and were usually not described in detail in the proceedings. The sixteen cases involving prostitutes for the entire province will seem, in this light, like a very small drop in a very large bucket. On the other hand, given that only serious crimes – such as murder, homicide, highway robbery, violent theft and burglary, child stealing, and "affray" attended by wounding or homicide – merited prose descriptions in the annual police reports, the fact that prostitutes were appearing in the records bears some social significance.

The Meerut District cases that merited prose description in 1855 were arranged as follows in Table 3.2:[28]

Table 3.2 *Major Meerut District crimes, 1855*

Number	Category	# of cases
1.	Murder	5
2.	Attempt at murder	1
3.	Wounding with intent to kill	3
4.	Culpable homicide	2
5.	Highway robbery with homicide	1
6.	Highway robbery with wounding	1

"Translation of the Confessions of Phoolwaree Shah," who was active for about ten years before being captured (originally deposed in 1853) and "Translation of the Confession of Buddyan." This gang operated in a belt that extended across northern Bundelkhand. Capturing such criminals was difficult due to their high mobility; hence they fell under the purview of the Department of Thuggee and Dakoiti.

[27] No. 533 of September 22, 1856, NWP-CJP: "Triennial statement of crimes and offences, and statement of convictions for the year 1855 in Zillah Meerut," by E. M. Wylly, dated February 9, 1856. In addition to the figures given in the table, the district report noted for the record 247 additional burglaries "unattended with aggravating circumstances," 522 "other cases" of theft, 649 cases of cattle stealing "unattended with aggravating circumstances," and 910 cases of "crimes and offences not specified in Table 3.2."

[28] No. 530 of September 22, 1856, NWP-CJP: "Narrative of crimes committed in 1855" [Meerut District], probably by R. H. Dunlop, officiating magistrate. It is not immediately clear what distinguishes burglary and theft, given the descriptions of the individual cases.

Table 3.2 (cont.)

Number	Category	# of cases
7.	Highway robbery without violence	1
8.	Burglary with murder	1
9.	Burglary with wounding	5
10.	Burglary with theft [simple burglary]	8
11.	Theft of property attended with murder	3
12.	Attempt at theft of property with wounding	5
13.	Theft of children	1
14.	Theft of property valued at Rs. 500 and upward	5
15.	Cattle theft	1
16.	Cattle theft attended with wounding	4
17.	Affray attended with homicide	3
18.	Affray attended with severe wounding	10
19.	Perjury	3
20.	Theft of property after administering deleterious drugs	1
21.	Cases in which from Rs. 100 to 300 Rs. value of property has been stolen	9

Interestingly, a large proportion of the cases that ended in death or serious wounding stemmed from what may be deemed illicit sexual-emotional relationships, whether in the context of marriage or extramarital relations. And in Meerut in 1855, the victims of the violent crimes emanating from such illicit relations were almost always women. For example, of the five murders described in Meerut District for 1855, two were wives murdered by their husbands for alleged infidelity; a third case involved a rich widow who had been poisoned by family members. Likewise, of the three woundings with intent to kill, one involved a man who inflicted a sword wound on a woman who refused to live with him, before killing himself; the other involved a husband who wounded his wife because she refused to come home with him. Of the two culpable homicide cases in Meerut District in 1855, one involved the killing of a mother by two sons who were enraged because she had arranged the marriage of their sister without their consent. Finally, the burglary with murder case (under category 8) turned out, upon investigation, to be not a case of burglary at all but a premeditated murder made to look as though it was the result of a property-owner defending his home from a burglar; the primary victim in this case was not a woman but rather a local chowkidar "who had for some time been engaged in an intrigue with one of the females" of the house in question. (One can imagine, however, that the woman with whom the chowkidar was carrying on the intrigue did not fare well at the hands of her relatives.) A similar pattern can be seen in

Agra District in 1855.[29] Of the twelve cases of murder or wounding with intent to murder, seven stemmed from illicit sexual-emotional relationships. Six of these clearly involved a "love-triangle" or "quadrangle" in which a man became enraged at the infidelity of either his wife or paramour. In four of these cases, the wounded or murdered victims were the rival male lovers; in two cases, the women were the victims. A seventh case involved the murder of a prostitute; the motive for the murder was unknown, but the features of the crime suggested a jealous rage.

We might conclude, then, that based on these glimpse of crime in Agra and Meerut districts, violence against prostitutes across the North-Western Provinces was a function of violence against women generally – particularly given the apparently high incidence of violent crimes resulting from illicit sexual-emotional relations. But of the fourteen cases noted here in which prostitutes were victims, only three can be said to have stemmed from jealousy (interestingly, of these three cases, two of the culprits were sepoys). In eight cases the motive for the crime was theft (in only one was the culprit a sepoy; however, in several cases the culprits escaped and their identities were concealed). In two cases the motive was unknown. And the final case was the murder of a woman who had the bad luck to visit the house of a client embroiled in a land dispute on the very night he was attacked by his enemies.

Whether or not prostitutes were overrepresented as victims of serious crime – and there seems to be good reason to think they were – there can be no question that the profession of sex in exchange for money made them particularly attractive targets. This is because prostitutes were more likely than most to find themselves inhabiting two dangerous worlds: the world of illicit sexual-emotional relations, and the world of property.[30] Of course, the picture of the prostitute as a two-dimensional victim is partly a product of the source material: It will be recalled that the nature of the records is such that petty crime did not merit sustained discussion. That prostitutes did dabble in petty crime is suggested by case of Jowala Devee, a murdered prostitute of Delhi, whose fate was said to have "excited little sympathy, as she had repeatedly plundered her customers

---

[29] No. 189 of July 10, 1856, NWP-CJP: "Extract cases no. 1 to 18 from the Agra Magistrate's narrative of crimes in connection with Police Report for 1855."

[30] Sometimes that property was considerable. Thieves broke into the house of one "Motee [,] a Tuwaif," and "stole property amounting to 820 Rs." No. 541E of September 22, 1856, NWP-CJP: "Abstract of Heinous Offences for the year 1855" (Allyghur), G. P. Money, Magistrate, March 13, 1856. The fact that she is referred to by Money as "Tuwaif" is, I think, an indication that she was perceived to be of an altogether different class than the "common" bazaar prostitute.

in the most shamefaced manner."³¹ We know from other records, moreover, that prostitutes in Meerut were also known to trade in kidnapped girls (more on which later), and they were involved in the illicit sale of liquor.³²

Another way of probing the significance of the sixteen cases involving prostitutes is to ask how those cases were dealt with by the authorities. Of the fourteen cases in the proceedings for 1855 and 1856 in which prostitutes were victimized, nine ended in the capture of the suspected parties. Of these nine cases, seven ended in conviction and punishment. The punishments ranged from execution in three cases of murder to various terms of imprisonment (six months to life) for wounding. In the one case of simple theft in which a suspect was captured, the prisoner was released "for want of proof." These figures would seem to suggest that the authorities tended to regard crime against prostitutes as a serious matter, and this impression is generally supported by the prose commentary. For example, F. W. Pinckney, the deputy commissioner of Jubbulpore, reported that his investigation of the case of the severe wounding of the prostitute Bussuntee began in the pre-dawn hours of October 8, 1855 at the hospital, where the victim had been taken by the police and her relatives. Bussuntee had been badly cut up by her companion the previous evening while returning from a local *urs melā* (an annual festival associated with the death anniversary of a Sufi saint) at the Rani *Tālāb* (tank). Pinckney arrived at the hospital with the civil surgeon, who tended to her wounds (including the amputation of her right hand). Despite her wounds, Bussuntee was able to describe her assailant to Pinckney: She told him that though she did not know his name she could recognize him and his mother, and also knew where they lived. Pinckney ordered Bussuntee to be put upon a *charpai* (stringed cot) and rode by her side while she directed her bearers to the house in question. Pinckney and the kotwal entered the house and seized the residents along with

---

³¹ No. 108 of August 6, 1856, NWP-CJP: S. Fraser, Commr. Delhi, to Sec. to Govt. in Agra, dated May 19, 1856.
³² On the involvement of prostitutes in the liquor trade, see No. 309 of April 22, 1853, NWP-CJP: Captn. G. R. Cookson, Cantt. Jt. Mag., Meerut, to Lt. Col. Steel, Sup. Cantt. Police. (Also see Chapter 1.) For the sale of kidnapped girls to prostitutes in Meerut, see No. 61 of June 10, 1850, NWP-CJP: G. H. France, Sessions Judge Saharanpoor, to M. R. Gubbins, Offg. Regr. to the Court of the Niz. Adt. North Western Provinces, Agra, February 6, 1850. I am grateful to Clare Anderson for directing me to this latter reference. These girls came mostly from the region around Coel, Etawah, and Mathura. I discuss this case in greater detail. Similar trafficking in girls was occurring in what is now Haryana; see no. 108 of August 6, 1856, NWP-CJP: S. Fraser, Commr. Delhi, to Sec. to Govt., Agra, dated May 19, 1856, para. 91.

corroborating evidence. The alleged assailant, Wazir Khan, was tried, convicted, and sentenced to life imprisonment.[33]

A more extensive report was provided in the case of the murder by poisoning of Hydree, a prostitute of Kydgunge in Allahabad, which occurred on February 4, 1855. The lead official on the case, Deputy Magistrate P. Carnegy, learned of the crime from Hydree's sister, Sahebjan, also a prostitute. Sahebjan had also been poisoned, but had regained consciousness within a few hours and had managed to make her way to the police post in the neighborhood. Carnegy soon received from Sahebjan "such a description of the murderers as enabled me to take active measure for their pursuit." They were arrested within twenty hours, on the road to Banda. The principal assailant turned out to be a notorious poisoner named Khanazad Khan of Patna, who had been preying on prostitutes throughout Bihar and the North-Western Provinces in recent years. According to his confession, he and his accomplice, a boy named Munee, had spent two nights with Sahebjan and Hydree in the former's house, during which time they had given money to the women to procure "bazaar spirits," overpaying on each occasion to gain their confidence. On the third night, Khanazad Khan slipped some drops of poison into the women's drinks; when they "became insensible" he began removing their ornaments and robbing them of their cash. Carnegy may have found this case particularly interesting because it emerged during the course of the investigation that the accused was a member of a gang of "reclaimed thugs" who many years earlier had been granted some land in Patna district so as to "[betake] themselves to honest pursuits."[34]

Of course, it is in the nature of police statistics to cast a generally positive light on the performance of the police. Still, if we look more closely, it is possible to see some cracks in the evidence that suggest a more conflicted picture of the prostitute's relationship to the world of officialdom. Most of the murdered and wounded prostitutes whose cases appear in the Criminal Judicial Proceedings were assaulted in or near their own houses, like Hydree and Sahebjan of Allahabad.[35] These

---

[33] No. 361 of September 13, 1856, NWP-CJP: "Abstract of cases of the 1st and 2nd class, during the past year" [Jubbulpore], signed F. W. Pinckney, Dep. Commsr., Jubbulpore, April 8, 1856.

[34] No. 59 of March 4, 1856, NWP-CJP: P. Carnegy, Dy Magstr., Allahabad Dt., to G. Chester, Officiating Commsr., Allahabad Dv., February 9, 1856.

[35] See e.g. the three cases listed for Meerut District in 1855. The first two occur in no. 530 of September 22, 1856, NWP-CJP: "Narrative of crimes committed in 1855" [Meerut District], probably by R. H. Dunlop, Officiating Magistrate; the third case is from no. 541E of September 22, 1856, NWP-CJP: 'Abstract of Heinous Offences for the year 1855' [Allyghur], signed G. P. Money, Magistrate, March 13, 1856.

houses were usually located in the city or cantonment bazaar with easy proximity to a police post, which should have meant prompt investigation by the authorities, as in the case of the Allahabad poisoners and the Jubbulporee attack. An additional example of such prompt investigation was, indeed, the 1853 murder of Nuseebun, a prostitute who lived in the sadr bazaar adjoining the Meerut cantonment. Ameerun Dhye, who lived with Nuseebun, deposed that she was roused in the night by the "moans and groans" of Nuseebun who was being murdered by a sepoy whom she recognized as Ram Singh of the Sappers and Miners. She bolted her door in "great terror" until daybreak, when she "gave intimation at the Kotwalee." The suspect was immediately seized; but despite damning evidence in the form of additional eyewitness testimony and a bloody footprint that matched his oddly shaped foot, the sepoy was eventually acquitted on the testimony of his fellow soldiers that he was not only in the lines during the night in question but on duty.[36] An aggressive police response did not always result in a conviction, even if the culprit was captured.

On other occasions, the proximity of the police post did not even translate into rapid action. For example, in the case of another Meerut prostitute murder, in late December 1855, the Cantonment Joint Magistrate R. Cookson complained that even though "women carrying on in the same trade lived on either side and below" the victim, they would not give "the slightest clue nor disclose the name or description of a single person who visited her, with some of whom they must be acquainted."[37] Cookson attributed the silence of the victim's neighbors to "the usual apathy of natives of this country" and gave the crime little additional thought. One of those reasons may indeed have been a form of apathy, or the sense that the prostitute victim was receiving her due. Such seemed to have been the case with the murder of Jowala Devee of Delhi, noted earlier, who was reputed to rob her customers.[38] Ironically, however, one sepoy of the 70th did provide a hint to the identities of the culprits in her case, one of whom was as a result speedily captured on the road to Aligarh with a wagonload of incriminating evidence in the form of

---

[36] No. 58 of June 5, 1854, NWP-CJP: Capt. G. R. Cookson, Cantt. Jt Mag, Meerut, to Lieutt. Col. J. Steel, Supdt. Cantt. Police, dated January 1, 1854. This was the only murder in the Meerut cantonment during 1853; there were no murders in the previous two years.

[37] No. 10 of April 2, 1856, NWP-CJP: R. Cookson, Cantt. Jt. Magstr. Meerut, to J. Steel, Suptd. Cantt. Police, January 1, 1856. Cookson concluded that because a box of clothes and some jewels were left untouched among the ruins of the house, which had been burned to the ground, the motive was not theft but jealousy.

[38] No. 108 of August 6, 1856, NWP-CJP: S. Fraser, Commssr, Delhi, to Sec to Govt, Agra, May 19, 1856.

stolen goods. This individual implicated three other sepoys. However, only the sepoy caught red handed with the evidence was hanged for the crime.[39]

But another reason prostitutes living near a police post might not report a crime is that they had little faith in the police on the spot, either because those police were thought to be incompetent or were known to be complicit. Local official complicity was the suspicion in the March 1855 murder of Beeba Jan, a prostitute of Agra city, who had her throat slit in addition to being strangled – an odd detail that suggests a kind of warning to others, namely, to avoid talking to the police. The murder was not discovered for two whole days even though someone had reported to the chowkidar on the day after that something was amiss. A suspect was identified, and though it was learned that he had fled toward Gwalior and Tonk he was not apprehended. Meanwhile the magistrate who visited the scene of the crime "immediately on its being reported" noted the "great neglect on the part of the chowkeedars" for failing to immediately break open the lock; he even harbored "some suspicions of accessoryship though not sufficient for conviction." In the end the chowkidar was dismissed.[40]

Suspicions of a different kind of malfeasance, percolating higher up the official and unofficial chains of command, distinguished the murder of another prostitute, "Bujjo of Furruckabad," in September of 1855. Bujjo, who lived alone in a house in the city only "a few hundred yards from the Kotwalee," had been stabbed repeatedly in her house on or about September 25. On September 30, by which time the stench from her decomposing body was overwhelming, the police finally broke open the lock. After some prodding, Ajooba, a nine-year-old daughter of a neighboring prostitute named Hooseinee, identified some men whom she had seen enter the house five nights earlier; these individuals were immediately arrested but eventually released for lack of evidence. The reporting magistrate, W. G. Probyn, was convinced of their guilt however and stated that he "never released any prisoners in the whole course of my experience with greater regret than I do these." Probyn added that he suspected that the kotwal, who was "intimately connected with one of the principal personages in Furruckabad," had purposefully neglected to register the official report of the crime because he did not wish to delay

---

[39] No. 126 of August 6, 1856, NWP-CJP: R. Robertson, Suptdt. Delhi, to S. Fraser, Commr. Delhi, February 21, 1856. The other three men involved were acquitted on a technicality.
[40] No. 189 of July 10, 1856, NWP-CJP: "Extract cases no. 1 to 18 from the Agra Magistrate's narrative of crimes in connection with the Police Report for 1855," signed R. Drummond, Magistrate, February 4, 1856.

his own departure to a better posting in Mirzapore District under one Mr. Lushington, Probyn's predecessor in Furruckabad. This allegation made its way across the province and led to several subsequent follow-up letters between himself, the commissioner of the Agra Division, the secretary to the lieutenant governor of the province, and Lushington himself; Probyn chose to stand his ground, however, and refused to retract his original opinion of the case that had the kotwal "exerted himself directly the matter came to his ears, the whole case would have come to light, and the perpetrators of the murder brought to justice."[41]

The vague involvement of Magistrate Lushington of Mirzapur in corrupting the expeditious investigation of Bujjo's murder raises a related question, namely, the absence of cases in the North-Western Provinces Criminal Judicial Proceedings from the 1850s involving Europeans directly victimizing prostitutes. Does this mean Europeans – particularly British soldiers – did not murder, wound, rob, or otherwise harm cantonment or regimental prostitutes? This seems unlikely in the extreme, given what we know about crime against prostitutes in Europe in the same period. More likely, rather, is that British soldiers did commit such crimes, but the cases were dealt with outside the normal magisterial channels – that is, by the regimental authorities in courts of inquiry and courts martial. Though one might suspect that the outcome of such cases were less than satisfactory from the plaintiff's point of view, a systematic investigation would need to be undertaken to arrive at any certain conclusions on this score.[42] The impression one is left with is that, the views

---

[41] No. 201 of July 10, 1856, NWP-CJP: "Extract entries 1 to 3 Theft with murder from the Abstract Statement of Heinous Crimes for the year 1855" [Furruckabad], signed W. G. Probyn. See also 232 of July 10: C. B. Thornhill, Sec to Govt, to G. F. Harvey, Commissioner of Agra Dvn (which identifies Lushington as the former magistrate in Furruckabad); and 318 of September 13, 1856, Probyn to Harvey, August 30, Furruckabad (in which the influential personage is identified as the uncle of the kotwal, the "naib" of the "nawab rais" of Farrukhabad). Lushington's views on the allegation were solicited by the lieutenant governor, but if he provided them they are among the records that are missing, perhaps due to the rebellion. Probyn is the same official who reported in the case of the attempted murder of the prostitute Bilaso, noted earlier, that though her mother and sister were wounded and a doorman killed, she seemed "to have had a most wonderful escape." See no. 363 of August 22, 1856, NWP-CJP: W. G. Probyn, Offtg. Mag. Furruckabad, to G. F. Harvey, Commr. Agra Dv., dated July 11, 1856.

[42] An example of such a case, not involving a prostitute however, is the July 3, 1856 killing in cold blood of one Mahomed Khan of Sopheepoor, near Meerut, by a British artilleryman. According to R. H. Dunlop, the magistrate of Meerut, two British artillerymen had gone out shooting and had bagged a pigeon that happened to belong to an individual named Ramdhun of Sopheepoor. Ramdhun and his friend, Mahomed Khan, demanded the pigeon and threatened to complain to the quartermaster of the regiment about the shooting, at which point one of the two artillerymen, who had quietly been reloading, suddenly lifted his weapon and killed Mahomed Khan. The men then fled to their

of the occasional upright officer notwithstanding, British soldiers welcomed the opportunity to leave the cantonment proper for the local "fleshpots" of the bazaar. If so, there would be an incentive for the regiment to punish any soldier who harmed a prostitute, since the frequency of such crimes could result in government proscriptions against regimental access to bazaar sex. What we do know is that British regiments regularly availed themselves of the services of Indian prostitutes in the cantonment and even city bazaars, often in very large numbers. On more than one occasion well into the 1860s the military and civil authorities found themselves at loggerheads on this issue – with the former insisting that diseased prostitutes be locked up or otherwise kept off limits to British soldiers, and the latter stating in no uncertain terms that enacting such prohibitions would not only be impracticable but illegal. The Allahabad magistrate in 1863 put it best: Confronted with a demand by the brigade major of Her Majesty's 77th regiment that some particularly infectious women be arrested, he coolly declined, observing not only that prostitution was not an offense but that the women had done nothing to render themselves "amenable to the Law."[43]

The Prostitute and the Raj

One may conclude, based on the foregoing, that Company officials in the mid nineteenth century deemed women engaged in the sex trade to be worthy of legal and police protection, even if the bureaucratic machinery

---

regimental barracks, where their fellow soldiers barred entry to the crowd of the villagers that followed them. The body of Mahomed Khan was eventually brought to the sergeant, who instituted a court of inquiry. The plaintiffs were unable to identify the guilty parties in a line up however. The two artillerymen later confessed to the sergeant in private, but they alleged that the "affray" was the result of a scuffle in which the victim was accidentally shot. No. 144 of August 6, 1856, NWP-CJP: R. H. Dunlop, Magistrate Meerut, to Greathead, Commr., July 10, 1856. A court-martial held on August 16 cleared the accused, Gunner Patrick Corran, of the charge of premeditated murder; he was released back to his regiment. I am grateful to Douglas Peers for locating and sharing the court-martial record, General Orders 535, recorded August 30, 1856 (IOLR L/MIL/17/2/305, BL, London).

[43] Ballhatchet, *Race, Sex and Class under the Raj*, pp. 36–38 (p. 37 for the quote), citing India Military Proceedings in the India Office Records. When the magistrate suggested that the brigadier simply restrict his men from going to the haunts of these women, the brigadier became apoplectic and called the proposal "absurd," noting that the regimental "[l]ines are surrounded in every direction by Bazars that are in the civil jurisdiction." The brigadier was reprimanded for his intemperate tone, and no action was taken – until the passage of the Indian Contagious Diseases Act of 1868. A similar scenario occurred when the Agra magistrate was asked by the regimental brigadier to have some "diseased women 'turned out' of their villages, and the local *zamindar*s ... heavily fined for harbouring them."

and a sometimes questionable level of official integrity – not to mention the imperial double standard of race – rendered this a task difficult of accomplishment. Indeed, in some cases, such as those of the severe woundings or murders of Beeba Jan of Agra, Bussuntee of Jubbulpore, Hydree and Sahebjan of Allahabad, and Bujjo of Furruckabad, the officials on the spot even seem to have made the successful investigation and prosecution a point of personal pride. There are many possible bases for such official "benevolent paternalism" toward women deemed prostitutes. One possibility that cannot be discounted is that such self-representation on the part of officials in the reports was a function of the desire to inflate the official record and thus gain the notice of superiors in the divisional and provincial headquarters; but even this supports the point that prostitutes were considered deserving of legal and police protections. Another possibility is that British officials recognized the implicit importance of the work that prostitutes did for the social and sexual contentment of soldiers in both Indian and British regiments, and they sought to protect them accordingly – especially when those soldiers abused the privilege of ready access to these women. A third possibility is that the commercial nature of prostitution inadvertently endowed it with a special status under Company rule, and thus violence against prostitutes was seen to bear a family resemblance to other crimes that threatened the peaceful conduct of commerce.

Whatever the cause, an official "benevolent paternalism" toward prostitutes is consistent with the tenor of British Indian legal reform in the first half of the nineteenth century. According to Radhika Singha, magistrates in the Bengal Presidency (which included most of north India in this period) were increasingly concerned with "wives, children and the female relations of [poor] families being seduced away from them for the purposes of prostitution," so much so that Regulation 7 of 1819 gave magistrates specific provisions to "punish any person who enticed and took away a married woman from her husband, or an unmarried female under the age of fifteen living with her parents or legal guardians, 'for the purpose of rendering [her] ... a prostitute or concubine, or otherwise disposing of her in an unlawful manner ... '."[44] This legal reform, aimed at protecting the inviolability of the family, was constructed, as Singha argues, around the increased rights and responsibilities of the male head

---

[44] Radhika Singha, *A Despotism of Law: Crime and Justice in Early Colonial India* (Delhi: Oxford University Press, 1998), pp. 147–148; Singha cites Bengal Criminal Judicial Proceedings, 31 of July 9 [or 10?], 1819: J. Eliot to Regr. Nizamat Adawlut, West Bengal State Archives, as well as the Regulation 7 of 1819

of household. As such, it made "the domestic more domestic."[45] It also had the perverse effect, however, of drawing attention to the prostitute as an object deserving of state consideration, even pity.

Despite a host of legal interventions, the traffic in women and girls continued to be a familiar phenomenon in the North-Western Provinces, especially the further west one traveled. As the Muzaffarnagar District magistrate, H. G. Astell, observed with regard to Banjara slavers in 1849:

> [T]heir jurisdiction extends I believe to the whole of the Upper Provinces, from one end of which to the other this trade of Kidnapping appears to thrive. Of the existence of this nefarious trade I believe all Magistrates are aware but from the above circumstances [the jurisdictional boundaries] find themselves unable to do much for its suppression. The populous district of the Doab lying between Ally Ghur and Cawnpore appears to furnish the Chief supplies whilst in this neighbourhood [near Muzaffarnagar] and in that of Lahore, seem to be the principal marts at which the Females are sold.[46]

William Henry Sleeman even delineated a distinct brand of "thuggee" devoted to a version of this species of crime throughout northern India, termed "*Megpunnaism*," the murder of indigent parents for their children, in which Banjaras and other mobile communities were often implicated.[47] S. Fraser, the commissioner of Delhi, reported a rash of

---

[45] Radhika Singha, "Making the Domestic more Domestic: Criminal Law and the Head of the Household, 1772–1843," *Indian Economic and Social History Review* 33, 3 (1996): 309–343.

[46] No. 261 of September 30, 1850, NWP-CJP: H. G. Astell, Magstr. Moozuffernuggur, to D. B. Morrison, Commr. Meerut Dv., June 12, 1850. I am grateful to Clare Anderson for alerting me to this file. For Bengal proper, see Chatterjee, *Gender, Slavery and Law*. Officials had a more positive view of the efficacy of British suppression of the slave traffic in directly ruled territories by the late 1860s. For instance, J. Forbes Watson of the *People of India* series claimed that "[t]he practice of purchasing children to be instructed as courtezans was commonly practiced some years ago, even in British territories, and is frequent at the present time in those of native Princes; but the stringent nature of the laws existent under the British rule against all practice of slavery, however it may be disguised, prevents any open violation of them, and the customs formerly existent can hardly now escape punishment." This passage is included in the text glossing the photograph of the "bazar woman," Wuzeerun – see Figure 3.1. J. Forbes Watson, *The People of India: A series of photographic illustrations, with descriptive letterpress, of the races and tribes of Hindustan*, vol. 3 (London: The India Museum, 1868–75), no. 165.

[47] W. H. Sleeman, *A Report on the System of Megpunnaism or, The Murder of Indigent Parents for their Young Children (who are sold as Slaves) as it prevails in the Delhi Territories, and the Native States of Rajpootana, Ulwar, and Bhurtpore* (Serampore: Serampore Press, 1839). Singha, *Despotism of Law*, pp. 161–162, cautions against discounting Sleeman as simply a sensationalizer. Though his work was clearly possessed of an "Orientalizing" dimension, one claim that he made, that many ascetics were involved in the enslavement of children, would seem to be borne out by the evidence: On *gosain*s see Pinch, *Warrior Ascetics and Indian Empires*, chapter 4, and on *bairagi*s see Indrani Chatterjee, *Gender, Slavery and Law*, pp. 222–223, 246; in both, however, women procurers were explicitly involved as well.

complaints in 1855 that thieves had carried off young girls in the Rohtuck District and had, with the connivance of the Jhujjur Nawab and other chieftains of the region, sold them to the "dancing women of the Jhujjur Ilaqua." One of the women even showed one of the girls to her parents, apparently with the idea of selling her back – to no avail.[48] In the same year, the Agra authorities were sent two individuals who had been arrested by order of the political agent at Gwalior for child theft in Mathura District.[49] By far the most detailed case, however, comes from the Meerut Division, and involved the capture red handed of a gang of Banjaras by an intrepid kotwal in 1849. The arrest occurred in a village near Muzaffarnagar where the Banjaras were putting up in the house of a local zamindar while they conducted sales in the vicinity. A total of fourteen women and girls were recovered, six of whom had already been sold and taken to prostitute establishments in Meerut and Sardhana. The women had been kidnapped from the districts of Aligarh, Etawah, and Mainpuri, all located 200 to 300 miles south of Muzaffarnagar. The authorities attempted to reunite the victims with their families but were only able to do so in the case of three of the fourteen – the three that were young girls. The remaining eleven, said to be "women of full age," were disowned by their friends because they were presumed to have become prostitutes. "They were allowed to go their own ways when the case was finally disposed of."[50]

It is difficult to know which way that was. Like stocked trout in season, they were probably too dazed to do more than swim in plain view against the current, ready to be caught again. Many surely ended up returned to the establishments from which they had been rescued, though this would have been complicated to some degree in the particular case cited earlier by the fact that the women that ran those establishments had been arrested and convicted.[51] Whatever their fate, the apparently docile behavior of

---

[48] No. 108 of August 6, 1856, NWP-CJP: S. Fraser, Commssr, Delhi, to Sec to Govt, Agra, May 19, paras. 91–94.

[49] One of them was described as a forty-six-year-old Gosain named Golab, the other a twenty-eight-year-old Brahmin named Bhowany. No. 220 of February 14, 1856, NWP-CJP: Cover Letter from G. F. Harvey, Offg. Commissioner Agra, to Sec. to Govt, January 31, 1856. See also 271–272 of January 19, 1856, describing a sixty-year old "Goshein" woman named Ghanee arrested for kidnapping a female in Jaipur and trying to sell her in Patiala

[50] No. 261 of September 30, 1850, NWP-CJP: H. G. Astell, Magstr. Moozuffernuggur, to D. B. Morrison, Commr. Meerut Dv., June 12, 1850.

[51] On the procuring of girls for regimental and sadr bazaars, see Chatterjee, "Colouring Subalternity," pp. 62–68. The close connection between female enslavement, female procurers, prostitution as sex-slavery, and the cantonments in British India is now widely accepted; see e.g. Ketan Mehta's film, *The Rising: The Ballad of Mangal Pandey* (2005), which features an early scene of a slave mart near the cantonment in which the local

these young women presented what Astell described as "the most curious circumstances elicited from the investigation," namely, the apparent ease with which the females were "captured" and conveyed about the province. Even though most of the victims were "women of full age," which Astell later specified as between fifteen and twenty years, and though they "appear[ed] to have been brought ... against their will," they nevertheless allowed themselves to be transported all the way from the Banjara slave "depot" in Aligarh District "without making the slightest attempt to make their situation known to the Travellers on the road, or at the Halting places." Even more astonishing for Astell, these women allowed themselves to be "tempted to go a little way from their village with the promise of sweetmeat," evincing a degree of gullible simplicity "one would think only applicable to that of a child of 4 or 5 years of age."

Two explanations seemed to compete for primacy in Astell's mind: the alarming suspicion that these young women wanted to run away from home, versus the conviction that the docility of these women was a mark of their race, not unrelated to "the usual apathy of natives of this country" invoked by Cookson of Meerut a few years later. The first response imagines the women as subjects, the later as objects, in the grammar of enslavement and prostitution. Astell may have been programmed to favor the latter conviction, given the racialist paradigms that increasingly structured British thought in the nineteenth century. Observers in the twenty-first century, on the other hand, are perhaps more likely to acknowledge the possibility that they were willing runaways, to interpret their flight as a bid for freedom – even as an embrace of prostitution as sex work, free of the modern moral stigma that much of the nineteenth and twentieth centuries placed upon it. In any case, it is possible to imagine that the docility and childlike simplicity that Astell saw in these young women was in fact a series of defensive masks that they put on after being rescued, the first steps toward a feigned innocence as they sought to navigate the unfamiliar moral shoals of Company law.

Assuming that a postmodern injection of agency into the action of mid nineteenth-century women is not entirely off the mark, we might ask what could prompt a young woman to let herself be taken from her home or (more likely) the home of her husband. In later depositions, some of the women stated that "they were beguiled under false pretences."[52] Perhaps

brothel owner is implicated (I am grateful to Indrani Chatterjee for first drawing my attention to this scene; personal communication, March 27, 2007).

[52] According to a later report of the actual trial by the Sessions Judge at Saharanpur, some of the women later deposed that "they were forcibly taken away by threats, and others that they were beguiled under false pretences." See no. 61 of June 10, 1850, NWP-CJP:

what some of these young women sought, not unlike already enslaved women in western India who fled their masters' homes,[53] was a new home and new kin – and that this is what the Banjaras offered them as a way of luring them into their net. Not all north Indian homes were happy ones, as we know not only from common sense but from the illicit sexual-emotional relations in Agra and Meerut glimpsed earlier. New marriages could be arranged, but they would have to be far enough away to evade the existing kinship webs in which the women were already enmeshed. Hence the willingness to travel long distances with the Banjaras with relatively little complaint or calls for help. Another motivating factor may have been more basic: simple destitution.[54] Astell suggested as much when he explained that the women could not return to their homes because the presumption of their having become prostitutes "made their *friends* disown them" (emphasis added). That he spoke of "friends" and not "family" suggests that these women had no family to turn to, perhaps due to death – though it is also possible that the presumption that they had fallen into prostitution prompted their families to sever ties.

It is also difficult to know whether and to what degree the turn to "sex work" in northern India began with a moment of enslavement. But the slave dimension does offer an additional insight as to the nature and evolution of a "benevolent paternalism" on the part of the Company. Perceiving this, however, requires rethinking slavery not in terms of the conjoined discourses of property and freedom that have dominated the historiography of Atlantic plantation slavery (not to mention the philosophy of British and British Indian law), but in terms of the social death and rebirth, or marginal kinship, that slavery in fact constituted in practice.[55] What did this mean for girls enslaved into prostitution? As the civil surgeon of Rangpur (in Bengal) noted in the early 1870s, "girls sold to elderly prostitutes 'generally look up to the woman who brings them up as their own mother'."[56] This was because, as the deputy magistrate of

G. H. France [?], Sessions Judge Saharanpoor, February 6, 1850, to M. R. Gubbins, Offg. Regr. to the Court of Niz. Adt., Agrah.

[53] Sumit Guha, "Slavery, Society, and the State in Western India, 1700–1800," in Chatterjee and Eaton (eds.), *Slavery & Society in South Asian History*, p. 179.

[54] Singha, *Despotism of Law*, p. 160; Pinch, *Warrior Ascetics*, pp. 80–81; Chatterjee, *Gender, Slavery and Law*.

[55] See the discussion in Chatterjee, *Gender, Slavery and Law*, esp. pp. 26–28; Guha, "Slavery, Society, and the State," pp. 162–165; Suzanne Miers and Igor Kopytoff (eds.), *Slavery in Africa: Historical and Anthropological Perspectives* (Madison: University of Wisconsin Press, 1977); and Orlando Patterson, *Slavery and Social Death: A Comparative Study* (Cambridge, MA: Harvard University Press, 1982).

[56] Judicial Proceedings, West Bengal State Archives (WBSA), no. B269 of October 1872: Civil Surgeon Rangpur to Commr. Rajshahi Divn, dated May 27, 1872, cited in Chatterjee, *Gender, Slavery and Law*, p. 222.

Tippera (also in Bengal) noted in the same year, the "old prostitutes" would "obtain children too young to know their parents" who were then "taught to call them [the old prostitutes] mamma."[57] As Indrani Chatterjee has argued, not only was marginal kinship central to slavery in south Asia but thinking about slavery in this way helps us see continuities and ruptures between the "pre-colonial" and the "colonial" in new ways. Sumit Guha, Ramya Sreenivasan, Richard Eaton, and Dadu Ali have elaborated on this key point, describing the centuries prior to 1800, by highlighting the fact that often the claimant kin of the slave was the corporate body of the king – in other words, the state.[58] Sometimes these royal slaves were soldiers; and sometimes they were concubines. The Nagpur state in the early nineteenth century even claimed low-caste widows at risk of falling into prostitution, deeming them *rājbeṭī*s, "daughters of the state," and selling them off to the highest bidder, often at a considerable profit.[59] The Company obviously chose a different tack, especially as the abolitionist movement gained steam. Instead of claiming destitute women at risk of prostitution and selling them, usually to wealthy men, nineteenth-century officials did the reverse: They sought to "rescue" women and girls sold into prostitution. But while the girls could usually be reunited with their families, the women were left, as we have seen, "to go their own ways." The Company was willing to be a "benevolent paternalist," but it would only allow the recipients of that "benevolent paternalism" to be free agents. Thus was the discourse of slavery reconfigured from kinship to freedom in the nineteenth century.

Were increasing numbers of prostitutes free agents in the nineteenth century? This is the flip side of the problem posed earlier, about the degree to which prostitution in northern India began with a moment of enslavement. Perhaps the expanding cantonment and regimental bazaars were attractive to some women – especially those captured in their teens whom the magistrates did not manage to rescue, and for whom the elderly prostitutes who purchased them could never be maternal figures – precisely because it was thought to be an arena where they could establish a degree of free agency and engage with Company officials as

---

[57] Judicial Proceedings, WBSA, no. B271 of October 1872: Dy. Magt. Brahmanberia to Magt. Tipperah, dated May 25, 1872, cited in Chatterjee, *Gender, Slavery and Law*, p. 222.

[58] Daud Ali, "War, Servitude, and the Imperial Household: A Study of Palace Women in the Chola Empire"; Richard Eaton, "The Rise and Fall of Military Slavery in the Deccan, 1450–1650"; Ramya Sreenivasan, "Drudges, Dancing Girls, and Concubines: Female Slaves in the Rajput Polity, 1500–1850"; and Sumit Guha, "Slavery, Society, and the State in Western India, 1700–1800" – all in Chatterjee and Eaton (eds.), *Slavery and Society in South Asian History*.

[59] Guha, "Slavery, Society, and the State in Western India," p. 167.

"benevolent paternalists." In other words, perhaps such women looked to the corporate military body of "John Company" as an owner-patriarch-parent, not unlike the way royal slaves in earlier regimes conceived of their kings. This is, of course, speculation, but it does present the beginnings of a logic whereby "Cashmerians" might look one way on May 10, 1857, while the wealthy elite who owned establishments, such as Mees Dolly, might look another. What we do know is that the conditions were ripe for an expansion of prostitution throughout northern India in the early nineteenth century. The cantonments of the Bengal Army, the single most potent embodiment of imperial legitimacy in the early nineteenth century,[60] grew exponentially after the Company's capture of Delhi in 1803.[61] The decisive military component of this new standing army was the infantry, which required large numbers of disciplined men willing to work for long periods of time away from home. That Banjaras and other slavers could undertake the outright kidnapping and sale of women and girls with relative ease and on such a large scale suggests that there was a growing demand for prostitutes. Perhaps it was being met by "free" women as well.

Whether or not we can perceive a transformational logic based on enslavement, kinship, and freedom to understand the choices prostitutes made in Meerut on May 10, what is interesting about all this is the degree to which prostitutes come out of the shadows prior to 1857. They appear as surprisingly visible figures in early British India, both at the level of ideology (as the strong shadow cast by a rising domesticity) and practice (as the resilient victims of crime). Prostitutes seemed to matter in different ways to different people. And because they mattered, it should not surprise us that they might have operated decisively on both sides of the political fence on May 10. Whether or not they actually caused the military revolt in Meerut, and by extension "1857" the event, they were very much part of the world that gave rise to it and gave it meaning.[62]

---

[60] Seema Alavi, *The Sepoys and the Company: Tradition and Transition in Northern India, 1770–1830* (Delhi: Oxford University Press, 1995).
[61] Peers, *Between Mars and Mammon*; T. Jacob, *Cantonments in India: Evolution and Growth* (New Delhi: Reliance Publishing House, 1994).
[62] Portions of this chapter draw on and update Pinch, "Prostituting the Mutiny: Sex-slavery and Crime in the Making of 1857," in Crispin Bates (ed.), *Mutiny at the Margins: New Perspectives on the Indian Uprising of 1857*, vol. I (New Delhi: Sage, 2013), 61–87.

Entr'acte
Zahir Dehlvi's *Tale of Treachery*

The claim that prostitutes of the sadr bazaar at Meerut sparked the premature military revolt at Meerut (and thus inadvertently saved the British from a synchronized rebellion across north India) originated with an English-language source: the report of J. Cracroft Wilson, written on December 24, 1858. In this report, Wilson described the women as the "frail ones of the Meerut bazaar." As Wilson put it, "the frail ones' taunts were heard far and wide" and "the spark which fell from female lips ignited it [the revolt] at once." Wilson's account was later bolstered by research done by Lieutenant-General George MacMunn in the early twentieth century. In 1912 or 1913, while posted in India, MacMunn stumbled upon a passing reference in a letter from W. Henry Norman, adjutant general of the force that besieged Delhi, written in August 1857 to his wife in the hills, describing a European woman hanged at Meerut for "being implicated in the arrangements for the first outbreak." At some point in the early 1920s, while again posted in India, MacMunn met an aged pensioner and "Mutiny" veteran who had taken part in the operations in and around Meerut. This individual remembered the European woman and identified her as one "Mees Dolly," a regimental widow who had gotten into trouble for theft and "drifted to the bazaar" at Meerut. Captured near Meerut, she had been wanted for "egging on the mutineers" and for helping in the murder of two Eurasian girls who also lived in the bazaar.

In 1914, soon after MacMunn had stumbled upon the letter from Norman to his wife, an Urdu book entitled *Tarāz-e-ẓāhirī*[1] was published from Lahore. Better known today as *Dāstān-e-Ghadr* ("A Tale of Treachery"),[2] the book's author was the poet and erstwhile Mughal

---

[1] A play on the author's first name, Zahir, this title may be translated as "the ornament's appearance."

[2] I prefer "treachery" rather than the usual "mutiny" for "ghadr" (غدر) because it better captures the shared sense of betrayal experienced by both Dehlvi and the Mughal emperor Bahadur Shah Zafar at the behavior of the sepoy rebels.

courtier, Zahir Dehlvi, who had passed away three years earlier in Hyderabad. Born about 1835, Dehlvi had grown up in Mughal Delhi, or Shahjahanabad, the scion of a family with long and distinguished administrative service to the imperial court. A frequent visitor to the palace from the age of eight, Dehlvi was appointed at thirteen or fourteen to the post of *dārogha-e-māhī-marātib*, or "superintendent of the fish insignia." This meant (as Dehlvi's recent translator Rana Safvi explains) that "he was in charge of the Mughal emperor's fish emblem, which was used on ceremonial occasions and processions."[3] Safvi adds: "As part of his duties, he had to accompany the emperor whenever he went out whether in official state processions or in public. On other days, he gave attendance at the jharokha [balcony] darshan and in court."[4]

Dehlvi was in Delhi when the rebels arrived from Meerut on the morning of May 11, 1857. The first half of his book details the events of that fateful day and the subsequent months in and around Delhi. Early in his account, Dehlvi described the initial confrontation between the rebel cavalrymen, who had forced their way into the palace, and the emperor, Bahadur Shah Zafar. The cavalrymen wished to enlist the emperor as their leader. For his part, however, the emperor was dismayed at the turn of events and demanded an explanation for the cavalrymen's conduct. In response, the men recounted the circumstances of the notorious cartridges, the refusal of the eighty-five skirmishers to perform the firing drill, the subsequent court-martial, and the punishment meted out to their brethren at the "ironing parade" on May 9. Then, according to Dehlvi, they added the following explanation:[5]

---

[3] Rana Safvi, "Translator's Introduction," in Zahir Dehlvi, *Dastan-e-Ghadar: The Tale of the Mutiny* (Gurgaon: Penguin, 2017), pp. xiii–xiv. Dehlvi's mother's uncle previously had held the position until his death in 1848 (Dehlvi, *Dastan-e-Ghadar*, trans. Safvi, p. 13). See also Dalrymple, *The Last Mughal: The Fall of a Dynasty, Delhi 1857* (New York: Knopf, 2007), pp. 17ff., 30.

[4] The *jharokhā darśan* was the daily public appearance of the sovereign on the balcony of the palace.

[5] My translation is from Zahir Dehlvi, *Dāstān-e-Ghadr* (Lahore: Sang-i Mīl Publications, 2007), pp. 47–48 (emphasis added). I follow my translation with the passage as it appears in the Urdu. Because previous translations (including Safvi's) of this difficult passage gloss over important details (see note 8), I endeavor here to stay as close as possible to the original. While refining the translation I consulted with several colleagues, to whom I am grateful. They include Sonal Singh in 2013; Rana Safvi and the late Shamshur Rahman Faruqi in 2017; and Seema Alavi, Dalpat Rajpurohit and – especially – Aftab Ahmad in 2018. I have italicized the sentence where Dehlvi describes the women and discuss it in greater detail in Chapter 4.

When we entered the jailhouse in Meerut camp there was total mayhem and there was speculation in and consultation among every household. *Especially among women, as they have always been foolish and short-sighted. The result [of their actions] never occurs to them. Among them the majority were women whose men had been imprisoned.* By using insulting language and taunts they fanned mischief and mutiny, and their sharp tongues worked like fuel on fire. At this point [as the old saying goes], ["]one only needed to say *hu* to provoke a crazy man["]came true.[6] Those women started to taunt the men, ["]you are all men and profess to be soldiers, but [in fact] you are shameless cowards, without honor. We women are better than you[.] Are you not ashamed that right in front of you your officers were shackled and handcuffed, and you stood by watching and could do nothing? Here, take these bangles and wear them, and give the weapons to us[;] we will liberate the officers.["] Those seditious words led to further escalation, and among the regiments of the entire army an impassioned fire of masculinity exploded, and [the men] were ready to kill and be killed, and together they decided that in the night they would break into the jailhouse and free the officers of the army. This is how it came to happen. In the night the foot soldiers and cavalrymen of the army girded for battle[7] and climbed onto the jailhouse and broke it open and rescued eighty-four officers and broke their handcuffs and shackles.[8]

---

[6] This sentence posed special challenges. The Romanized Urdu is "*is mahal par dīvānah ra hu e bas ast kā mazmūn sadik̤ āyā.*" The underlying idea is that when a *dīvānah*, a madman (whether crazy with the love of God or his beloved), hears the syllable "hu" (not unlike being snuck up on by someone who surprises you with the word "boo!"), it transports him into an uncontrollable frenzy. I am especially grateful to Aftab Ahmad for making this sentence clear to me (emails and conversation of February 27–29, 2018, with additional sharpening in January 2023).

[7] Lit., "tightened their belts."

[8] Safvi translates the italicized passage as follows: "There were conspiracies being hatched in every house with group discussions and debates everywhere, *especially amongst the womenfolk who have less power of reasoning and don't think of long-term consequences. There were many women whose inheritance had been confiscated*" (Safvi, *Dastan-e-Ghadar*, p. 59, emphasis added). Safvi adds the following speculative endnote (p. 314n59) after "confiscated": "Under the Doctrine of Lapse, adopted children were not considered legal heirs and many women and their adopted children lost their inheritance after the husband's death. However, these women were wives of erstwhile rulers, many of whom joined in the War of Independence. Here the reference may be to the employees and serving mother of the dispossessed women." Thus Safvi would seem to have interpreted the term *wursa* as "inheritance." As noted later, and in the introduction to Chapter 4, I translate this as "men" or "husbands."

Rizvi's translation of the same passage: "In every house there was a discussion about this. *Particularly the ladies were most zealous and those whose men were sent to gaol were most vociferous, (in their protestations).*" S. A. A. Rizvi and M. Bhargava (eds.), *Freedom Struggle in Uttar Pradesh* (hereafter *FSUP*), vol. 1 (Lucknow: Government of Uttar Pradesh, 1957), 406 (emphasis added).

The Urdu text as it appears in Dehlvi's *Dāstān-e-Ghadr* (2007 edition) is provided as follows. I am grateful to Aftab Ahmad who checked my Urdu typing and made some corrections.

جب ہم داخلِ جیل خانہ ہوئے تو کمپ میرٹھ میں تہلکہ عظیم بر پا ہو گیا اور گھر گھر کھچڑی پکنے لگی اور باہم صلاح و مشورہ ہونے لگی۔ خصوصاً فرقہ مستورات میں ہمیشہ سے ناقص العقل کوتہ اندیش ہوتے آۓ ہیں۔ ان کو ہر گز اپنے انجام پر نظر نہیں ہوتی۔ ان میں اکثر عورتیں تھیں کہ جن کے ورثاء محبوس ہونے تھے۔ انہوں نے زبان طعن و تشنیع سے پنکھا جہل جہل کر نائرہ فتنہ و فساد کو بھڑکانا شروع کیا اور ان کی چرب زبانی آتش فساد پر روغن کا کام کر گئی۔ اس محل پر دیوانہ را بوۓ بس است کا مضمون صادق آیا۔ ان عورا ت نے مردوں کو طعنے دینے شروع کیے کہ تم لوگ مرد ہو اور سپاہ گری کا دعویٰ کرتے ہوۓ مگر نہایت بزدل اور بے عزت اور بے شرم ہو۔ تم سے تو ہم عورتیں اچھیں، تم کو شرم نہیں آتی کہ تمہارے سامنے افسروں کے ہتھکڑیاں بیڑیاں پڑگئیں اور تم کھڑے کھڑے دیکھا کیے اور تم سے کچھ نہ ہو سکا۔ لو یہ چوڑیاں تو تم پہن لو اور ہتھیار ہم کو دو، ہم افسران کو چھڑا کر لاتی ہیں۔ ان کلمات فتنہ انگیز نے اور اشتعال طبع پیدا کیا اور تمام فوج کے دلوں میں جوش و خروش مردمی اور مردانگی کی آگ بھڑک اٹھی اور مرنے مارنے پر تیار ہو گئے اور باہم یہ صلاح قرار پائی کہ شب کو چل کر جیل خانہ توڑ کر افسران فوج کو چھڑا لاؤ۔

Dehlvi's 1914 memoir appears to confirm, at least in general terms, Wilson's 1858 claim that the women's taunts were the spark that prompted the military revolt at Meerut. Both accounts feature women who invoke the image of "bangle-wearing men" to shame the men of the 3rd Light Cavalry.[9] There are key differences, however. The most important of these concerns the identity of the women. Wilson calls them the "frail ones of the Meerut bazaar," which (as noted in Chapter 2) was a common Anglo-American euphemism for "public women" or prostitutes. Dehlvi, by contrast, describes them as the "women [*aurateṁ*] whose men [*wursā'*] had been imprisoned." The full sentence is: *in meṁ aksar aurateṁ thiṁ kæh jinke wursā' mahbūs hue the*, or "Among them the majority were women whose men had been imprisoned." Furthermore, he precedes this sentence by describing women in general using the term *masturāt*, a term that derives from Arabic that also means "veiled" or "chaste" women.[10] So, at least as far as Dehlvi was concerned, the cavalrymen who were humiliated on the night of May 9–10 did not regard their female tormentors as prostitutes.[11]

---

[9] Note, however, a slight difference: Whereas Wilson's "the frail ones" harangued the men with the image of their disgraced and imprisoned comrades being forced to wear "anklets" (a humiliating euphemism for shackles), in Dehlvi's account the women shame the cavalrymen of the 3rd by instructing *them* to don bangles.

[10] Platts, *A Dictionary of Urdu, Classical Hindi, and English*, p. 1033.

[11] The following discussion is confined to the possibility of independent sources for each account. It is remotely possible, however, that Dehlvi was the source for Wilson (see Chapter 5: Conclusions, Reflections).

How to assess the reliability of these two similar yet conflicting accounts? The first issue to be confronted is how Dehlvi and Wilson learned of the claim that women sparked the men's decision to revolt. Unfortunately, Wilson does not identify a source. He begins his report with the theory (see Chapter 1) that a synchronized uprising across north India had been planned for May 31, and that only Carmichael-Smyth's ordering of the firing drill and the fateful taunts of the "frail ones" saved the day by sparking a premature eruption of violence in Meerut. The only reference he makes to his sources is the prefatory phrase: "Carefully collating oral information with facts as they occurred."[12] He does add, however, that rumors of the complete massacre of the English at Meerut had begun to reach Moradabad (seventy-files miles west of Meerut) on May 12, and that on the following day "positive and authentic information of the massacre and outbreak was received." On that day, May 13, having obtained the permission of the military officers at Moradabad, he "went into the lines, and conversed freely with the Native officers and men of the 29th Regiment Native Infantry." According to Wilson, "[t]hey listened attentively, and it was easy to see that there was a great majority of the regiment in favor of peace and order."[13]

Thus it is likely that Wilson was told the story of the "frail ones of the Meerut bazaar" during his conversation with the men of the 29th Native Infantry on May 13, though there may have been glimmers of the account in the rumors that arrived on the previous day. There are, however, other possibilities. For example, on May 14, Wilson rode to Rampur to consult with the nawab, Yusuf Ali Khan, and his younger brother, Kazim Ali Khan – ostensibly because he was concerned that rival claimants to the Rampur state might use the opportunity presented by the chaos of the revolt to assassinate the nawab and seize the throne. But his real purpose was to ensure the nawab's support in putting down any impending revolt in the district. Wilson concluded from his

---

[12] J. C. Wilson, Commissioner on Special Duty, to G. F. Edmonstone, Secretary to Government, Allahabad, dated Camp Calcutta, December 24, 1858, reproduced in *FSUP*, vol. 1, 404.

[13] Ibid. Wilson's rapport with the sepoys is confirmed in a private letter of May 24 from Matilda ("Tilly") Saunders (the wife of the Magistrate of Moradabad, C. B. Saunders), who wrote that "he [Wilson] is a great favorite with the sepoys - talks to them in their own way – and they thoroughly understand each other – he had been to them repeatedly talking and entreating [? ill.] them and at this juncture they took their oath of allegiance on the Ganges water to remain true to their salt." See "Incomplete letter from Mrs. Saunders to England, dated May 24, 1857," in *Saunders Correspondence*, vol. 1 (Moradabad, May and June 1857), Mss.Eur.C93, Asia & Africa Collection, British Library, f. 6.

interviews that "both appeared loyal and true," though he was far less sanguine about "the whole Pathan race."[14] Wilson was in frequent contact with the Rampur nawab despite later abandoning Moradabad for Meerut District and, later still, the Gangetic belt between Aligarh and Farrukhabad. It is thus possible that Wilson heard the story of the "frail ones" during his visit to Rampur.

Dehlvi provides significantly more detail about how he learned the details of his version of the story. Though he recounts the interview between Bahadur Shah Zafar and the men of the 3rd Light Cavalry as though he were an eyewitness to it, in fact he was not present in the court in the early morning of May 11 when the cavalrymen stormed into Delhi, forced their way into the palace, and were confronted by the emperor.[15] This is because, as Dehlvi informs the reader, May 11 was Ramadan and he had risen late, at 7.25 am. As he was performing his morning ablutions a maidservant rushed in and announced that "there is a ghadar [revolt] taking place in the city!" Dehlvi, stunned and incredulous, interrogated her. She insisted that "sawars [cavalrymen] are roaming the streets and the dust of destruction is blowing all over the city." Soon after, a messenger from the royal quarters of the palace arrived and informed Dehlvi that he had been summoned – along with all members of the court – to attend the emperor. Upon his arrival at the *Diwān-e-Khās*, or special audience hall, he sat down amid some other courtiers to await the emperor's entrance. It was here that Dehlvi learned that seven Europeans had been killed, including the Resident. The news sent him reeling: "I lost my senses when I heard this, but after a while I regained some semblance of order." It was only then, he added, that "I heard an account of the morning's events from those present in the court."

To summarize: The source for Wilson's account was probably the collected officers and men of the 29th Native Infantry, with whom he conversed in the infantry lines on May 13 and who had been hearing rumors since the previous day about the circumstances that led to the violence in Meerut. The source for Dehlvi's account were the Mughal courtiers, with whom he spoke on the morning of May 11 in the palace and who themselves had witnessed the emperor's interrogation of the men of the 3rd Light Cavalry earlier that very morning. Thus, both Wilson and Dehlvi were one step removed from the initial actors – the soldiers who revolted.

---

[14] Wilson, p. 401.
[15] This paragraph is based on Dehlvi, *Dastan-e-Ghadar*, trans. Safvi, pp. 71–79.

The information chain for each may be represented thus:

Soldiers who revolted → Officers and men of the 29th Native Infantry → Wilson
Soldiers who revolted → Mughal courtiers in the palace → Dehlvi

It is worth noting, also, that Dehlvi received his information on the same day and in the same location – that is, on the grounds of the palace – where it was first transmitted to his immediate interlocutors, whereas Wilson's information would have traveled seventy-five miles over two days. Thus, it would not be unreasonable to regard Dehlvi's account as the more reliable of the two. However, it should also be noted that Wilson drafted his report immediately in the wake of the revolt, whereas Dehlvi's account was part of a memoir that was composed nearly a half century after the rebellion. Indeed, mindful of the passage of the years, Dehlvi insisted in his preface that "This is an absolutely truthful account of the events which took place in my lifetime, presented without artifice, exaggeration or dishonest manipulation ... I have used words that I heard from people during these events, and have not changed them. The incidents which occurred during this period, I have seen myself and jotted down faithfully." He added, for emphasis, that "I have written down everything that happened during the mutiny and not relied on market gossip."[16] It is even possible that Dehlvi kept notes to aid his memory. At one point in the mid-1890s, after he had shifted from Jaipur to Tonk, he described being robbed by a gang of highwaymen while traveling with his wife. The next day, when he returned to the scene to collect whatever he could find, he discovered that the robbers had taken all their money, jewelry, and clothes. But, he added, they "had done me a huge favour. They had left behind my most precious possessions – my ghazals, qasidas [long poems] and *other writings*."[17]

~ ~ ~

Dehlvi remained in Delhi through the summer, attending the emperor's presence. Meanwhile rebel soldiers from across north India streamed into the city, elevating it to the center of the rebellion – and elevating the emperor as its symbolic leader.[18] By June the British had regrouped and

---

[16] Dehlvi, *Dastan-e-Ghadar*, tr. Safvi, p. xx.
[17] Dehlvi, *Dastan-e-Ghadar*, tr. Safvi, p. 243 (emphasis added).
[18] The following two paragraphs, recounting Dehlvi's flight from Delhi, up to his arrival in Rampur, is based on Dehlvi, *Dastan-e-Ghadar*, tr. Safvi, pp. 144–167.

were commencing their prolonged siege from the ridge on the northwestern edge of the city.[19] After the British finally broke through the city's defenses in mid-September, Dehlvi made the decision to abandon his home. Even though he, like most of those in the service of the emperor – and indeed the emperor himself – did not support the rebellion and were severely critical of the behavior of the rebels, and especially the indiscriminate killing of Europeans, Dehlvi realized that his family could be in danger should they encounter rampaging Company forces. Gathering what belongings and valuables they could carry, Dehlvi's family headed south, exiting the walled city via the *Dilli Darwāzā* (Delhi Gate). They paused for a few days, along with several hundred other refugees, at the *barfkhāna* or "ice house," located outside the southern wall. There, on the fourth or fifth day, they learned of the execution of the head of the emperor's bodyguard, Mir Nawab – even though his father-in-law had been head of the British elephant stables and a key supporter of the British throughout the rebellion. This news convinced Dehlvi that not only were any servants of the emperor in mortal danger but that his presence could endanger the lives of his loved ones. Consequently he along with his brother and brother-in-law set out on foot in the direction of "Khwaja Sahib" (Nizammudin), which they reached in the evening after being repeatedly harassed by robbers. On the following day, joining a caravan of 15,000 to 20,000 refugees protected by a bodyguard of hired Gujjars, they reached the "*sarāi* of Sol Basant."[20] Two or three days later the caravan reached Farrukhnagar, thirty miles to the west.

At Farrukhnagar, Dehlvi and his kinsmen "were faced with roads leading in different directions."[21] They opted for nearby Jhajjar, where Dehlvi's uncle lived. They covered the sixteen miles in one day. However, after eight days in Jhajjar, they were forced to flee yet again as British forces were starting to threaten the town. They set their sights on Panipat, seventy-five miles to the north/northeast, where they arrived several days later – by then reunited with Dehlvi's father, mother, other brothers, sister, and wife, who in the meantime had arrived in nearby Barsath. Dehlvi does not provide clear dates, but at this point it would have been early October 1857. The family settled down in Panipat,

---

[19] See Dalrymple, *The Last Mughal*, for a detailed, captivating account.
[20] Possibly this is identical with the Basant Lok complex in present-day Vasant Vihar, and if so they only had managed to cover seven or eight miles. Dehlvi reported that "there was no food in sight" and "the soles of our feet were blistered, our throats and lips parched." This, the massive caravan, the heat, and the fact that they were unused to physical hardship, likely slowed their progress.
[21] Dehlvi, *Dastan-e-Ghadar*, tr. Safvi, p. 147.

rented a small shop, and earned a meager livelihood as traders. They remained in Panipat for about five months. However, the authorities began arresting refugees from Delhi – including one of Dehlvi's brothers, an uncle, and a brother-in-law. Sometime around March or April of 1858, Dehlvi along with several younger relatives decided to make their way east, to explore the possibility of settling the family in Lucknow. They managed to get as far as Bareilly when they learned that Lucknow "had met the same fate as Delhi" – that is, that Mughal refugees were being rounded up and executed in the wake of the British capture of the city. After two weeks in Bareilly, Dehlvi and another refugee, a cavalryman from the emperor's royal guard, were captured by rebel soldiers and accused of being British spies. They were saved from execution at the last minute by a former royal official of Delhi who had made common cause with the rebels. After some deliberation, Dehlvi decided to head northwest again, but this time his destination was Rampur. After a circuitous journey on back roads, he arrived in Rampur in late April 1858. Dehlvi and his party were soon introduced to the nawab, Yusuf Ali Khan, who immediately recognized his family name and assured them of his protection and eventually secured for them an official certificate of pardon. Dehlvi and his family would settle in Rampur for four years, where he found employment with the "Sahibzada," Muhammad Raza Khan, the son-in-law of the nawab.[22] The following decades would see Dehlvi shift back to Delhi briefly (1862), then to Alwar (for four years), Jaipur (nineteen years), and Tonk (fifteen or sixteen years); finally, after wandering in search of patronage, he settled in Hyderabad, where he died in 1911.[23]

---

[22] As noted, Wilson remained in touch with the Rampur nawab during his movements across the region in 1857–1858, therefore it is possible that this was his source for the Meerut "frail ones" account. I take up this issue along with other, related possibilities in Conclusions, Reflections.

[23] See Dehlvi, *Dastan-e-Ghadar*, tr. Safvi, p. 273.

4   ... Women Whose Men

> [T]he majority were women whose men had been imprisoned.
> Zahir Dehlvi, *Dāstān-e Ghadr* (1914)

When Zahir Dehlvi looked back on the sequence of events that led to his escape and exile from his beloved Delhi in 1857, the words of the rebel cavalrymen from Meerut echoed in his memory. Central to their explanation of why they had risen up in revolt were the humiliating taunts leveled at them by local women – or, more precisely, the "women whose men had been imprisoned." As first noted in Chapter 2, Cracroft Wilson had heard a similar story, though he described the women in question as "the frail ones of the Meerut bazaar," a mid-century euphemism for prostitutes. Bolstering Wilson's account (and terminology) was a separate source about the execution of a British woman who was wanted for her involvement in egging on the soldiers and, in addition, for the murder of two Eurasian girls in the bazaar – a story that was confirmed, many years later, in the recollections of an old "country-born" veteran in the early twentieth century. George MacMunn, who recorded this tale, concluded that the executed woman was identical to the veteran's "Miss Dolly," a down-on-her-luck British widow who had found a second career as a brothelkeeper in the cantonment bazaar.

Chapter 3, following on the accounts of Wilson, MacMunn, and the old veteran, explored the place of prostitutes in the cantonment bazaar. This chapter, by contrast, takes Dehlvi's claim that the *bāghī*s [rebels] were driven to take up arms against their officers by women "whose men had been imprisoned" (*jinke wursā mahabūs hue the*) as its point of departure. For Dehlvi – or, more pointedly, for Dehlvi's *bāghī*s – it was clear that these women were neither prostitutes nor brothelkeepers. The key term here is *wursā*, which I have rendered simply as "men." But the word is more complex. *Wursā* is the plural of the Arabic *wārat*, which means "the one who remains behind when all others have left." It conveys a sense of steadfastness and is even considered one of the names of God. In Urdu, in the context of women, the term *wursā* refers

125

to husbands, guardians, inheritors, or protectors. Thus Dehlvi, in saying that the women "were those whose men had been imprisoned," was also indicating that they were the wives, wards, or otherwise under the protection of the men who had been imprisoned – that is, the men of the Bengal 3rd Light Cavalry.[1] In other words, the men belonged to them and they belonged to the men.

To summarize, then, from Dehlvi's point of view these were mostly married women – or at the very least, they were perceived to be in relationships of mutual obligation and attachment with the imprisoned men. As we shall see, it was not uncommon for such women, whatever term we use to describe them, to live in or near the cantonment. But here things get blurry. While the social world of the Company Army has received some attention in the historical literature, particularly with respect to British women and, secondarily, the Indian wives of British soldiers (especially in the late eighteenth and early nineteenth centuries), we know next to nothing about the Indian wives and female dependents of Indian soldiers. Fortunately, sources do exist in the form of military pension records, though these have remained untapped till now. In this chapter I examine such records in order to fill out a picture of who the women of Meerut *may have been*; additionally, these sources begin to suggest why the wives and female dependents of Indian soldiers – and the soldiers themselves – might have begun to feel alienated from Company authorities by the mid-1850s.

"Fraudulent Wives"

A particularly attractive feature of Company military service was the regular pay it offered as well as pensions for "invalided" soldiers.[2] Initially these took the form of land, but eventually, as the supply dwindled, a monthly stipend system was instituted (see Figures 4.1 and 4.2 depicting veteran pensioners). If soldiers were killed on active duty, moreover, their named dependent would be awarded a "family pension." As a result, before deployments all soldiers were instructed to register their immediate relations on a pension roll that traveled with the regiment. The family members who could be so named were restricted to the immediate relations, that is, the mother, father, wife, son, and daughter

---

[1] For their comments on the layered meanings of *wāris/wārat/wursā*, I am indebted to Shamsur Rahman Faruqi (email communication of June 16, 2017), to Rana Safvi for additional insights and assistance, and especially to Aftab Ahmad for additional clarifications (emails of December/January 2022–2023).

[2] See esp. Alavi, "The Company Army and Rural Society," pp. 147–178.

Figure 4.1 "An old pensioned sepoy, wearing a medal," Calcutta (?), 1840, by Emily Eden
Source: Victoria Memorial Hall, accession no. R435-30. By kind permission of the Trustees of Victoria Memorial Hall, Kolkata, India.

(images of family pensioners are harder to come by, but see Figure 4.3). Each soldier would have to indicate the order of preference. Upon the death of the soldier in battle or on foreign service, the named beneficiary would come forward to claim his or her pension. After the identity of the family pensioner was confirmed, this individual would be paid a pension on a regular basis by "pension paymasters." The pension paymaster would travel to central locations of "pension circles" to distribute the pensions; the beneficiaries would likewise travel from their villages and towns to receive their pensions. Consequently, certain locales at or near pension circle centers and cantonments became attractive to pensioners as places of residence.

In the late 1840s, pension paymasters began to notice, or rather *assert*, that numerous "fraudulent" claims were being made on the pension

Figure 4.2 "A pensioned sepoy who had distinguished himself in the time of Lord Lake, and one of the police Chaprassees at Moradabad," North India, 1836–1842, by Emily Eden
Source: Victoria Memorial Hall, accession no. R435-67. By kind permission of the Trustees of Victoria Memorial Hall, Kolkata, India.

fund. Such alleged fraud took a variety of forms. The most common form consisted of women claiming pensions who were either reported to be outright imposters or near relations and not, in fact, wives or mothers. The precise cause and timing of the uptick in "pension fraud" is unclear. One precipitating factor may have been a general desire to cut costs: The Company frequently experienced phases of retrenchment, particularly in the wake of major military campaigns.[3] With the Anglo-Sikh Wars finally concluded in 1849, there would have been ample desire to find cost-saving measures across the military establishment, especially in the

---

[3] Peers, *Between Mars and Mammon*.

Figure 4.3 "Two old women who stationed themselves near the entrance to the camp on each day's march and accompanied 'our' camp for three successive years," Simla (?), 1840, by Emily Eden
Source: Victoria Memorial Hall, accession no. R435-95. By kind permission of the Trustees of Victoria Memorial Hall, Kolkata, India.
Note: Figures 4.1–4.2 are the only pre-1857 images I have come across of Indian military pensioners. Figure 4.3 merits comment since the two women are not explicitly identified as family pensioners by the artist, Emily Eden. Unfortunately, no mention is made of them (or of the veteran pensioners) in Eden's letters (compiled in Emily Eden, *Up the Country: Letters Written to her Sister from the Upper Provinces of India*, ed. Edward Thompson [London: Oxford University Press, 1930]). Eden does mention in a letter of November 12, 1837 two women who approached their entourage (she had joined her brother, the governor general, Lord Auckland, as he made a long tour of north India, from Calcutta to Simla and back, between 1837 and 1840). They appeared at the ghat in Ghazipur and appealed for a pardon for a husband of one who had been convicted of murder, loudly proclaiming his innocence (p. 19). However, Eden describes these two as having been "carried down [the steps of the ghat] in covered palanquins ... very much enveloped in veils," and making their petition "without showing their faces." They were later "carried off," never to be mentioned again. So they are unlikely to be identical to the women in the painting. Though the pension controversies described in the present chapter increased dramatically in the 1850s, it is possible that earlier cases had occurred and that the women in Figure 4.3 were rejected family pensioners hoping for an award or restitution of stipends. Another possibility is that they simply felt an affinity for the Company Army, perhaps in part due to pensions, and enjoyed the opportunity to travel with the entourage as camp followers.

Bengal Army (which was both the largest Presidency army and the one that had expanded the most during the 1840s). However, one official noted that the Afghan war of 1842 was a principal factor. Thomas Moore, pension paymaster of Meerut and Haupper, observed that the fraud was "almost entirely confined to Pensioners admitted since the disasters in Affghanistan [sic] whose claims were investigated by Special Committees assembled in the principal stations of the Army." Moore claimed that "it is now evident that advantage was taken of the difficulty which then existed in procuring correct information regarding the families of the men who belonged to Regts [sic] which had been destroyed and also perhaps of the general feeling of compassion which at that time existed throughout the country." The report of the pension paymaster at Allahabad supported this claim, citing the numerous fraudulent claims among family pensioners from the 37th Native Infantry, "destroyed in the retreat from Cabool." Two witnesses alone provided evidence backing up the claims of over thirty pensioners, "of whom several have proved impostors."[4]

As will be seen in the pages that follow, events in Afghanistan in 1842 (especially the retreat from Kabul and its aftermath) appeared frequently in investigations of fraud.[5] However, the nature of the fraud varied considerably, as did other military engagements. Casualties from the Anglo-Sikh wars between 1845 and 1849 also loomed large. Furthermore, sometimes the survivors knowingly made what would be deemed a "fraudulent" claim – that is, they seemed to be guilty of attempting to deceive the authorities and take advantage of the pension system – whereas at other times the claimants seemed to be innocent of any wrongdoing. And there was plenty of gray area in between. A typical example is the case of "Luchmee," who from 1842 to 1852 received 3 rupees and 8 annas per month as family pensioner no. 4150. Luchmee first arrived in the cantonment at Deyrah (now known as Dehradun) with Goor Singh Newar in the early 1820s. They lived together in the cantonment as he rose up the ranks to the position of naik. In 1840, Goor Singh

---

[4] R. Walker, Acctt Mily Dept, to A. S. Banks, Offg Secy to the GoI, Mily Dept, dated December 20, 1851, no. 132 of March 24, 1853, Military Consultations, National Archives of India (hereafter MC).

[5] The "Afghanistan Disaster" generated an outpouring of pension claims from surviving dependents. For a taste of this, see the Index to the Military Proceedings for the first six months of 1842, vol. 1 (A–B), under the heading "Adjutant General." I counted approximately thirty petitions for pension support by surviving dependents, usually forwarded by commanding officers of regiments; usually each correspondence referenced multiple requests for pensions. For the officially sanctioned generosity in adjudicating these claims, see nos. 52–53 of March 2, 1842 and 56–58 of April 6, 1842, Military Proceedings, National Archives of India (hereafter MP).

Newar was sent to Kabul and Luchmee went him. He was among the thousands of British and Indian soldiers that died in the "Disaster in Afghanistan." As Luchmee reported to pension paymaster Thomas Moore, "after his death [she] suffered the severest hardships in that country, [and] begged her way back to Deyrah, where she was told she was entitled to a pension." She accordingly "applied for it, and received it, but she was totally ignorant that she had no legal right to it."[6] In any event, the pension of 3 rupees and 8 annas per month, awarded her in May of 1842, did not provide sufficient funds for her upkeep so she "subsisted by working as a servant in the lines of the Battalion at Deyrah for her food." Moore recommended not prosecuting her in either the civil or criminal court, as she was too poor to pay a civil fine and "if convicted [of a criminal offense] she would be sentenced to imprisonment, during which she must be supported at the expense of Government thereby adding to the loss already sustained."[7]

What made Luchmee unworthy of any right to a family pension in Company eyes was the fact that, as Moore put it, "she had never been married to the late Goor Sing Newar" despite having lived with him for twenty years. She readily acknowledged her unmarried status both to Moore and to the junior officer in Deyrah, Lieutenant Aubert, who initially had alerted Moore to the Luchmee's case. But she also insisted that "she was guiltless of any fraud." Moore's superiors ultimately agreed to not prosecute Luchmee, though they originally had felt "she should be punished in some way or other."[8]

Luchmee's case did not end there. The Company military authorities, increasingly sensitive to fraudulent claims by the late 1840s, had instituted procedures to encourage their detection and discourage future "abuse." These were announced in series of circulars in 1849–1850 and 1850–1851. Circular 218 of 1850–1851 made provisions for the reward of 20 rupees to any soldier or pensioner who reported cases of fraud. A havildar of the Sirmoor Battalion, unnamed in the records, had alerted Aubert to the case of Luchmee. He was, accordingly, awarded the prize of 20 rupees. Additional reforms, noted in circular No. 8010 of 1849/50, required receipt of all continuing pension payments to be supported by "securities" or "sureties," witnesses among the soldiery or pensioner class who could attest to the identity of the claimant and

---

[6] Acct Mil Dept summary, dated March 5, 1851, no. 152 of March 14, 1851, MC.
[7] Thomas Moore to R. Walker, dated January 27, 1851, encl. in no. 152 of March 14, 1851, MC.
[8] See the notation to the cover note on p. 4, signed "WM," dated September 11, 1850, no. 151 of September 13, 1850, MC.

legitimacy of the claim.[9] When Luchmee had received her pension installment in 1850, she was supported by "Dillaram," pensioner no. 3681. When later confronted with the facts of the case, Dillaram reportedly stated "that the woman had always been looked upon in the light of Goor Sing [sic] Newar's wife, and that as she had been in receipt of a Pension from Government for so many years he did not consider he was doing wrong in stating what he did." Nevertheless, "he at the same time confessed that he was aware the woman had never been married."[10] Moore recommended he be struck permanently from the pension rolls. Ultimately the Council in Calcutta, worried about the effect such draconian punishments might have, chose to reduce the penalty to the forfeit of six months of pension.[11]

Luchmee's case had yet another twist. Her initial 1842 claim to a pension had been supported by two securities, men of the regiment. One had subsequently died at the Battle of Aliwal in 1846; the other, however, was still alive. His name was Naick Kesur Singh Rohilla, no. 5158, and he was receiving a pension of 8 rupees, 15 annas per month (over a third of which was for wounds received in battle). As this veteran resided in the vicinity of Deyrah, a popular settlement for pensioners, Moore called him in for an interview. According to Moore, the pensioner "stated that Goor Sing Newar was in the Sirmoor Battalion, whom he enlisted, that 'Luchmee' was then living with him, and he supposed her to be his wife, and under this impression gave evidence before the court." Moore felt that Kesur Singh was "as much, if not more to blame than the woman herself, as he was at the time holding the situation of pay havildar of his company." Moore recommended withholding six months of his pension as well, similar to the penalty meted out to Dillaram; this punishment was upheld by his superiors at Fort William.[12]

---

[9] The terms "security" and "surety" were used interchangeably in the correspondence.
[10] Letter from Thos. Moore, Major, Pension Pay Master, Meerutt and Haupper, to R. Walker, Accountant General, Mily Dept, Ft William, dated August 21, 1850, no. 151 of September 13, 1850, MC. Moore recommended Dillaram's removal from the pension roll, but Government opted to only deprive him of six months worth of pension. The final punishment is confirmed in the reply from Fort William in no. 152 of September13, 1850, MC.
[11] I return to the question of official anxiety over draconian punishments at the end of the chapter.
[12] Thos. Moore, PPM Meerut & Haupper, to R. Walker, AMD, dated January 27, 1851, no. 152 of March 14, 1851, MC. There were, of course, other "mistress" cases. See e.g. nos. 160–161 of June 18, 1852, MC, describing the situation of Moonia, who since 1842 had received a pension as the widow of Bhowanny Deen, a sepoy in the 37th Regiment Native Infantry who died in Afghanistan. In 1850 Moore received information that Moonia was, in fact, married to Bhowanny Deen's brother, named Banee, but she had left Banee to live with Bhowanny Deen and had two children by him. After

A second revealing case, also emanating from the "Disaster in Afghanistan," was that of Shah Begum and Neaz Begum, the two surviving wives of Mahomed Noor Khan, Ressaldar of the 3rd Irregular Cavalry (the very regiment that would refuse to fire the greased cartridges at Meerut in late April of 1857). This officer had died in October of 1842 during the retreat from Kabul to Jalalabad. The case involving his widows came under official scrutiny a decade later, in May of 1852, after the elder wife, Shah Begum, approached Moore while on his pension distribution rounds at Moradabad. According to the petition by Shah Begum, she had been fraudulently deprived of the pension by the younger wife, Neaz Begum, who in 1843 had gone to Umballah Cantonment (where the regiment was then headquartered) to make her claim to the pension. Shah Begum had initially intended to contest the award of the pension to the younger wife, but her relatives persuaded her to desist as it "would bring disgrace on the family." She relented, content with an informal arrangement whereby Neaz Begum would share half the 26 rupees per month pension with her. As it turned out, Neaz Begum failed to live up to her end of the bargain after the first installment. Despite this Shah Begum remained quiet, as she was able to survive on the proceeds of a house and some property left to her by her husband. However, according to the petition that she presented to Moore in 1852, Neaz Begum had recently attempted to relieve Shah Begum of that meager inheritance as well. It was at this stage that the elder wife decided to lay her case before the pension paymaster. Meanwhile, the younger wife, having gotten wind of the petition, also wrote to Moore, urging him to ignore Shah Begum's story, "as it was false." As both parties resided in Bareilly, which was where the regiment was also quartered in 1852, Moore ordered that the commanding officer institute a formal committee of enquiry. This was headed by Lieutenant S. G. Hire; it heard the testimony of three senior Indian officers of the regiment who confirmed the elder wife's account in all its essentials. Upon reviewing the evidence, officials in Calcutta decided that henceforth the pension should be awarded to the elder, Shah Begum, "without disturbing the payments heretofore made to Neeaz [sic] Begum."[13]

Bhowanny Deen went to Afghanistan "she rejoined her husband [Banee] at Kurnaul and has resided with him since." In June of 1852, following an investigation by the magistrate at Panipat, Moonia was struck off the pension roll.

[13] The information in this case is contained in nos. 130–132 of February 11, 1853, MC, which include letters from Th. Moore to R. J. H. Birch, Secy to the GoI in the Mily Dept, dated August 13, 1852; Hire to Moore, dated July 1, 1852; the report of the committee of enquiry; the copy of the pension roll from 1843 (noted); the departmental notes by Birch; and the final disposition of the case.

What made this case remarkable, in part, was the very fact that it found its way into the records. Many Afghan cavalrymen seemed to have had more than one wife, though in many cases the second marriage was of a different and more temporary sort than the first. We learn this from a later exchange between the officer who commanded at Moradabad, Colonel John Coke, and the Adjutant General of the Army (AGA) Lieutenant Colonel W. Mayhew, regarding an inquiry from the viceroy on the subject of the practice of "intermarriage of Pathans and Punjabee Mussulmans with Mahomedan women." Coke wrote:

> Doubtless many of the Pathans of the 1st Punjab Infantry and Mooltanee Cavalry married kept women at Moradabad, but there is nothing unusual or extraordinary in this, as they do so wherever they go. When the 1st Punjaub Infantry left Moradabad on the 10th November to return to the Punjaub they may have taken some 30 women with them as wives and concubines but I do not see that there is anything to apprehend on this account. The concubines after having relieved their men of their plunder will return and many of the wives will do the same. Those that are foolish enough to accompany the Pathans to their homes will lead a sorry life.[14]

It is possible that Neaz Begum was one of these "kept women" and, furthermore, that the "disgrace" the family of Shah Begum wished to avoid may have been in part related to the perceived ignominy of their ancestor having contracted a marriage of this sort.[15] Of course, this is speculation, as the records do not afford more information on this particular case.

There is, however, one additional detail of note from the case of the Begums Shah and Neaz. Also archived with the papers is a copy of the original pension roll that identified Neaz Begum as the claimant widow. In addition to recording her age as twenty-six years at the time of receiving the pension, in September of 1843, the pension roll noted the following information:

Religion, caste or tribe: Pattanee.
City or village: Jellalabad.
Pergunnah or Zillah: Shajehanpore.
Province: Shahjehanpore.
Indelible marks at the period of being pensioned: Has a small black mark about the size of a pin's head, on the palm of the left hand close to the thumb[.] rather fair.

---

[14] Memorandum by Col. John Coke, dated January 8, 1859, encl. in no. 1100 of April 29, 1859, MP. Based on this memorandum, the government concluded "that an undue importance seems to have been attached to these so called marriages" (Lt Col W. Mayhew, AGA, to Secy to GoI, Mily Deptt, d/ Allahabad January 27, 1859, no. 1100 of April 29, 1859).

[15] I return to the question of second marriages later in the chapter.

Leaving aside the interesting fact that Neaz Begum hailed from "Jellalabad" (Jalalabad) – which suggests that she and Mahomed Noor Khan met during the 1839–1842 occupation of Afghanistan – the descriptive details in this pension roll point to a matter that plagued the family pension system, namely, the heightened sensitivities attendant upon the identification of female relatives. Indeed, this may also have been a source of the "disgrace" Shah Begum's family wished to avoid. Neaz Begum, for her part, was willing to tolerate the indignity of physical inspection for identification purposes. (Of course, as noted earlier, part of the family "disgrace" that Shah Begum's relatives wished to avoid may have been that Neaz Begum was one of the "kept women" described by Coke.) In any case, the problem of identification became especially pronounced in the then western reaches of Bengal Presidency, that is to say, in the Punjab, which came under Company rule after the Anglo-Sikh wars of the 1840s. Moore himself alluded to this dilemma in December of 1850, when he observed that "[t]he female relatives of the native soldiers generally have a very great objection to prefer [*sic*: proffer] their claims for pension or to attend to receive it, and many in consequence, tho' in indigent circumstances, make no claim, and from this, result many of the frauds."[16]

A further gloss was put on this "objection" to identifying female relatives by Lieutenant Colonel C. T. Chamberlain, commanding the 1st Irregular Cavalry in Lahore, who was tasked with compiling the pension roll for his regiment. Chamberlain prefaced his remarks with the observation that "[t]he men of the Irregular Cavy [*sic*: Cavalry] are generally considered of a different class to those of the Regts of the line and of 611 men borne on the Rolls of this Regt 590 are Mahomedans." He then observed that "the ladies and women of respectable Mahomedans are never permitted to leave the precincts of the harem, and therefore could not enjoy a pension unless for identification they personally attend in the Court of the disbursing officer." Chamberlain provided two examples. The first involved the wife of Meer Bahadoor Ally, the Ressaldar of the Regiment until his death at Dadur in 1841. "[H]is widow has never enjoyed a pension, which she would have done had her friends permitted her to attend for payment 10 years past by [*sic*] and the sum of (6000) six thousand Rupees has consequently lapsed to

---

[16] Major Thos. Moore, PPM Meerut & Hawper, to R. Walker, AMD, dated December 19, 1850, encl. in no. 211 of February 7, 1851, MP. Moore was "convinced that in this circle there are many frauds of this kind as yet undiscovered, though I have reason to suppose that at the next half yearly payment [as the news of stricter pension rules regarding fraud became more widely known] a good many will be exposed."

Govt." The second was the current Ressaldar, Mirza Azim Beg Sirdar Bahadoor, who refused to name either his wife or daughter, even though they were his only surviving relatives – his father and mother and son having already died. Chamberlain "explained that it was for the benefit of his family that he should do so, but he respectfully declined stating that he considered the credit of his family of more importance than a pension from Govt."[17]

Chamberlain did not give up, however. He suggested to the officer in charge of the Adjutant General's office, Lieutenant Colonel H. T. Tucker, that "instead of their being obliged to name their female relations that they be permitted to say daughter of so and so and that in lieu of appearing in court, they be permitted to draw the pension by power of attorney." He even suggested the further precaution that "the lumburdar or head authority [in the pensioner's village] could easily find out all information and be held responsible to Govt for the same." Tucker looked favorably upon Chamberlain's suggestion, though he was not keen on the idea of relying on the *lambardār*. He forwarded the correspondence to the governor general's office for final determination. The further up the chain of command the idea went, the less sympathy it received. By the time it reached Simla, it was rejected outright. "[T]he means of fraud upon the Govt and occasions for it are already too numerous and unavoidable to admit of His Lordship consenting to any relaxation of a rule which was well considered at the time [1847] and is, in the Governor General's judgment, wholesome and necessary."[18]

The governor general's decision on Chamberlain's appeal in 1851 was not without precedent. A similar decree had been handed down in 1850 in a different case, from Moradabad, involving the heirs of Sepoy Seearam Doobey in the Grenadier Company of the 36th Regiment Native Infantry. Doobey was killed in action on January 13, 1849 at Chillianwalla, one of the bloodiest battles of the Anglo-Sikh wars. In November of 1849 a committee of four British officers was formed to investigate the fate of the pension. Doobey had named his father,

---

[17] Lt Col. C. T. Chamberlain, Commdg the 1st Regt Irregr Cavy, to Brevet Major Major J. D. McPherson, Brigade Major, Lahore, dated March 13, 1851, enclosed in no. 83 of June 13, 1851, MP. Chamberlain noted that he was compiling the pension "long roll" in pursuance of Adjutt. Genl's Circular No. 2606 of November 23, 1847.

[18] Lt Col H. T. Tucker, AGA, to Major R. Wyllie, offg secy to GoI, Mily Deptt, dated April 30, 1851, no. 83 of June 13, 1851; and Col. J. Stuart, Secy to GoI, Mily Dept., to the Secy to the GoI in the Mily Dept Calcutta [?] [*sic*], Simla, dated June 2, 1851, no. 84 of June 13, 1851, MP. Governor General Dalhousie, who appears to have just arrived in Calcutta, concurs in no. 85 of June 13, 1851, MP.

Girdharee Doobey, age fifty-six, subadar of the 54th Regiment Native Infantry, as his nearest relation. However, Doobey's wife, Gaineea, age seventeen, appeared in person to claim the pension. The problem was that Doobey had not listed her name in the pension roll. Despite this deficiency, two native officers of the regiment gave evidence attesting to the legitimacy of Gaineea's claim. Subadar Gungadeen Opudeiah insisted that he "has known her since her marriage which took place three years ago." Similarly, Havildar Pokah Sing stated "that he has known the claimant between two and three years and has seen her frequently." Both added that Doobey "had an objection to mention her name, therefore it was not entered in the Book." The British officers therefore agreed that she should be awarded the pension and their decision was transmitted to Calcutta. However on February 22, 1850, the Calcutta Council recorded its decision to disallow Gaineea's claim, noting that "as Government permit their Native Troops to name an heir for Family Pension from five degrees of relationship [wife, father, mother, son, and daughter], and do not allow any interference with such nomination."[19]

Matters remained thus for five years. In 1855, however, the government began to bend on the issue. The occasion for this apparent shift was the increasing numbers of Punjabis, especially Pathans, recruited into the Company Army in the wake of the Anglo-Sikh wars. A detailed letter from then Major (or Captain?) John Coke,[20] commanding the 1st Punjab Infantry, opened on a similar note to that of Chamberlain's, quoted earlier: The men who objected to naming their female relations did so not out of any opposition to the orders of government; to the contrary, "the men most sensitive on this point, are in all probability, the best soldiers in the Regiment." Coke acknowledged that "this may seem very silly to European ideas" but added that, in his opinion, "they are more worthy to be considered honorable men, than those, who for the sake of the pension, mention the names of the female portion of their families, for it most certainly is considered a disgrace in the eyes of all respectable natives, more especially among Pathan tribes 'Trans Indus'." He editorialized further: "I consider the soldier who will not

---

[19] Nos. 97–98 of February 22, 1850, MC. Gaineea's claim should not be interpreted as an affront to the claim of her father-in-law. Given that she was only seventeen years old whereas Girdharee Doobey was fifty-four, the family could have reasoned that it would be better for the wife to receive the pension as the father was likely to die sooner (at which point the pension would be resumed by the government). Both claimants hailed from Mujawan Kote village, Chillie [pargana or thana?], Allahabad District.

[20] We met Coke earlier on the subject of second wives and concubines among the Pathans and Punjabi Muslims, in 1859.

sell what concerns his honor for money, is more likely to be a good soldier, than he who does so."[21]

To get around the problem, Coke recommended that the government simply confirm through witnesses the existence of female heirs without the naming of names. He pointed out that "[t]he fact of writing the name, does not appear to me, to establish the truth, or falsity of the case, as the soldier who wished to defraud Government, would not be deterred by the want of a fictitious name." Of particular concern was the fate of the deceased soldier's mother. Coke asked, with respect to mothers, "whether the certainty or otherwise, of a soldier, having a mother alive, is at all increased by knowing her name." What mattered was "whether the soldier has a mother alive, or not, not to find out what her name is." Coke also pointed out that after the soldier died, the difficulty of identification would resolve itself, "as the man who objected to mention the names of the females of his family would be beyond the reach of these feelings, and his heiress would have to appear before the committee, or relinquish her claim, which very few *if any* would do."

Brigadier N. Chamberlain, commanding the Punjab Irregular Force, supported Coke's recommendation and emphasized that this was not a matter restricted to the Punjab frontier:

However much the Trans Indus Mahommedan may differ from the Rajpoot of India, still when death is upon him, a provision for those he leaves behind becomes an engrossing thought, and the Havildar of the 1st Punjab Infantry, who told his Commanding Officer with his last breath that his old mother had been dependent upon him for her livelihood, and that if Government would continue to support her, he would die happy, merely said what many under similar circumstances would feel.

Chamberlain also noted that fully 35.8 percent of the Punjab Infantry, or 417 of the full strength of 1,162 men, were "Trans-Indus Pathans" who "object to give the information required to complete their kindred rolls." He added:

[T]hese tribes are yearly learning better to appreciate the advantages of our service; and the more we can draw them towards us, whether it be by the benefits of the pension establishment, or from any other cause, the more likely are we to find them true to their engagement. ... If the widow receives a monthly stipend for the loss of her husband, or the parent for his child, wives and parents will be the less ready to oppose their husbands or children entering our service.[22]

---

[21] J. Coke, Captn, commanding 1st Punjaub Infy, to Capt Adams, Major of Brigade, Kohat, dated June 24, 1855, enclosed in nos. 82–83 of February 4, 1856, MC.

[22] N. Chamberlain, Brigadier, Commdg Punjaub Irr. Force, to the Mily Secy of the Chief Commsnr of the Punjaub, Camp Kussmore, dated December 21, 1855, enclosed in nos. 82–83 of February 4, 1856, MC.

Chamberlain was less sure about Coke's other point, that women claiming pensions would readily present themselves to the pension committees, but he was willing to grant the possibility. He may have been concerned about a related issue: As many of these women were "*pardānaśīn*," that is, veiled and generally subject to guarded restrictions when it came to relations with men beyond the immediate family, the witnesses from among the class of pensioners serving as security at the time of awarding the pension to the women and surety when they appeared for periodic pension distribution would likely not be sufficiently acquainted with the women to be able to identify them by sight. This very problem had been noted by the pension paymaster of Meerut and Haupper in 1853.[23] In any case, in February of 1856 Calcutta decreed that a committee be constituted to investigate the matter and make recommendations.

The results of that investigation are not known. In the meantime, another issue had come to the fore: the meager nature of physical descriptions of claimants in the pension rolls. We have already seen an example of this in the description of Neaz Begum, the younger wife of Ressaldar Mahomed Noor Khan. The "indelible marks" recorded at the time of her admittance to a family pension in 1843 consisted of "a small black mark about the size of a pin's head, on the palm of the left hand close to the thumb." In addition, she was described as "rather fair." Neaz Begum's case was not one of impersonation, of course. Rather, she had attracted official attention in 1852 due to the petition of the elder wife of Mahomed Noor Khan, whom the younger woman had defrauded and was later trying to dispossess. But one can easily imagine someone impersonating pension claimants on the strength, or rather weakness, of such flimsy marks of identification.

The military authorities had come to the same conclusion. In November of 1855 the military auditor general and the accountant in the Military Department wrote to the Calcutta Council that "many of the frauds which are now practiced are attributable to the very casual and superficial nature of the examinations which are undergone by pensioners when attending for the payment of their stipends, encouraged also doubtless by the very limited and indefinite description given of them in

---

[23] Thomas Moore to C. H. Lushington, dated November 26, 1853, enclosed in no. 230 of December 9, 1853, MC. Moore also noted that "[t]he identity of Family as well as all other pensioners is proved at each payment by requiring them to exhibit the marks entered on their Rolls before paying them their stipend." It is worth noting, however, that Neaz Begum, the younger wife of Mahomed Noor Khan, had readily presented herself at Umballah in 1843, whereas the elder wife, Shah Begum, had not. See earlier in the chapter.

their rolls." They therefore urged "a careful and minute description" of the claimant by the investigating committee when awarding the pension, and "a personal examination by the Pension Pay Master *himself* [emphasis in the original] of the pensioner with his roll aided by a diligent inquiry in each case concerning the claimant" – particularly when there was any suspicion of fraud. They even recommended that a "respectable European or East Indian" (i.e., Eurasian) clerk, with a beginning salary of Rs 100 per month, be appointed to assist the pension paymaster "in preparing cases for their examination, and generally superintending the establishment when the Pay Master is engaged in personally paying the Pensioners."[24]

Government sanctioned these recommendations and added one of its own: Pensioners should not be given copies of the full descriptive roll, which "contains full particulars in respect to peculiar marks, scars from wounds, etc.," as impersonators "representing deceased pensioners have inflicted wounds, and otherwise marked themselves, so as to correspond with the description given in the roll." Rather than "placing in their hands the means of enabling parties to commit frauds, Government are of opinion that a simple certificate containing a mere general description of the person would answer every purpose." The detailed roll would only be kept with the pension paymaster and amended as appropriate with "any further particulars coming under his observation after carefully comparing the roll with the pensioner's person."[25]

This all must have seemed perfectly reasonable to officials in the provincial and presidency headquarters. However, it must have been obvious to those serving in the bureaucratic bowels of the military that the addition of more staff, howsoever "respectable," and the keeping of close guard over the detailed descriptive rolls would not guarantee that fraud could or would be checked. A further glimpse of the challenges that bedeviled the pension system is afforded by the remarkable case of Rutton (sometimes spelled "Rattan"). Rutton had received a family pension in 1845 as the widow of Cassee Misser ("Kashy Misr"), a jemadar in the 5th Regiment Native Infantry, who had (along with his entire regiment) perished in Afghanistan. In 1853 one Shakh Salub Alee, pensioned naick of the 8th Regiment Native Infantry, presented a petition to F. C. Tombs, the recently appointed pension paymaster of

---

[24] A. Goldie, Coll. Mil Aud Genl, and E. Drummond, Acct, Mil Dept, to J. A. Dorin, President of the Council of India in Council, dated November 17, 1855, no. 639 of November 30, 1855, MC.

[25] F. D. Atkinson, Offg Sec to the GoI in Mil Dept, to A. Goldie, Mily Auditor Genl, dated November 29, 1855, no. 650 of November 30, 1855, MC.

Dinapore, Benares, and Monghyr, stating that Rutton had fraudulently obtained the pension as she had never been the wife of Cassee Misser but rather his mistress. Tombs had been on his rounds at Benares at the time and took down testimony of several witnesses (including Rutton) in the case, most notably Subahdar Major Bahadoor Adheen Pandy, pensioner of the 73rd Regiment Native Infantry, and a family pensioner named "Bunnoo" (sometimes spelled "Bannoo").[26]

According to the evidence collected by Tombs, especially from Bunnoo, Cassee Misser's first wife had died in 1829 or 1830 in Delhi.[27] In the following year Misser's regiment had been posted to Nusserabad. While accompanying a detachment thence to Ajmere, "he took the woman Rutton into his service ... for the purpose ostensibly of attending upon his infant children." Bunnoo informed Tombs that Cassee Misser was never married to Rutton, but that after his death in Afghanistan she endeavored to get a pension as his widow from two separate pension committees, "assembled at Ferozepore and Jaunpoor." However, because "she could not produce witnesses or securities to support her claim," she was unsuccessful. Bunnoo added that Rutton "eventually obtained a pension before a committee at Dacca thro' the connivance of Subehdar 'Adheen Pandy' and the Drummer 'Shamshair Khan,' since dead."

Not surprisingly, Rutton insisted that she and Cassee Misser were married at Ajmer, that at the time she was sixteen and he was seventy, and that he was "a high caste Brahmin" and she a "Mahruttin Brahminee, a native of the country of Ajmere." Rutton seems to have offered this last sociological detail in order to underscore her respectable rank and the caste propriety of their marriage. Ironically Tombs, in reporting this fact, inclined to the view that "no marriage could consequently I believe have been performed between them." Apparently, for Tombs, though they were both brahmans, the difference in their place of origin was enough to discount the legality of their marriage.[28] Rutton

---

[26] Tombs to C. H. Lushington, Acct, Military Department, dated July 1, 1853, enclosed in no. 139 of July 22, 1853, MC.

[27] This date, and much of the other facts narrated in 1853 by Tombs in this paragraph, would be revisited in 1854, on which see later in the chapter.

[28] Tombs seems to have had an extraordinarily inflexible "caste of mind" (cf. Nicholas Dirks, "Castes of Mind," *Representations* 37 [Winter 1992]: 56–78.) Cases of caste disparity occasionally cropped up, prompting the pension paymaster to conclude that the women were mere "mistresses" and not wives. See the case of Jeynee, determined by the paymaster of Meerut and Haupper to be the "mistress" of Surnam Singh of the 54th Native Infantry, detailed in a letter from Thos. Moore to E. Drummond, dated July 22, 1854, encl. in no. 149 of August 18, 1854, MC. Jeynee had received a pension as widow in 1842 but her claim was invalidated: whereas he was a "Chuttree" (kshatriya) she was a

further admitted, according to Tombs, that she had never had a child with Cassee Misser, but she elsewhere insisted that she was the mother of his son, Sunkur Misser, who was also killed at Kabul.

Tombs then related Subehdar Bahadoor Adheen Pandy's testimony. Pandy acknowledged that he had never seen Rutton before becoming her surety, "which he was induced to do in consequence of the representations of the deceased Drummer 'Shumshair Khan' and the Family Pensioner 'Bunnoo'." This was not all. Tombs added, with incredulity: "he cannot say whether 'Rutton' was married to 'Cassee Misser' or not, and that he personally knows nothing about her, her caste, her parents or her home, that he was not present at her marriage, and that he does not know when or where the committee was held before which 'Rutton' substantiated her claim to Pension." Despite all this, on May 19, 1844 Adheen Pandy "deposed before the Asstt Adjutant General at Benares" that he "recognize[d] Rutton ... as Cassee Misser's widow" and "always understood 'Sunkur Misser' late Sipahee of the same corps [as] the son of the Jemadar, and 'Rutton' his wife." This affidavit was then transmitted to Dacca (where the 5th was then stationed), where Rutton presented herself before a committee assembled on May 20, 1845 in order to make a third and ultimately successful attempt at claiming the widow's pension.

In his lengthy report of July 1, 1853, Tombs professed himself to be at a loss to explain Adheen Pandy's conduct:

I know not what the motives of a native Commissioned Officer of his rank and service (enjoying as he does a most liberal Pension) could have been in thus becoming surety for an utter stranger, whose appearance[,] conduct and language alone should have led such an experienced person as the Subehdar to doubt the possibility of Rutton's having ever been the married wife of a respectable native officer.

He flatly disregarded both Rutton's and Adheen Pandy's testimony and believed the case to be "one of clear fraud." In his view, "the woman appears to have effected her object by sheer importunity"; and he regarded the conduct of Adheen Pandy as "most culpable." The

---

low caste "Noonia" (or "saltmaker") and this was "sufficient to shew that no legal marriage could have taken place." According to her testimony, "many years ago a detachment of the 54th Regiment Native Infantry then stationed at Benares was proceeding on command to Jaunpore, and halted at the village of Sindorah, ... she met Surnam Sing then a sepoy of the Detacht., and formed an intimacy with him, and... having no relatives he took her to live with him, ... she had three children by him, and lived with him up to the period of the Regiment proceeding to Cabool." For another such case, adjudicated by Tombs, see the discussion of the "Koormin" Punnah later in the chapter.

government agreed and noted as well the "apparently very reprehensible proceedings held at Dacca on the 20th May 1845." On July 22, 1853 both Rutton and Adheen Pandy were struck from the pension rolls.[29]

The case did not end there, however. In late August of 1853, the governor general received two lengthy petitions, dated June 6, 1853 and apparently transmitted directly to Calcutta, bypassing Tombs. One was from Rutton, written from confinement in the Benares cantonment sadr bazaar *kotwali* or police station, and the other from Adheen Pandy. Though they differed in particulars, both leveled serious accusations against Bunnoo and, more importantly, one "Moonshee Badoolah, in the service of Captn Toob [*sic*]." Rutton detailed how when she was trying to claim her pension in the 1840s she sought out the aid of Bunnoo, who took her to Adheen Pandy. Bunnoo and the drummer Shamsher declared to Adheen Pandy that they knew Rutton well and had been present at her marriage in the regiment. "When they made this declaration before the subadar others were present, and equally bore witness to the truth. Among them were Khema Jevalar a woman who receives a pension, and resides in the lines and Hingoo a tailor, Sojeearee a woman." Adheen Pandy, supposedly (according to Rutton) satisfied of the truth of her claim, then went before the brigade major and provided his affidavit. "The Brigade Major got the papers, and sent them to the Regiment [then at Dacca] and I obtained my ticket."

Rutton reserved the juiciest details for the latter part of her petition, details that implicated Tomb's assistant in the Benares office, Moonshee Badoollah. Bunnoo, she claimed, was motivated by "spite and malice towards me." She explained:

The fact is as follows, the moonshee is the lover of Bannoo's grand daughter, and the Moonshee receives bribes through Bannoo. She said to me, the Moonshee is a very powerful man, you better give me some bribe for him, else he will bring you into difficulties and you may lose your pension. I refused to give her any bribe for the Moonshee, upon this ___ [*sic*] the Moonshee called some female pensioners and Bannoo, and wrote down false testimony, and brought me into my present melancholy position ... In opposition to the usage of public officers, the Moonshee wrote down the deposition of the witnesses which he himself suborned, and whom he examined in my presence, in his own words, and through I objected to his writing whatever he liked, my objections were not listened to.[30]

---

[29] General Order no. 584 of 1853, dated July 22, 1853, MC.
[30] "English translation of the Persian Petition from Rutten, widow of the late Kashee Misser," dated June 6, 1853, no. 249 of August 26, 1853, MC.

In short, Rutton, insisted, "they [Bunnoo and the Moonshee] want to ruin me, and to make ladies who receive pensions afraid of them, in order to compel them to pay them bribes."

Adheen Pandy's petition followed a similar narrative arc, but with more detail and rhetorical flourish.[31] He began by noting his forty-nine years of loyal service, during which he had seen combat in no fewer than thirty-three times, had twice volunteered for additional duty, had received medals and a gratuity for wounds, and had been raised to the rank of subahdar. After retiring to Benares he had received furthermore "a number of certificates and letters from officers in expression of their satisfaction with me." The remainder of the petition is worth quoting in its entirety:

I am not initiated in the intrigues and rogueries of courts of justice. Moonshee Badoollah is with Captn Tomb, and pays the pension, [and] tries now in my old age to outwit me. The circumstances are as follows. It is about eight years since Bannoo who receives a pension, and Shamsher brought Rattan the wife of the late Kashee Misr Jamadar of the 5th Regt to me and declared that she was the widow of the said Jemadar, and that her husband had been killed in battle, and that she was therefore entitled to a pension. She went in and out in my house for six months. I was aware that the Jemadar had contracted a second marriage, this circumstance had been attested by his mother in the presence of Jamadar Sree Misr and Bohount Singh and Subadars Mota Deen and Gunga Pundah of the same regiment. I was a friend of the late Jamadar, and acquainted with most of his circumstances. When I asked him regarding the marriage, he told me that he had contracted another marriage, and when Bannoo and Shamshera were asked they declared that the lady whom they brought to me had been his wife. After I had well ascertained the fact I went with Shamshera to the Brigade Major, and deposed to the fact and stood security. On this Rattan received a pension which she has drawn during eight years. Bannoo used to go with her to the pay office to fetch it. Her pension was eight rupees a month. This year [1853] I was called by Badoollah to his Bungalow, and he asked me regarding Rattan. I have been in the habit of talking to the officers, and therefore know how to speak, I gave him a correct statement of what had happened eight years ago. He cross examined me and it appeared to me that he was making fun of me. I am an old man, and have been honored by my superiors, and his ridiculing me was therefore very much out of place. I was much grieved, and said what do I know regarding her. [This and the previous sentence are marked with a penciled asterisk.] Having bad intentions towards me he wrote whatever he liked and laid it before the

---

[31] "An English translation of the Persian petition from Audhun Pandee, Subadar, stating the circumstances under which Rutten ... widow of ... Kashee Misser ... 5th NI, [was] deprived of pension," dated June 6, 1853, no. 251 of August 26, 1853, MP.

Captain [Tombs], who immediately ordered that Rattan be taken to the Kotwalee. I was much surprised at these proceedings, and left the Bungalow. I heard that there had been a quarrel [sic] between Bannoo and Rattan. The grand daughter of Bannoo is a sweetheart of Badoollah, and he therefore is in the interest of the family, and they all wish that the Jamadar's widow should lose her pension. With the intention of depriving her of it they conspired with several persons. During the quarrel [sic] Bannoo publicly said that Badoollah her grandson-in-law would support her, and threatened her that she would with his assistance deprive her of her pension and ruin the honor of "her" Subadar. Out of spite she made a deposition contrary to that which she at first had made and she suborned witnesses who attested that Rattan is not the widow of the late Jamadar. These witnesses are Janabe her son-in-law and one or two bad women.

My Lord what she now deposes is in opposition to what she formerly said. She came for six months every day to my house, and said that Rattan the widow of the Jamadar, who had been my friend, was in great distress, and requested me to interest myself in her behalf that she might obtain a pension. [penciled *] What she does now she does out of spite. [penciled *] If the case is well investigated, it will turn out that the Moonshee is in the wrong. I have therefore the honor to request that you will order that the case be thoroughly sifted. Three points require investigation – first [penciled *] Is Rattan the widow of the late Jamadar Kashee Misr or not? Witnesses to prove this fact are at Benares. [penciled *] Secondly, has Bannoo, who now contradicts her own statement brought her up out of spite or not. Thirdly. Is it true or not that Bannoo threatened her in the excitement of the quarrel that she would deprive her of her pension by the help of Moonshee Badoollah, who was her son in law, and that she would ruin the good name of the subadar. Also, is it a fact, or not, that Moonshee Badoollah is a lover of Bannoo's grand daughter? It is on account of this affair-de-coeur that he has contrived to deprive Rattan of her pension. All these points can be proved by trustworthy witnesses, if your Lordship will order an enquiry. In hope that you will not allow that my good name be blemished in my old age. I hope you will send order to the Magistrate at Benares to take up the matter.

Unfortunately for Rutton and Adheen Pandy, by the time the governor general in council reviewed these petitions, in late August of 1853, the two had already been struck from the pension rolls. The governor general accordingly ordered C. Hugh Lushington, the head of the Accounts section in the Military Department, to conduct a follow-up investigation. Lushington was the officer to whom Tombs routinely reported. Sadly, no report from the investigation appears in the files. Still, Pandy's petition seems to have had some effect: His first-class "Order of British India" insignia was ordered returned in November of 1853.[32]

---

[32] No. 122 of November 25, 1853, MP.

No change was made, however, to the decision to remove Rutton from the pension roll.[33]

The case did not end in the summer of 1853. Adheen Pandy, laboring under the cloud of disgrace, to say nothing of the loss of his pension, had sent in two subsequent petitions – one on September 13, 1853 and the second on July 27, 1854. Unfortunately, the September petition did not make its way into the records but, based on Pandy's July 1854 petition,[34] it would seem that the reply from Calcutta was less than what he had hoped for. It would also appear that the governor general had requested yet more information on how he had come to assist Rutton in securing a pension. In the third petition, consequently, Pandy "solemnly declare[d] that he had no hand in helping Ruttna [sic] in obtaining a pension as the widow of Kashi Misser Jemadar of the 5th Regiment N. Infantry." This declaration seemed to contradict the narrative in his first petition, so Pandy elaborated: "[Y]our Petitioner according to his custom of visiting Gentlemen with whom he is acquainted in his rounds, one morning called on Captain Lydiard the Adjtt. General of the Benares Division." This would have been in 1845. The drummer Shumsher and family pensioner Bunnoo "unfortunately" happened to be at Lydiard's office at the time, with Rutton in tow; they insisted to Lydiard that the Subadar Bahadur could attest to Rutton's status as the wife of the deceased Casee Misser. Lydiard then proceeded to question Pandy on the matter. Adheen allowed that "your Petitioner told him that he knew Kashi Misser and his friends[,] that in company with some native officers he had visited Kashi Misser at Saugor in 1819[,] that Kashi Misser mentioned to them that his wife was dead that he had married again and that the woman Ruttna then present had called on your Petitioner a few days ago and mentioned some of the incidents of that day[.]" But he explained to Lydiard, as he had to Rutton, that "as he had not seen her it was impossible for him to certify whether she was the identical person the said Jemadar had married on the death of his first wife." Pandy then stated that subsequent to his encounter with Lydiard, the pension paymaster at the time, one Major Boileau, had, despite Pandy's reluctance, urged him to act as a security for Rutton, "that [as Boileau put it, according to Pandy's retelling] there could be no harm in it as the woman had already been 7 or 8 years on the Pension list." This suggests that the encounter with Boileau occurred in 1852, just before that officer died and Tombs

---

[33] See nos. 495–496 of December 2, 1853 (regarding no change to Rutton's punishment), and 161–162 of December 9, 1853 (concerning the "irregular" and "unsatisfactory" proceedings of the Dacca committee from May 1845), MP.

[34] Pandy mentions his September 1853 petition in his July 1854 petition.

took over the office.[35] Pandy, "not wishing to act against the Gentleman's request[,] agreed to be security for the money he advanced her but not for her being the lawful wife of the said Jemadar." Pandy then added more detail about the "quarrel ... between Bunno and her Protégé [Rutton] about money matters," and how "Bunno to avenge herself told Captain Tombs the present pay master that Ruttna was not the lawful wife of the said Jemadar which statement she was of course afterwards obliged to maintain and of which fraud your poor petitioner is the victim."[36]

Upon reviewing this new information, the government relented and restored to Adheen Pandy a monthly pension of Rs 25. This was, however, far less than the original monthly amount of Rs 70. It would have been a severe blow for so distinguished and long-serving an officer. Perhaps the contradictory details that emerged in his petitions had undermined his case. And officials in the accounts section may not have taken well to the insinuations leveled at the late Major Boileau, the former pension paymaster. The curious fact that no report appears in the archives, despite the orders from Calcutta, suggests that matters may have been swept under the rug. Especially glaring is the absence of any mention by Tombs, or his superiors, of Tombs' (and, no doubt, Boileau's) influential assistant in Benares, Moonshi Badoollah, who was alleged by both Rutton and Pandy to have been entangled in a love affair with the granddaughter of Bunnoo, herself a pensioner, and to have orchestrated together with Bunnoo a shadow network that preyed on the fears and fading memories of old age pensioners with threats and bribes.

~ ~ ~

It is useful to pause here and reflect. Cases of pension "fraud" proliferated in the records between 1850 and 1857. Some involved, as in Luchmee's case, with which we began, women who were commonly thought to be married to soldiers killed in action but who, upon investigation, were deemed to lack sufficient legal standing as "wife" and therefore widow. Sometimes these women were described as mistresses, sometimes dependent wives of an unsanctioned type (more on this later). Less often, but not infrequently, the "fraud" involved multiple claimants to the status of "wife," as in the case of Shah Begum and Neaz Begum. Sometimes the claimants were children later deemed to be either adopted or

---

[35] See nos. 5–6 of October 1, 1852, MP. More on Tombs later in the chapter.
[36] Adheen Pande, late pensioned Subadar Bahdaoor, to Lieutt Coll R. J. H. Birch, Secy to GoI, Mily Dept, Govt House, Calcutta, dated July 27, 1854, no. 289 of August 25, 1854, MP.

"illegitimate." Cases of outright imposture, where women (and less often children and sometimes parents) claimed pensions in others' names, what today would be regarded as "identity theft," were far less frequent. And, as Rutton's case suggests, sometimes the fraud was being perpetrated by officials in the pension paymaster's office itself, with the connivance (and perhaps instigation) of family pensioners themselves.

Though the cases seem straightforward on the surface, especially when first encountered by the researcher in the military archives, most of them – when examined in detail – possessed a layered complexity that hinged on the very definition of legitimacy and respectability. As has become increasingly evident in recent years, notions of both legitimacy and respectability were firming up in British India in the early nineteenth century – even as (or, in fact, *because*) policies to detect "fraud" were being implemented. The upshot of the hundreds of cases that came forward in the 1850s was, invariably, that many survivors of Company soldiers killed in action were accused of being "fraudulent" and were often tried, convicted, and sentenced to imprisonment. Usually this resulted in the punishment of not only the "fraudulent" pension claimants (usually women) but also the sureties and securities (usually veteran or "invalided" pensioners) upon whom their claims to and receipt of pensions were based.

We began this and the previous chapters with the 1857 uprising at Meerut – and the taunts leveled by women at the soldiers of the Bengal 3rd Light Cavalry for not defending the honor of the men who had been imprisoned. Indeed, this book orbits around this key event. Zahir Dehlvi, it will be recalled, described these women as "women whose men had been imprisoned," using a term for "men" – *wursā* – that suggests they were the women's husbands. Wilson described the women, by contrast, as the "frail ones of the bazaar" – as women who would today, in a less euphemistic lexicon, be described as "prostitutes" or "sex workers." The pension records of the preceding seven years allow us to perceive these women according to less abstract, and less polarized, categories. Most importantly, John Coke reminds us that the women of the cantonment often occupied a gray area between prostitute and wife: as concubine or "kept woman." We are not far removed, it would seem, from Golab Jaun, the respectable "Cashmerian" woman who resided with the veteran surgeon Dr. T. Smith in the Meerut cantonment. Smith, it will be recalled, chose to disregard Golab Jaun's warning and was massacred by the mob on the evening of May 10, 1857.[37]

---

[37] See Chapter 2. I return to Dr. Smith and Golab Jaun in "Conclusions, Reflections."

Let us stay with Dehlvi for a moment. The women "whose men had been imprisoned," he informs us, taunted the men of the regiment for not defending the honor of their fellow soldiers, imprisoned due to their refusal to touch the greased cartridges. What has emerged in these pages so far is the fact that the question of honor was not restricted to men: The procedures being instituted to support bereaved survivors of those killed in action or on foreign service themselves required that women married to or otherwise dependent on these men sacrifice their own honor as well. British Indian regulations, being crafted in the early 1850s, were demanding that they step out from behind the veil for their own good, as it were.[38] We may conclude, therefore, that the tangled question of gender and honor was already in the air in the years immediately preceding the introduction of the Enfield rifle and its notorious ammunition.

How many cases of fraud were pursued in the 1850s? It is difficult to answer this question with any degree of certainty. During my research in the National Archives in New Delhi in the winter and spring of 2012–2013, I recorded notes on about 100 cases dated between 1850 and 1857. The peak years for such cases were 1853 and 1854. As I delved into the files, it became clear that part of the reason for the upsurge was the initiation of rewards offered to witnesses for the reporting of fraud, which had taken effect in 1850. The instigator of the rewards system was the pension paymaster of Lucknow and Cawnpore, one Captain Mariott. Apparently frustrated with what he regarded as the dubious claims being made upon his office, he had decided to pay – out of his own pocket if necessary – a reward of Rs 50 for information on one of two cases (though which one is not specified). One involved a woman (named Sewbundee) receiving a pension as the mother of a deceased sepoy; the other involved a boy (Seamloll Awasthee) receiving a pension as the son of another. Both had been receiving pensions since 1842 – the year of the retreat from Kabul. Upon investigation, the mother turned out to be the sepoy's aunt who had raised the sepoy from infancy after his own mother died; the boy was revealed to be not a natural-born son but adopted. Neither thus fell "within the degrees of relationship to entitle them to pension" and were stripped of their pensions. The Calcutta authorities agreed to cover Mariott's costs but sanctioned future reward amounts at Rs 20, noting that "[i]t is indispensably necessary to put a stop to these

---

[38] There is a resonance here with veiling controversies that brought French politics to a boil in the early twentieth century. See Joan Wallach Scott, *The Politics of the Veil* (Princeton: Princeton University Press, 2010).

frauds on the Pension Paymaster as soon as possible."[39] For his part, Mariott decided to retire in the following year, noting, "I have striven hard both to detect and prevent fraud ... as the duties of this office have been unusually heavy these last two years."[40] Again, this suggests that the late 1840s were the years when military authorities began directing their gaze toward questions of "pension fraud."

Given time constraints, I restricted my attention to "pension fraud" cases between 1850 and 1857. Also, because my attention was focused on the position of women in the cantonment, I concentrated my search on pension files that involved female-sounding names. In the foregoing I have provided a thematic sampling of these cases, mainly from the western half of Bengal Presidency, that is, from Benares to Meerut, including much of Awadh. In the following pages I focus on cases from Benares to the east, mainly involving the Dinapore Pension Paymaster's office (covering Bihar and eastern Uttar Pradesh). Sadly, space does not allow for a prose treatment of all cases that I examined, but Appendix 2 provides a complete listing.

It should be emphasized, however, that many more cases occurred than the 100 or so that I recorded in 2012–2013. Furthermore, the cases that made their way into the archives do not represent the entirety of the "fraudulent" claims adjudicated by the pension paymasters and the Adjutant General Accounts office in the Bengal Military establishment. This point is based on the following logic: Moore, the pension paymaster of Meerut and Haupper, calculated that, as of October 31, 1852, there were in his jurisdiction (which extended from "Futty Gurh [Fatehgarh] to Peshawar on one side, and Indore to Nepal on the other") 545 family pensioners (i.e., survivors of those killed in action or who died on foreign service). Of these, 321 (or nearly 60 percent) were females – mostly wives, but also daughters and, more infrequently, mothers.[41] All told, there were five pension paymaster "circles" for the Company's Bengal Army from

---

[39] See nos. 112–113 of April 26, 1850, MC. R. Wyllie, secretary to government in the Military Department, expresses doubt in his covering letter "whether, under the circumstances, the [Cawnpore] magistrate would punish them if brought to trial." This was likely due to the fact that the civil authorities tended to view the prosecution of such "frauds" as both a waste of the court's time and perhaps even morally unjustifiable. This was especially the case for "frauds" investigated by the pension paymaster of Dinapore, Tombs. See later in the chapter.

[40] Mariott is quoted in no. 6547 of March 21, 1851, encl. in no. 380 of August 8, 1851, MC.

[41] Thomas Moore to C. H. Lushington, dated November 26, 1853, enclosed in no. 230 of December 9, 1853, MC. Moore made this observation in the context of a different quandary faced by the pension office, namely, the fact that many of the women were "pardanishin" or veiled and that consequently the soldiers who stood security for them could not be expected in most cases to be personally acquainted with the women.

the 1830s to the 1850s: from west to east the circles were (1) Meerut-Haupper, (2) Cawnpore-Lucknow, (3) Allahabad, (4) Dinapore-Benares, and (5) Barrackpore-Chittagong. The density of pension paymaster offices in the central and eastern tracts of the North-Western Provinces (what today would be eastern Uttar Pradesh and Bihar) reflects the fact that the lion's share of military recruitment came from Awadh and Bhojpur – famously targeting men who were generally known as *"purbiās"* or "easterners" in Hindi-Urdu.[42] If we assume that each of these pension "circles" contained roughly 545 family pensioners (following Moore's estimate), then there would have been roughly 2,725 beneficiaries receiving family pensions at any given time. Again, based on Moore's estimate, about 60 percent of these, or 1,635, would have been female.

How many of these cases would have prompted a fraud investigation? In a not uncommon moment of bureaucratic editorializing, pension paymaster F. C. Tombs of the Dinapore office opined in 1853 that "about one fourth of the Family Pensioners on my Rolls are not lawfully entitled to their Pensions as not being within the prescribed degrees of relationship."[43] If we assume that Tomb's estimate reflects the emerging consensus among the pension paymasters, then we might conclude that approximately 681 claimants were suspected of being fraudulent in 1853, of whom 409 would have been female.[44] Admittedly, Tombs (who joined the Benares-Dinapore-Monghyr office in October of 1852) would become – as we shall see – well known in bureaucratic circles for his energetic attempts to ferret out and prosecute "fraudulent" claimants, so his numerical claims regarding "fraud" should be taken with a grain of salt and may not reflect the level of cases that were investigated and prosecuted in the early 1850s. Still, it would seem that the 100-odd cases that caught my attention in the archives in 2012–2013 represent a moderately small fraction of the total caseload. Furthermore, the fact that the fraud investigations invariably implicated the sureties (usually veteran soldiers) who backed up the pension claims, the total number of individuals impacted was substantial.

~ ~ ~

[42] On Company military recruitment, see esp. Dirk H. A. Kolff, *Naukar, Rajput and Sepoy: The Ethnohistory of the Military Labour Market in Hindustan, 1450–1850* (Cambridge: Cambridge University Press, 1990); and Alavi, *The Sepoy and the Company*.

[43] Tombs to Lushington, dated November 10, 1853, encl. in no. 225 of December 16, 1853, MC.

[44] The figures of 681 and 409 are derived by beginning with the 1,635 number arrived at in the previous paragraph and first dividing by four (based on Tombs' claim of a quarter being fraudulent) and then taking 60 percent of that figure (based on Moore's claim that 60 percent were female).

Tombs took over the Dinapore office, which handled pensions in Bihar and eastern Uttar Pradesh, in October of 1852. Formerly a lieutenant in 18th Native Infantry, and prior to taking over as paymaster, Tombs served in the commissariat branch. In that position he had attracted the attention of Governor General Dalhousie while the latter was on tour through north India. One Captain Maitland, the brigade major at Sialkot, had been in line for the Dinapore paymaster position, but he had been badly wounded at Multan and withdrew his application. Dalhousie took the occasion of Maitland's withdrawal to note that "[a]mong the many other candidates I find none preferable to Lieut. Tombs, now in the Commissariat Dept. He bears a high character; and having had an opportunity of observing his conduct in my own camp I can bear personal testimony to his able, conscientious, and successful performance of his duties."[45] So Tombs came into the office with a reputation for energy and zeal. He did not disappoint: Between 1852 and 1856 he generated more "fraud" cases than any other pension paymaster.[46]

The case of Rutton and Adheen Pandy in the Benares pension office, described earlier, was among the first that Tombs confronted. Another case, similar in certain respects (particularly in that it involved a widow later deemed a mistress), was that of Punnah, the wife of Aumunt (also referred to as Amunt and Aunint in the files) Singh, a sepoy in the 54th Regiment Light Infantry. Punnah had received her pension in February of 1843, after the death of Aumunt in Afghanistan. In his June 1853 report to Lushington in the Accounts Military Department, Tombs wrote that Punnah "confesses that she was the mistress and not the wife of the late 'Amunt Sing'." However, Tombs also enclosed in his report a note to the cantonment joint magistrate in Benares, requesting that he arrest the two sepoys who had stood as her surety in claiming the pension. In this note, Tombs added that the deceased soldier "was a Chuttree or Rajpoot Thakoor whilst 'Punnah' is a Koormin and hence it is evident that she cannot be the lawful wife (or widow) of the sepahee on whose account she has fraudulently obtained a Pension from the state."[47] The cantonment joint magistrate, who was none other than George

---

[45] Minute by Dalhousie on Bt. Captain F. Tombs, no. 5 of October 1, 1852, MP.
[46] See Appendix 2. Tombs accounts for all the Dinapore cases between 1852 and 1856, representing approximately 48 percent of the cases in the table.
[47] Tombs to G. B. Malleson, Cantonment Jt Magistrate of Benares, dated May 31, 1853, encl. in no. 130 of July 8, 1853, MP. See the other enclosures for Tombs to Lushington and Malleson to Tombs. The original pension roll was also included with the correspondence, in which Punnah's caste was reported as "Lackooe." She had received a pension of 2 rupees, 12 annas per month.

Bruce Malleson,[48] wrote back to Tombs on the following day, informing him that he had "found the woman 'Punnah' guilty of the fraud *therein imputed to her*, [and] sentenced her to six months imprisonment with a fine of twenty rupees" (emphasis added). In short, Punnah seems to have been convicted on the strength of her "confession" that she was a Kurmi married to a Rajput and thus guilty of an intercaste union.

To be sure, some of Tombs' cases involved outright imposture. A striking example concerned the pension of Sewnarrain Misser of the 15th Regiment Native Infantry. In June of 1854 Tombs received a tip that the person who had been receiving Sewnarrain Misser's pension was in fact an old soldier named Ramjeewun. The manner in which Ramjeewun had been able to accomplish this imposture reveals some of the logistical challenges confronting surviving family members seeking to present themselves in person to claim their pensions. According to Tombs' informant, Sewnarain Misser had died in 1842 or so, probably in Afghanistan. Soon after, Misser's mother, named Doolsunee, had set out for Benares, "to claim arrears of pension," Tombs presumed, "due to the Estate of her late son Sevnarrain [*sic*] Sing (Misser)." En route Doolsunee stayed at the house of an acquaintance, one "Musummut Sahujeh," and during the night she "seemingly placed the Roll inside the thatch of the roof of the hut for security." When Doolsunee departed the following morning, she forgot to take the roll with her. A year later, Sahujeh decided to get her roof repaired, and while this was being done "the parcel containing the Roll dropped out." Sahujeh showed the parcel to Ramjeewun, who recognized it for what it was and, "being an old soldier, determined to palm himself off as the original holder, a feat which he unfortunately accomplished. And thus carried on successfully a glaring fraud for some 10 or 11 years past."[49]

---

[48] Malleson would soon become a household name as the author of the scandalous account, *The Mutiny of the Bengal Army: An Historical Narrative* (London: Bosworth and Harrison, 1858), which began with a denunciation of numerous high-ranking military officials, including Colonel R. H. Birch, secretary to the government of India in the Military Department; and later as editor of Kaye's multivolume *History of the Sepoy War in India*, eventually reissued as *History of the Indian Mutiny of 1857–58*. In the early 1890s he would publish another controversial volume, *The Indian Mutiny of 1857* (London: Seeley & Co., 1891), in which he argued that the rebellion was the product of a widespread conspiracy (see Chapters 1 and 2). Nowhere in his writings does Malleson reflect on the role that the explosion of pension fraud investigations in the early and mid 1850s might have played in causing disaffection among the class of veterans and their families who had formerly been among the Company's most staunch loyalists.

[49] Tombs to Drummond, dated August 4, 1854, no. 356 of September 8, 1854, MP. See also the letter from Birch to Drummond, dated September 8, 1854, communicating the congratulations of the government.

Tombs did not detect this imposture on his own. In fact, he seemed to have been fooled by Ramjeewun's ploy. When Ramjeewun presented himself for Sewnarain Misser's pension, Tombs noted the identification marks of smallpox but also observed a discrepancy in the height of the claimant. Therefore he "examined the man rather narrowly and inserted some additional marks of identification." Though troubled by the height issue, Tombs put it down to the fact that "these men after the lapse of years become bent and decrepit from old age and infirmity and their measure does not correspond with that inserted in the rolls as the height at the time of a pension being invalided." Tombs added that "as the imposter Ramjeawun had been in the service[,] he was enabled to reply to such questions as are usually put by me in cross examination and to make a mily [abbr: military] salute, go through his pacing, etc." Luckily for Tombs, he was later tipped off to the imposture, probably by an informant desirous of the Rs 20 reward, and immediately wrote to the magistrate in Mirzapur, requesting that the culprit be apprehended. He concluded his report with the observation that this was the third such instance of veteran imposture that he had encountered, and that "[j]udging from these instances I doubt not therefore that other cases of fraud amongst even invalided Pensioners still exist and many probably of those men who have absented themselves since I received charge of this office or who have been reputed as being dead, were impostors." The government communicated to Tombs its approbation "at his activity in bringing to light so many cases of fraud."

Most of Tombs' efforts were directed not at detecting and punishing fraudulent veteran (or "invalided") pensioners but rather family pensioners. Cases of impersonation among family pensioners appeared to be fairly common and most often involved sisters, sisters-in-law, or aunts, who were not included among the acceptable "degrees of relationship," presenting themselves as either mothers or wives (widows). Sometimes the impersonation was simply one of convenience. An example is the case of Hanso, the sister-in-law of the deceased soldier, Hunnooman Sing (*sic*) of the 26th Regiment Native Infantry, who had been drawing the widow's pension since 1827. The widow, who is not named, was still living and according to the information received by Tombs, together they "have lived upon the proceeds of [the pension]" and "the fraud must therefore have been effected with her [the actual widow's] connivance." The reason for the fraud, it was presumed, was either that the widow, who was older, did not wish to subject herself to the inconvenience of travel to receive the pension, or that the family had decided to present the younger woman as the widow so as to extend the pension beyond the death of the actual widow in the event that the latter died first. Regardless, Hanso was struck from the pension roll and tried in the Patna court. But "[i]n consideration however of the age and infirmity of the defendant, she was sentenced to only seven days imprisonment without labor."[50]

Another case of this sort was that of Judoee and Purbuteeah, sisters-in-law. Judoee was married to one "Pudaruth Opudiah," a still active sipahi in the 46th Regiment Native Infantry, but since 1843 she had been collecting Purbuteeah's widow pension. Purbuteeah was the widow of the deceased Ramphul Opadia of the 5th Regiment Native Infantry, which had been destroyed in Afghanistan. Tombs discovered the impersonation in June 1853 when Judoee "kept aloof" and Purbuteeah instead appeared to collect her own pension. Tombs had just taken over from the deceased Boileau, and his reputation for strictly adhering to the rules was no doubt becoming well known. Possibly Judoee and Purbuteeah decided to own up to the impersonation, not realizing that Tombs would regard it as a case of "fraud" and use it as a pretext to remove both of them from the pension roll. This is suggested by the fact that no fewer than twenty-two invalided and family pensioners resident in the village Gahnur (or Gunbur?) gave evidence in support of the fact that Judoee had been collecting Purbuteeah's pension, including the two women themselves. The papers do not offer any specific reason for the practice, though it may have been simple convenience. In any case, they seem to have regarded it as a fairly routine matter, an innocuous bending of the rules. Tombs, however, was of the view that a "double fraud has thus been perpetrated." Both women were sent to trial.[51]

More often cases of impersonation involved a surviving family member not within the prescribed "degrees of relation" claiming to be a parent or widow or child of the deceased soldier. As with all the types of cases being surveyed here, there are far too many to recount in their entirety. What is interesting about these cases, however, is that they prompted Tombs to request that he be granted the power of a magistrate so that any statements made under oath in his presence would have the force of law. The case that prompted this plea was that of Cheejah, the sister of Dulloo Singh of the 35th Native Infantry, who had been receiving a pension as the mother since 1842 (Dulloo had been killed at Ghazni in Afghanistan). Cheejah had, according to Tombs, readily admitted in

---

[50] Tombs to Drummond, dated August 26, 1854, enclosed with Drummond to Birch, dated September 5, 1854, no. 161 of October 13, 1854, MP.
[51] Tombs to Drummond, dated August 5, 1854, no. 106 of September 22, 1854. See also no. 108 of September 22, 1854, MP, in which Birch recommends that both women be tried.

his office on January 1, 1853 that she was not really the mother of Dulloo Singh, as she was named and described in the pension roll, but his sister. Later in the month, when the case was investigated by the local *thanadar* of Beireah (in Ballia District), where Cheejah resided, Cheejah and eleven of her relatives insisted that she was in fact the mother. The magistrate of Ballia reviewed the report and concurred in this opinion. Tombs was convinced otherwise, however, so he wrote to the magistrate of Ghazipur requesting that evidence be taken from additional relatives (including Cheejah's brother and nephew) in other villages, and "of investigating the case in his [the magistrate's] own court and presence." This resulted in the conviction of Cheejah of "fraud and personation." She was sentenced to four months imprisonment and a fine of Rs 80 or an additional four months.[52]

Tombs concluded his report with an observation:

I take this opportunity of bringing to the notice of Government the all but impossibility of proving a case of fraud of this nature especially where the parties reside in the District and where they pertinaciously assert that they really are parents, children or widows (as the case may be) tho' it may be known that they are not so. The pensioners can of course always produce Friends and relatives in their respective villages to support their assertions and disinterested parties are unwilling to incur enmity and vengeance of the Families of the Pensioners by giving evidence against the latter – particularly when residing in the same village.

Cheejah had, according to Tombs, readily confessed in his office. But later, "when advised by her Friends I presume subsequently to deny the admission she almost succeeded in evading punishment." Tombs thus requested that "all Pension Paymasters be vested with the powers of a Magistrate in order that depositions taken in their presence may be legally formal." His reason was not simply that the utterances of family pensioners in his presence would themselves thus carry legal weight in court. Rather, his focus was on the inside information possessed by the sureties and securities among the veteran (or "invalided") pensioners:

There are generally speaking some one or more Pensioners who have some knowledge of the facts of each case as brought forward and tho' these people may not object to give their evidence on the spot and in the presence of the P. Pay Master [*sic*] they will frequently assert total ignorance of the matter rather than suffer the inconvenience of tedious attendance at a Magistrate's court with its concomitant expense and necessity of separation from their families and interruption to their domestic pursuits.

---

[52] Tombs to Lushington, dated June 13, 1853, encl. with no. 138 of July 8, 1853, MP.

Pension paymasters would be able thereby to summon witnesses, who "would not then be so much under the influence of the zemeedars [sic] and Head men of villages or the Friends, and relatives of the Pensioners implicated." Further, pensioners and their sureties and securities would "not be tempted to deny in a magistrate's court any confession which they might have previously made in the presence of a Pension Paymaster before they had the opportunity of consulting with their relations and tutoring their witnesses."

Lushington forwarded Tombs' request to the governor general in council, though he himself was opposed to it. Alternatively, he suggested that magistrates "give immediate attention to cases of fraud on the part of Pensioners."[53] Birch, acting for the Council, forwarded Tombs' request and Lushington's alternative recommendation to the civil branch in Bengal and the North-Western Provinces for consideration. In mid-August 1853, while these suggestions were being weighed, Tombs reported six additional cases "of fraud in which the pensioners concerned have admitted the fact and that several others are under investigation."[54] Many of the pensioners with suspicious claims, he added, "have absconded" and the district officers report that they "are not forthcoming in their villages[,] their securities having probably induced them to keep out of the way and thus prevent enquiry and investigation on my part." He therefore added another request: that securities be given six months from the date of the claim to come forward in cases where they suspect fraud, in which case they would be granted a full pardon for standing surety. In mid-September, word came down that both of Tombs' requests had been denied, as had Lushington's alternative that magistrates take immediate action on pension cases. With respect to the latter, the governor of Bengal Province had observed that an order giving priority to cases in which the government was concerned, "even if legal, would have an appearance of unfairness which nothing but extreme necessity could justify."

As to Tombs' request for magisterial powers, Bengal authorities felt it was impracticable: Even if Tombs were to take evidence under oath, the case would still have to go to a sessions or district judge for adjudication. The witnesses would have to be examined all over again, as "[n]either the judge nor the magistrate could legally decide a case upon evidence taken

---

[53] Nos. 141–142 of July 8, 1853, MP. See also Birch's summary note initialized by the Council members, dated June 29, 1853, included with no. 132 of September 30, 1853, MC. Lushington would soon begin drafting new procedures for prosecuting cases of pension fraud. These would be approved in March of 1854. See later in the chapter.
[54] Tombs to Lushington, dated August 16, 1853, no. 253 of September 16, 1853, MC.

before another officer."⁵⁵ And, finally, as for Tombs' recommendation to grant pardon to pensioners who come forward with new information about those for whom they had stood surety, thus encouraging them to discover frauds, Birch felt that "[i]t is so very delicate a matter, interfering with Pensioners, unless where fraud is plainly thrust upon the notice of Govt, that perhaps it may be thought inexpedient to dive any further than had already been sanctioned, into the secret history of cases now on the Rolls." The governor general in council, along with the other councilors, agreed: Dalhousie (using the letter D) initialed Birch's summary; another member, one "JS," penned, "I was incline [sic] to let bygones be bygones and be more cautious for the future"; and a third, "J,L" added, "I concur in the foregoing remark."⁵⁶

Tombs was undeterred. There were many cases to keep him busy – especially cases that he regarded as impersonation. Cheejah's case, described earlier, was important in that it prompted Tombs to attempt a legal innovation. It was not a typical case, however, in that Tombs did not include in his report Cheejah's motivation for impersonating Dulloo Singh's mother. Earlier we described some cases where the motivation seemed to be logistical convenience, or – less charitably – a desire to invest the youngest family member with the pension so as to extend its longevity. Either may have been the case with Cheejah. But there is another and more likely possibility. It was noted by Lushington that Dulloo Singh had listed Cheejah as the mother when he had filled out his pension roll before proceeding to Afghanistan. The official presumption was, no doubt, that Dulloo Singh was not simply complicit in the fraudulent impersonation but had actually masterminded it. However, it is also possible that Cheejah's birth mother had died in his infancy and that Cheejah, assuming she was sufficiently elder to him, had raised him in his mother's stead. He thus would have thought of her as his mother, and she would have thought of him as her son. Let us assume this is an accurate description of Cheejah's case. While a strict reading of the pension rules would enable Tombs to prosecute her as a fraudulent

---

⁵⁵ Cecil Beadon [?], Secy to the Govt of Bengal, to Birch, Offg Secy to the GoI, mily dept., dated Fort Wm, dated July 29, 1853, no. 154 of August 5, 1853, MC. The government's final disposition in the matter was conveyed in Birch to Lushington, dated September 15, 1853, no. 254 of September 15, 1853, MC. Also valuable are the summaries provided by Birch for the governor general in council, initialized and briefly annotated by council members, of July 29, August 5, and August 29, encl. with 132 of September 30, 1853, MC.
⁵⁶ Summary note by Birch, dated September 22, 1853, initialed and annotated by members of the council on the 23rd (D), 28th (JS), and 29th (JL) of September, encl. with no. 132 of September 30, 1853, MC. (JW also initialed and added a comment, but it is illegible and undated.) I have not been able to ascertain their identities.

"Fraudulent Wives" 159

impersonator, a more generous interpretation of the rules – an interpretation that focuses on the spirit of the pension system, namely, to provide support for the close family members upon the untoward death of the soldiering breadwinner in battle or on foreign service – would allow a case such as Cheejah's to be regarded as perfectly legitimate.

Many such cases emerge in the files. Sometimes they involved sisters, sometimes sisters-in-law. One such case was that of Tallewindee, who was granted a pension in March 1844 as the mother of Ghureeb Pandy of the 53rd Regiment Native Infantry. According to Tombs, "[i]t has been proved however, by her own confession and by the evidence of her surety and eleven other pensioners at Dinapore, that she is the Sister-in-Law and not the mother of the deceased Sepoy."[57] The government ordered that she be tried in the civil court. To Tombs' and Lushington's dismay, the magistrate of Patna, W. Ainslee, found her innocent. He reported his decision in a letter of April 3, 1854:

There is no doubt of the Pensr [sic] being the aunt and not the mother of the deceased sepoy Ghureeb Pandee. On the other hand there is no reason to doubt that, as alleged, she brought up as her own child the said Ghureeb Pandee from the age of 2 months when his parents died. She is not as aunt, entitled to the Pension[;] whether in consideration of the circumstances it should be continued or not is a matter with which I have nothing to do but I must say that I cannot impute a deliberate and intentional fraud to her and have therefore acquitted her.[58]

Tombs and Lushington were disappointed by this decision. The latter described it as "remarkable." For his part, Tombs recommended sending all future such cases to the cantonment joint magistrate rather than the district magistrate in the relevant jurisdiction, "as it will have a bad effect if impostors convicted of fraud escape with impunity when sent before the Civil Courts for trial."[59] Birch subsequently wrote to W. Grey,

---

[57] Tombs to Lushington, dated September 30, 1853, encl. in no. 188 of November 25, 1853, MP.
[58] W. Ainslee, Magistrate of Patna, to Tombs, Captn, Suptdt and Pension Pay Master of Native Pensions, Dinapore, dated April 3, 1854, encl. in no. 179 of May 26, 1854, MP.
[59] Tombs to Lushington, Dinapore and April 6, 1854, and in C. H. Lushington, Offg Acctt Mily Dept, to R. J. H. Birch, Offg Sec GoI, Mil dept, dated April 19, 1854, no. 179 of May 26, 1854, MP. While this case and others like it were being decided upon, Lushington had drafted formal procedures for the investigation and prosecution of pension fraud. They are too lengthy to quote here in their entirety but essentially capture the procedures that were evolving as a result of the numerous cases coming forward, especially from Tombs' office. See C. Hugh Lushington, "Draft General Order," February 22, 1854, encl. in no. 439 of March 17, 1854, MP. These were approved by the governor general in council on March 17, 1854. The draft was circulated for comment to the paymasters in Meerut, Allahabad, Lucknow, Dinapore, and Barrackpore. Very slight amendments were made, including the suggestion that cantonment joint magistrates be availed of in addition to district magistrates (as

secretary to the governor of Bengal Province, to convey Dalhousie's disapproval of the Patna magistrate's decision, which he deemed "singular."[60]

An especially revealing case is that of Gangia (also known as "Gungi" or "Gungoo" according to the transcript copies in the proceedings volume), who obtained her pension in 1844 as the mother of the deceased Atmaram ("Atruck Sing" in the first mention in the proceedings), a sepoy in the 30th Regiment Native Infantry. According to Tombs, Gangia admitted to him that she was the sister-in-law and not the mother of Atmaram. Her three securities also readily admitted the fact, as did four pensioned veterans and two family pensioners that were questioned. Tombs recommended striking her from the pension roll and trying her in the civil court.[61] He also recommended punishing two of the securities, pensioned sepoy Doman Singh and pensioned Havildar Persaud Singh, as they had "become sureties for no less than 17 and 20

---

suggested by Moore of Meerut). The consultation file included the departmental notes from the Calcutta Council, including a note initialed "JS" that "Mr. Lushington has given due attention to the suggestions of Pension Paymasters and perhaps more than was due to those of Captn Moorhouse, whose opinions are not entitled to much weight." This suggests that Moorhouse was deemed relatively ineffectual as a paymaster, at least when it came to detecting fraud. Or perhaps he was too sympathetic to the claims of pensioners? Prior to working in the pensions office, Moorhouse was a member of a rifle company in the 35th Regiment Native Light Infantry and earned campaign medals for Ghuznee (1839), Jellalabad (1841–1842), and Kabul (1842). He became pension paymaster at Allahabad in 1845 after serving brief terms as acting paymaster at Meerut, Jubbulpore, and Saugor from 1843. He held the position of paymaster at Allahabad until his death there of heat stroke and exhaustion in 1857. This information comes from the metadata accompanying an 1855 portrait of Moorhouse, held by the National Army Museum, London (https://artuk.org/discover/artworks/major-thomas-moorhouse-18071857-35th-bengal-regiment-light-infantry-182999).

[60] Birch to W. Grey, Secy to the Govt of Bengal, dated May 20, 1854, no. 182 of May 26, 1854, MP, NAI. The Patna magistrate became something of a thorn in Tombs' side. See e.g. the cases of Dooktee and Nunkee, nos. 253–256 of June 2, 1854, MP. Dooktee was, Tombs alleged, actually the sister-in-law of a soldier killed in action, but Ainslee felt she was still entitled to be regarded as the wife. Nunkee was not the real mother of a soldier killed in action, according to Tombs, but had adopted him as an infant. Ainslee felt this was sufficient to regard her as the actual mother. The skepticism of civil magistrates with regard to such cases was not restricted to the Patna court; see the case of Beesah/Bessah/Beesa, nos. 173–75 of July 11, 1856, MP, in which the deputy magistrate of Benares (unfortunately not named in the file) held that no guilt attached to a surety witness named Suddoo Sing, a pensioned sepoy, who was consistent in his belief that Beesah was the bereaved daughter of late Teeluck Sing, havildar, 42nd Light Infantry. Predictably this inspired incredulity on the part of the military authorities, who opted to fine Suddoo Sing regardless, for "an amount equal to that which accrued to her since he became surety." ("Benares Circle" pensioners fell under the jurisdiction of the Dinapore Pension Paymaster's office.)

[61] Tombs to Lushington, dated September 30, 1853, encl. in no. 188 of November 25, 1853, MP.

family pensioners respectively." By contrast, the third security, pensioned sepoy "Adjoodhea Doobay," appeared "to be willing to atone in some measure for his misconduct and offence by endeavouring to gain information of similar cases of fraud." Tombs suggested that he be pardoned if he could "bring to notice and prove at least 3 cases in which family pensioners may now be in the receipt of pensions, obtained under false pretenses."

Tombs was especially anxious to inflict a stern punishment on Gangia's two "obstinate" securities, Persaud Singh and Doman Singh. His views on them were identical, in one key respect, to his opinion of a surety in a previous case in the file, "pensioned Naick Ruggoonauth of the 20th Regt NI [Native Infantry]."[62] Ruggoonauth, Tombs reported, had

> been allowed ... to become security for no less than 35 family pensioners of all classes and castes, scattered all over the country of whose identity and actual degree of relationship it is impossible that he can have any knowledge and he appears to have made it his occupation to become the nominal surety of those Family Pensioners who could not I presume find sureties elsewhere, which he doubtless found to be a profitable speculation.

Tombs wished to grant Ruggoonauth pardon on the condition that he deliver no fewer than five cases of pension fraud. Ruggoonauth, like Doobay mentioned earlier, appeared willing to do so.[63] But Doman Singh and Persaud Singh refused this offer, and moreover were "obstinate to decline [*sic*] giving any information regarding the numerous fraudulent cases in which they must be doubtless implicated, and in short to throw obstacles in the way of enquiry and investigation." Tombs thus recommended their pensions be stopped and they be sent to the sessions judge so that they "may be punished for their disgraceful conduct."

What makes this case remarkable is that Persaud Singh and Doman Singh did not receive their punishment with quiet resignation. Not only did they refuse to become, in effect, Tombs' "approvers,"[64] they drafted a lengthy petition to Governor General Dalhousie, which they themselves carried to Calcutta, expressing dismay not only at their own punishment

---

[62] The 20th was one of the regiments that revolted at Meerut in May 1857.
[63] As noted later, the government frowned upon this course of action.
[64] This is the term used by the Department of Thuggee and Dacoitee, not by Tombs. Tombs seems to have drawn inspiration from Colonel William Henry Sleeman, who pioneered the practice of turning criminals into providers of what in the US context is called "state's evidence" by offering them with pardons or lighter sentences. See the discussion in Shahid Amin, *Event, Metaphor, Memory: Chauri Chaura, 1922–1992* (Berkeley: University of California Press, 1995).

but the abusive treatment being meted out by the government to an elderly woman that the deceased soldier regarded as his true mother.[65] They began their petition by reminding the governor general that "the pensionary support bestowed upon the soldiers and sepoys in the Hon'ble Company's service" is designed "to enable them to pass comfortably or without trouble the remainder parts of their respective infirm ages, prime parts of which they devoted in serving Gov't with faith and fidelity." Now, however, they were confronted with the prospect of "being stopped the payment of their pensions" and being left "unkindly to the insufferable violence of starvation." More importantly, they stated unequivocally that "Atmaram Sepoy of the Native Infantry ... having at the time of going on the Affghan expedition appeared personally before the Regt Committee stated that excepting Gangia his mother he had no other heir or heiress, and she having been according to his own declaration believed to be his mother, her name was penned in the book." She may have been his sister-in-law, but "he had himself actually called her his mother." Moreover, they added, "the Hindoos agreeably to the ever existing custom of their caste always esteem their eldest brothers as fathers and their wives as mothers with regard to the respect to them, on account of their being the greatest in age or first born by same parents."

Dalhousie, Birch, and the Council were not moved. They ordered that the two securities as well as Gangia be "be made over to the civil authority for trial."[66] Moreover, they "consider[ed] it *inexpedient* to authorize the entering into such compacts with the sureties as is proposed by Captn Tombs" (emphasis added). Adjoodhea Doobay and Ruggoonauth were thus also sent to trial. In the end, Tombs reported that Adjoodhea Doobay was pardoned as he "has been security for the Family Pensioner Gungoo only and as he has exerted himself to prove this case." The trial of Gangia, meanwhile, never occurred – or rather she was probably found guilty in absentia. She was reported to have absconded in Shahabad District.[67]

One final case of this sort is worth noting, even though it long preceded Tombs' appointment as pension paymaster. In 1850 "Soodhoo" was charged by pension paymaster Marriott of Oudh (Lucknow/Cawnpore)

---

[65] Petition of Pensd Havildar Persaud Sing and Pensioned sepoy Domun Sing, dated October 30, 1853, delivered to Dalhousie through Birch, no. 189 of November 25, 1853, MP.

[66] Birch to Lushington, dated November 19, 1853, no. 189A of November 25, 1853, MP.

[67] See nos. 416–418 of September 15, 1854, MP, including Tombs to Lushington, dated August 15, 1854. Shahabad District would become a center of the rebellion under the leadership of Kuar Singh and, as noted later, the canceled pensions of mothers and widows were a significant bone of contention in local memory.

with fraudulently drawing a pension as the mother of a deceased havildar of the 54th Native Infantry, "Mayaram Tewarry," another casualty of the retreat from Kabul in 1842. Soodhoo had supposedly "confesse[d] to be [ing] an imposter," as she was technically only Tewarry's aunt. She had begun receiving her monthly pension of 4 rupees and 8 annas in July of 1844, at the age of sixty. According to the pension roll, she usually received her pension in early July and mid-November. When questioned in 1850 about her relationship to the deceased havildar, she stated that "when Mayaram was a child of 2 months old its mother died and I suckled it and took charge of it until it was old enough to take care of itself. Mayaram having no other relative but myself, and I was his aunt and looked upon him as my own child." This, it would seem, amounted to her "confession."[68] R. Walker, the military accountant, noted that "[i]t seems doubtful whether, under the circumstances, a magistrate would punish the woman, but these cases have become so frequent that the fraud should perhaps not be passed over without further notice than the mere removal of her name from the Pension List." She was accordingly deprived of her pension in late April 1850 and sent to trial in the civil court.

The case did not end here, however. Walker suggested that the commander in chief of the army, Charles Napier, reprimand the securities in the case, so the file was forwarded to him. Napier, as it turns out, was appalled and instructed his subordinate, Captain W. H. Mayhew, to convey his extreme displeasure at the proceedings against Soodhoo and her securities. Mayhew wrote that "HE ["His Excellency," referring to Napier, in caps in the original] cannot for a moment suppose any intentional fraud has been committed, either on the part of the poor old pensioner herself, or on that of the only witness in the case, Merie Tewarry, pensioned Havildar of the same Corps." He continued:

The Commander in Chief conceives that the pensioner, whose whole dependence seems to have been on the late Havildar, whom under the circumstances she very naturally considered as her own child (and I am ordered to observe that in Sir Charles Napier's opinion, she was justified in so doing, having suckled him in infancy and supported him to maturity) ought to have the pension continued to her, the more especially as her adopted son's life was sacrificed on that lamentable occasion, when the greatest misfortune which our Arms have ever sustained in the East, fell on the Government of India.

Notwithstanding Napier's repudiation of the proceedings of the Accounts office and the Calcutta Council, the governor general upheld

---

[68] See nos. 118–120 of April 26, 1850, MC, comprising notes and correspondences between Walker and Wyllie, along with enclosures (including the pension roll).

the decision to strike Soodhoo from the pension rolls and send her to trial. One member of the Calcutta Council, initials RW, even went so far as to pencil a note on the consultation file that "[t]here is nothing whatever to shew, nor does the woman even assert, that she was dependent on the Havildar for her maintenance."[69] Napier resigned in disgust in November 1850 (this is usually attributed to a reprimand he received from Dalhousie for his manner of dealing with a regulation concerning food allowances for Indian troops, a matter of some controversy at the time, but it is clear that pension deprivations also played a role in his disaffection) and was replaced by a commander in chief more amenable to Dalhousie's administrative high-handedness.[70]

The procedures for investigation and prosecuting cases of pension fraud were firming up during the latter months of 1853 and the beginning of 1854, even as many of the aforementioned cases were working their way through the bureaucracy. The main instigator of this process was C. Hugh Lushington, the military accountant. Tombs made two additional suggestions. Since the government declined to invest pension paymasters with magisterial powers, he

> venture[d] to suggest that the Civil authorities in charge of Districts be instructed to call upon all Landholders, and Heads of Villages, to prepare and give in lists containing the names of all Family Pensioners who may reside within their respective Domains or Villages and to give information of the cases of those Pensioners whom they may know or suspect to be impostors.

As for the military side, Tombs similarly recommended that all commanding officers notify their commissioned and noncommissioned officers and men that they should "bring to the notice of their Commanding Officers the cases of all Family Pensioners residing in their respective villages, who may be in the receipt of Pension to which they are not duly entitled." As a penalty for noncompliance, Tombs recommended that soldiers and officers from those villages be made ineligible for a pension in the event that pension paymasters were to discover through their own

---

[69] For the order confirming the denial of a continued pension to Soodhoo, see nos. 158–159 of June 14, 1850, MC.

[70] On Napier's criticisms of Dalhousie's administration, see Charles James Napier, *Defects, Civil and Military of the Indian Government*, 2nd ed. (London: Westerton, 1853). Curiously, he only mentions pensions in the context of the seniority promotion system in the Bengal Army and the need to replace it with a system that affords "equality between Native and European gentlemen" in the military as was "being ceded in the civil service" (pp. 257–258); however, he earlier points out (p. 237) that "the Bengal Sepoy ... honourably and bravely ... devotes his life to duty, under promise of a pension and decorations after long years of service. To break faith with him would be infamous!" On the controversy regarding regulations for food purchases, see Robert Hamilton Vetch, "Napier, Charles James," *Dictionary of National Biography*, vol. 40, pp. 52–53.

investigations cases of fraud.[71] Lushington did not include these suggestions in his draft procedures.

Tombs would pursue one more question of law during his tenure as Dinapore pension paymaster. Some of the cases of sisters-in-law who were claiming pensions as widows were complicated by the fact that the women in question had undergone legal marriages to their brothers-in-law after their own husbands' deaths. This type of marriage was termed *sagāī* (or "sugaee"). In April of 1854 Tombs sought clarification from his superiors on the legality of *sagāī* for pension purposes. He was prompted by the case of "Nahallee," who had received a pension in 1827 as the widow of the sipahi "Kurrug" of the 40th Regiment Native Infantry.[72] Nahallee acknowledged to Tombs, however, that she had been earlier married to Kurrug's elder brother, "Bhoodun." Tombs' phrasing reflects his dim view of the matter: "The Family Pensioner herself admits this and owns that she was lawfully married to 'Boodhun' a Brother (elder) of the Sipahee 'Kurrug' *with whom she lived* after the death of her Husband Boodhun" (emphasis added). Tombs thus sought to cast Nahallee's bond with Kurrug as less than respectable, as a kind of "live-in" relationship devoid of any social (to say nothing of legal) sanction. However, "a relation" of Nahallee's "urged that the ceremony of 'Sugaee' was performed with 'Kurrug'" and that she was "therefore entitled to claim the Pension."

Tombs thus inquired as to the legality of *sagāī*, noting: "The custom of 'Sugaee' is I believe allowed amongst low caste Hindoos but as *adopted* [inserted in the margin: 'and illegitimate'] children cannot claim Pensions, I fancy that women with whom the ceremony of 'Sugaee' (if Hindoos) and of 'Nikah' (if Mahomedans) may have been performed cannot be looked upon in the light of lawfully wedded wives?" As it happens, and (as we shall see) much to Tombs' dismay, just a few months earlier, in January–February 1854, *nikāh* had been deemed a "valid form of marriage ... to qualify for the benefits of the Family Pension Establishment."[73] This determination arose out of a case from Meerut, which is revealing in its own right. Moore, the pension paymaster, had prosecuted a "Chumarin" (*chamārīn*) claiming to be the widow

---

[71] Captn F. C. Tombs, Suptt and Pay Master Native Pensioners, Benares, Dinapore, and Monghyr, to Lushington, dated January 16, 1854, encl. with no. 439 of March 17, 1854, MC.

[72] Nahallee was listed as family pensioner no. 88, Dinapore Circle, which meant she was an early beneficiary of the family pension system. Tombs to Lushington (?), dated April 5, 1854, no. 233 of July 21, 1854, MP.

[73] Government Letter no. 362 of February 13, 1854, as noted in the margin of Edmund Drummond to R. J. H. Birch, dated July 4, 1854, no. 233 of July 21, 1854, MP.

of a "Mussulman Classie" (*khalāsī*, tent pitcher) He ultimately "failed to obtain a conviction in consequence of the woman stating that she had been originally a Chumarin but that she had been made a Mussulman by the Classie who then performed the ceremony of Nikah with her." Based "on the woman's character," Moore was inclined to regard her statement as "untrue." He further acknowledged that in pursuing the case he "had simply gone on the fact that her *so called husband* having been a Mussulman and she a Chumarin the ceremony of Birjah or Shadee would not have taken place, and she was not therefore what amongst the natives is called the Hukkeeke or true wife."[74] Due to his failure to secure a conviction in the civil court, and "there being many similar cases in this circle," Moore sought the opinion of the government on the legality of *nikāh* for pension purposes. Lushington forwarded the question to Birch, who forwarded it to Bengal. The reply from C. F. Buckland, registrar of the Sudder Dewanny Adawlut, was unequivocal – in favor of the legality of *nikāh*:

In the case out of which this reference has arisen, there appear to have been some doubts, in Major Moore's mind as to the legality of the claim of the Nickahee wife, because she, one of the contracting parties[,] was originally a chumaren, but she alleged that she had become a Mussulman and then contracted marriage with the classie. This fact being established or rather the contrary not being proved, the Mahomedan Law applies to the case, and under the exposition of the Chief Law Officer of the Court, a translation of whose Futwa is herewith submitted, she is the widow of the deceased, and as such entitled to pension.[75]

As noted, enclosed with Buckland's letter was the chief qazi's *fatwa*: "According to sharia (Mahomedan Law) a woman married by the Nickah form, is like a woman married by the Shadee form. Their right and title to become heirs being similar, both are entitled to receive a pension."

Meanwhile back in Bihar, awaiting a response from his superiors on the question of *sagāī* legality, Tombs made his own inquiries with the civil authorities. He received a reply from the officiating magistrate of Shahabad District, Nahallee's place of residence, in late June. The magistrate had "investigated the case of Mussmt. Neehulee widow of Boodhun and Kurrug Sepoy deceased," and reported that:

---

[74] Thomas Moore to C. H. Lushington, dated December 3, 1853, encl. in no. 156 of January 6, 1854, MP, emphasis added.

[75] C. F. Buckland, Registrar of the Sudder Dewanny Adawlut, to Cecil Beadon, Secy to Govt of Bengal, dated January 30, 1854, encl. in H. Pratt, under Secy to the Govt of Bengal, to Col. J. Stuart, Secy to the GoI in Mily Departt., dated February 4, 1854, encl. in nos. 379–380 of February 17, 1854, MP. (This file is wrongly numbered in the Military Department Index as 378–379 of February 17, 1854.)

"Fraudulent Wives" 167

It is the custom in this District among the lower castes for the younger Brother, if unmarried[,] to marry the widow of his elder brother and this marriage called Sugaee is held perfectly binding and legitimate. This Sugaee appears to have been celebrated in the above case, and I am of opinion that Musummat Nehalee is the legitimate heir of Kurrug the sepoy deceased.[76]

Tombs, in relaying this information to his superiors, added with disappointment and alarm: "I presume that she is entitled to any property which may have been acquired and left to her by the deceased 'Kurrug'?" He added that, if *sagāī* be ruled legal, "I fear it will be almost impossible hereafter to prevent concubines amongst the lower castes of Hindoos from claiming and obtaining Pensions as the widows of men who may die, or be killed on service as it now is in cases where Mahomedans are concerned since it has been ruled that 'Nikah' constitutes a valid Form of marriage."[77]

Tombs' harsh opinion of *sagāī* wives was based, in part, on the fact that he was, like Moore in Meerut, confronting new cases that suggested that the ceremony of *sagāī* was starting to be employed for second marriages generally (as with *nikāh*) and not simply between brothers-in-law and sisters-in-law. He reported on two such cases in the very same week (late June 1854): the first regarding "Kissona," who had obtained a pension in the previous year as the widow of "Hurree Ram," a drummer in the 5th Regiment Native Infantry (the whereabouts of his death was not reported); and the second "Oodassee," who had obtained a pension in 1844 as the widow of "Lowton," a sipahee in the 41st Regiment Native Infantry who had died while on foreign service in China. According to Tombs' report on the latter, Oodassee (a resident of Awadh) had previously been married to Lowton's brother, "Joraee," but claimed to have performed the *sagāī* ceremony with Lowton following Joraee's death. With regard to Kissona, Tombs reported that she had previously been married to one "Bhoodun" of Saugor – "on whose death the ceremony of 'Sugaee' was, it is asserted, performed between her and the deceased Drummer, when the latter was stationed with his Regt at Saugor."[78] Based on the details of Kissona's case, it appears that the ceremony of *sagāī* was being utilized to legitimize marriages beyond the constraints of in-law relationships. Be that as it may, these cases were forwarded to

---

[76] Copy of letter no. 157 of June 20, 1854, from the Officiating Magistrate of Shahabad, to the Superintendent and Pay Master of Invalids, Dinapore, encl. in no. 233 of July 21, 1854, BMP, NAI.
[77] Tombs to Lushington (?), dated June 26, 1854, no. 233 of July 21, 1854, MP.
[78] Tombs to Lushington (?), dated June 28, 1854, no. 234 of July 21, 1854, MP.

Birch in Calcutta, who accordingly sought an opinion from the Sudder Court in July 1854.

In September a third case emerged, concerning one "Runneea," a recipient of a pension in the Benares circle since 1843. According to Tombs' investigation, Runneea had originally been married to "Bulraj" and was then married subsequently by the ceremony of *sagāī* to "Gunnase," a naik in the 30th Regiment Native Infantry. Her testimony was supported by one of her sureties, but the other one, along with three additional witnesses (a family pensioner and two pensioned havildars), claimed that "she was the mistress and not the wife of the late 'Gunnase'." As with Nahallee's case, however (and despite the countervailing evidence of the four witnesses), the local magistrate upheld the marriage and the legality of her claim.[79] The matter was forwarded up the chain of command (Drummond had taken over from Lushington as officiating military accountant); Birch in Calcutta renewed his request for an answer from the Sudder Court (as he had as yet had no response to his July inquiry).

A decision on *sagāī* was finally forthcoming in November 1854. According to General Order no. 1132, passed on November 14, 1854, "future marriages of Native Soldiers, under the ceremony termed 'Sugaie' will not be recognized as valid."[80] It was a victory for Tombs, though the provisional nature of the ruling would have caused consternation. In any case, it was a short-lived victory. All general orders had to pass muster with the Court of Directors in London. General Order no. 1132 of 1854 came under special scrutiny. On July 1, 1855 the official reply from London to Calcutta was entered into the official proceedings, as follows:

This question having been maturely considered, by your Government, you have resolved that no woman *now* receiving Pension as a widow shall be deprived of it, because her marriage with her deceased husband was only by the ceremony, called 'Sugaie,' but that the validity of that ceremony shall not be hereafter recognized. We should concur with reluctance in any change of a recognized practice, as regards the Pension to families of soldiers dying on Foreign Service, and if, as seems probable, the validity of the ceremony be recognized by the caste to which the soldier belongs, we are of the opinion that the right of the widow to a pension should be preserved.[81]

---

[79] Tombs to Drummond (?), dated September 12, 1854, no. 120 of September 29, 1854, MP.

[80] As recounted in F. D. Atkinson, Offg Secy to GoI in Mily Dept, to Adj Genl Army, dated July 14, 1855, no. 1 of July 20, 1855, MC.

[81] Extract from Military Letter from the Hon'ble the Court of Directors to the Government of India no. 56, dated May 2, 1855, no. 1 of July 20, 1855, MC (emphasis in original).

Thus, on September 14, 1855, General Order 1132 of 1854 was rescinded. All past and future *sagāī* marriages would be deemed legal for pension purposes.[82]

As it happens, London's 1855 review of the *sagāī* matter was not the first instance of official caution on the aggressive prosecution of fraud in the family pension system. In responding to one case in 1853, Birch noted that "the President in Council is disposed to think that much mischief may be done by dealing too harshly with sureties for Family Pensioners, who are themselves enrolled on the Pension lists," and added: "The confidence of the Native Army in the stability of Pensions will His Honor in Council fears be much shaken if they see so many sureties struck off and tried in the Civil Courts."[83] In another case, involving Tombs' prosecution of "Jumnie," an "illegitimate" daughter who was receiving a family pension, R. Walker, the military accountant, wrote to Tombs to "impress upon you the necessity of great caution in prosecuting enquiries of this nature as they are likely to give great offence to Natives of high caste." Tombs had also suggested that a general order be published prohibiting illegitimate children from receiving family pensions and hoped that it would be retroactive, "as there are doubtless many illegitimate children borne on the Pension Rolls and who receive Pension Pay." The members of the Calcutta Council agreed to issue Tombs' general order, but they shared Walker's concerns and consequently instructed Birch to write that "it will be sufficient if such cases of illegitimate daughters now enjoying pension be taken up as are forced upon the notice of Pension Pay Masters, without their originating enquiries as to their claims." And, just to punctuate the point, Governor General Dalhousie allowed Jumnie to retain her pension.[84]

~ ~ ~

---

[82] Nos. 139–140 of September 14, 1855, MC. There is no record of Tombs' view on the matter. In any case, he was soon transferred to the Benares pay office. We do, however, have some inkling of pensioners' perceptions of Tombs: One family pensioner whom Tombs had been investigating, "Odassee" (alias "Sewbuchna," not to be confused with the Oodassee of 1854, mentioned earlier), who claimed to be the mother of a fallen sepoy but was, allegedly, the sister, avoided the Benares pension office in 1855. Upon learning that Tombs was no longer the paymaster, she came to Benares in 1856 to claim her pension. Based on information Tombs' successor, Lieutenant C. L. Brown, had received in the interim, she and her securities were tried and convicted. See nos. 200–202 of January 23, 1857, MP.

[83] Birch to Lushington, dated December 16, 1853, no. 224 of December 16, 1853, MP. This was the case of Tallewindee, described earlier.

[84] Nos. 179–180 of March 18, 1853, MP, comprising letters from Walker, Tombs, and Birch. Jumnie was a resident of Awadh ("Oude") and daughter of sepoy Kalka Singh of the 26th Native Infantry. Tellingly, however, Dalhousie ordered Tombs (via Birch) to prohibit the awarding of such pensions going forward.

Dalhousie and Birch seem to have sensed that the aggressive pursuit of "fraud" cases by Tombs and his colleagues had gone too far. It is difficult to gauge the wider effect of the upsurge in prosecution of "fraud" cases during the 1850s, though it is clear that many pensioners generally had become disillusioned by 1857. A report drafted early in 1859 to assess "the Conduct of Native Pensioners during the Mutiny" found that the most glaring examples of questionable pensioner "loyalty" were at Meerut, Dinapore, and Cawnpore.[85] At Meerut, of the 275 pensioners singled out for investigation, fully 107 were found to have "not only rendered no aid but were suspected of either directly or indirectly assisting the rebel cause." Consequently their pensions were discontinued. Of the remaining Meerut cases, only sixteen pensioners "had distinguished themselves for loyalty" whereas 137 were found to have "had no opportunity to shew active loyalty." Of the remaining pensioners, six "provided good certificates" (presumably indicating that though they weren't able to come to the aid of the British, they were able to obtain testimonials in their favor from well-regarded members of the elite), eight were "objects of charity" (indicating that they were too infirm and near death to have taken part on either side in the rebellion), and one had died.

In contrast to Meerut, far more cases were investigated at Cawnpore and Dinapore. This may have been due to the fact that Meerut was not a major scene of rebel activity after the initial revolt on May 10, 1857. Whereas only 275 pensioners were investigated at Meerut, over 2,900 were investigated at Cawnpore. Of these latter, 1,591 pensioners were found to be "old, infirm, diseased, blind, and otherwise physically incapacitated." Consequently they retained their pensions. A total of 1,325 pensions were "declared to have been forfeited, because the holders of them though not *proved* to have joined the rebels, had opportunity of which they failed to avail themselves for rendering assistance to the State." Twenty-two pensioned native officers – mostly at the subadar rank, with one subadar major and one risaldar – had their pensions reduced to 10 rupees per month "on the grounds that they did not assist

---

[85] Nos. 213–229 of November 25, 1859, MC. Unfortunately, this file, entitled "Committees held at Dinapore and other stations, to investigate into the conduct of Native pensrs during the mutiny," consists mainly of summaries by Drummond. The original committee reports are not included in the consultation file. The Dinapore and Meerut numbers were tabulated together with Benares, Monghyr, and Bareilly. As the pensioner numbers reported for the latter three stations were very low, they are not discussed here. The Cawnpore report was based on the proceedings of a separate committee, convened in 1858.

Government with their influence." No Cawnpore pensioners were identified who actively came to the aid of the British.

A total of 1,365 pensioners were investigated at Dinapore Cantonment. Of these, twenty-five "had been remarkable for their loyalty," three "were related to those who had proved loyal," twelve "produced certificates of good conduct," two "were very young," and 117 were "objects of charity." The vast majority, fully 1,027, were found to have "had no opportunity to exhibit active loyalty." They did not lose their pensions. By contrast, fifty-nine pensions "were forfeited because all of the holders having opportunity still gave no aid, and many were under suspicion of aiding the rebels." Furthermore, 120 pensioners fell into a gray zone, whose fates would be determined by the government: "These men are not under suspicion of taking part with the rebels, yet they failed to present themselves in the manner and at the time required; but they plead ignorance, sickness, or physical incapacity."

Unfortunately there is no equivalent numerical tabulation of pensioners from Lucknow, another major scene of rebel activity. This is probably because the pension paymaster's office at Lucknow was destroyed, including all furniture, records, and even stationery. In reporting this fact, however, Marriott (the pension paymaster) noted the "unfaithfulness" of the native pensioners.[86]

The investigations into pensioner "disloyalty" in 1857 were mainly concerned with the behavior of pensioned soldiers and officers, not "family pensioners" as such. A different kind of archival trace, found in folk songs (or *lōkgīt*) popular in the decades after 1857, suggests that the stripping of pensions from widows was a significant factor in the revolt – or at least in how the revolt was remembered. This emerges in a "heroic lullaby" sung in Bhojpuri (a Hindi dialect spoken in western Bihar and eastern Uttar Pradesh) by village women to their babies (*babuā*) in southwestern Bihar that celebrated the warrior-rebel "Babu" Kunwar Singh of Jagdishpur, recorded sometime in the first half of the twentieth century. The song, which consists of four stanzas, opens with the following:

> Oh Babua! On that day our grandfather took up his sword,
> Oh Babua, to defend our wealth, religion, honor, and cows,

---

[86] See IOR/E/4/854, p. 971 (Asia, Africa, Pacific Collection, British Library, London). Unfortunately, I was unable to consult this proceedings file as it was part of a large collection of India Office Records documents that had been sent for digitization by the Adam Matthew Group.

... Women Whose Men

> Oh Babua, to defend *the pensions of our widows, young and old,*
> Oh Babua, to defend the honor of our mothers and sisters,
> Oh Babua, to defend us from the approaching calamity,
> Oh Babua, that day our grandfather took up his sword.[87]

> *Babuā ohī din dādā le lī tarvariyā ho nā*
> *Babuā dhanvā dharam ābarū gāyā par nā*
> *Babuā* bidhvā o rāṇḍī ke vṛtti *par nā*
> *Babuā māī o bahaniyā ke ijatiyā par nā*
> *Babuā āil rahe bipatī ke ghariyā par nā*
> *Babuā ohī din dādā le lī tarvariyā ho nā*

> बबुआ ओही दिन दादा ले ली तरवरिया हो ना
> बबुआ धनवा धरम आबरू गाया पर ना
> बबुआ *बिधवा* ओ राँडी के *वृत्ति* पर ना
> बबुआ माई ओ बहनिया के इजतिया पर ना
> बबुआ आइल रहे बिपति के घरिया पर ना
> बबुआ ओही दिन दादा ले ली तरवरिया हो ना[88]

I have italicized a phrase in the third line – "the pensions of our widows, young and old" – to draw particular attention to two words: pensions and widows. First, with respect to the term translated as "pensions": P. C. Joshi, who received the Bhojpuri text from Kuar Singh's descendant Durga Shankar Prasad Singh, noted that the term used was

---

[87] See Rag, *1857: The Oral Tradition*, p. 29 (also pp. 27–28 for additional verses and the refrain); P. C. Joshi, "Folk Songs of 1857," in P. C. Joshi (ed.), *Rebellion 1857: A Symposium* (New Delhi: People's Publishing House, 1957), 280–281; and P. C. Joshi, "Folk Songs of 1857," file no. 216, draft typescript (including footnotes to key terms and some additional introductory text not included in the published version), Archives on Contemporary History, Jawaharlal Nehru University (JNU) Library, New Delhi, see esp. p. 16 (folio 101). Joshi refers to the song as a "lullaby." Rag describes it as an example of *virhā* or "song of separation." Joshi does not provide the Bhojpuri rendering; Rag does, but in Romanized script. Joshi's source was Durga Shankar Prasad Singh, "a descendent of Kuar Singh who has collected and published material on the life and struggle of his great ancestor" (this is from the typescript version in the JNU archive; the published version also includes the reference but is more terse). Joshi provided no additional bibliographic information, though he later, for another poem, cited a 1955 article by Ras Biharilal, "*Lokgeeton Men Babu Kuar Singh* [Babu Kuar Singh in Folk Songs]," *Bhojpuri* 3, 7 (published from Arrah in April 1955) – which I have been unable to locate. Rag relies on Joshi's translation in his own rendering but also cites the 1955 Biharilal article, which is presumably his source for the Bhojpuri text.

[88] The Devanagari rendition provided here is based on Rag's Romanized Bhojpuri version of the stanza (*1857: The Oral Tradition*, p. 29). The only difference is that while Rag uses *biriliā*/बिरिलिया) in the third line, I use *vṛtti*/वृत्ति (following Joshi). I explain the implications of this usage in the following paragraphs.

"*vriti*;"[89] however, Pankaj Rag in his 2010 collection uses "*biriliaa*." Despite this discrepancy, both Joshi and Rag translate the word in question as "rent-free lands."

I have not found *biriliā* in any dictionary.[90] However the term *vṛtti* appears in many standard Hindi dictionaries and translates as, among other things, "means of subsistence," "stipend," "allowance," or "pension."[91] Specialized agricultural encyclopedia and lexicons from Bihar give meanings that are closer to the "rent-free lands" in Joshi and Rag. The administrator-linguist George Grierson, in the "land tenure" section of his late nineteenth-century volume *Bihar Peasant Life*, described *birit* as a generic type of "free grant" and the holder of such a grant as *biritiha* or *biritdar*. Notably, Grierson included here grants that are "given to the family of a man killed in the Raja's service in an open fight"[92] – or what in later military parlance would be referred to as "killed in action." A more recent multivolume *Kṛṣikoś* (agricultural dictionary), published in 1956, similarly defined *birit* as "tax-free land," *birta* as "tax-free land given for expenditure for religious works," and *virit* as "tax-free land given as a gift."[93]

However we might translate the term, what matters is that women in western Bihar who were memorializing Kunwar Singh's 1857 rebellion in songs for their children did so in a way that recorded the significance of a perceived assault by the British on the means of subsistence of widows.

---

[89] Joshi provides this information in a footnote to the typescript in the Archive of Contemporary History, JNU, p. 17. Cf. the published version of Joshi's essay, which does not include the note. See note 88 for bibliographic details. Joshi does not provide a Bhojpuri text of the song. I am grateful to Dr. Sonal Singh for double-checking the Joshi typescript at JNU for me during my absence from Delhi.

[90] However, H. H. Wilson defined "*bira*" and "*beera*" to mean "[r]ate of rent of lands according to the quality of soil and value of the crops." H. H. Wilson, *A glossary of judicial and revenue terms and of useful words occurring in official documents relating to the administration of the government of British India, from the Arabic, Persian, Hindustani, Sanskrit, Hindi, Bengali, Uriya, Marathi, Guzarati, Telugu, Karnata, Tamil, Malayalam and other languages* (London: Wm. H. Allen and Co., 1855), p. 88. I am grateful to Kailash C. Jha for locating this reference and for his assistance with clarifying this and other terms used in this song.

[91] Syamasundar Das, *Hindi Shabdasagar* (Kashi: Nagari Pracharini Sabha, 1965–1975), 4587, defines it first as "means of subsistence" and "daily wage," and second as "pension" or "fellowship" (वह धन जो किसी दीन, विधवा या छात्र आदि को गुबारा, कुछ निश्चित समय तक उसके सहायतार्थ दिया जाय । उपजीविका।, or "That amount which any needy person, widow, or student etc. is given for his/her support. Means of support"). Scholarship stipends are still referred to as *chhātra vṛtti* today (I am grateful to Dalpat Rajpurohit for this point). Neither dictionary, it should be noted, translates the term as "rent-free land."

[92] George A. Grierson, *Bihar Peasant Life, being a discursive catalogue of the surroundings of the people of that province* (Calcutta: Bengal Secretariat Press, 1885), pp. 322–323.

[93] Vishwanath Prasad, *Kṛṣikoś* (Patna: Bihar Rashtrabhasha Parishad, 1956), s.v. birit, birta, virit.

But not simply "widows." The second part of the phrase that I italicized in my translation of the Kuar Singh lullaby refers to "widows, old and young." The Bhojpuri is *bidhwā o rāṇḍī* (बिधवा ओ राँडी). A literal translation of this would be "widows and widows."[94] However, the term "widow" fails to capture the different inflections of the two terms. The first term, *bidhwā* (बिधवा),[95] communicates a sense of respect and compassion due an elderly widow – in part due to her presumed sexual inactivity. The second term, *rāṇḍī* (राँडी), conveys a more layered set of meanings. The exact spelling of the term (with the terminal 'ī') does not appear in most Hindi or Bhojpuri dictionaries but is derived from or related to the term "*rāṇṛ/ rāṇḍ*" (राँड़/राँड), which means both "widow" and "promiscuous woman or prostitute."[96] It was often used for women of middle and lower caste, especially for women whose husbands had died while they (the women) were still young and sexually active (or at least potentially so). Not infrequently *rāṇḍī* would be used as a term of disrespect. This is still the case. As a Rajasthani widow named Somi remarked in 2007 to a member of an academic research team, "people see little difference between a widow and a prostitute." Another widow from Rajasthan, Kamala, frustrated by the lack of employment opportunities, asked, "[w]ho will give work to a widow? Everyone thinks she is searching for a man." The principal investigator, Harsh Mander, added, parenthetically: "In Hindi, the pejorative terms for both are 'raand' [राँड] and 'randi' [रंडी], respectively."[97]

The Kuar Singh lullaby seems, then, to acknowledge a distinction that we have glimpsed in the "pension fraud" records from the 1850s, namely,

---

[94] Given the repetition, Joshi and Rag opted to compress the two words into one, "widows," in their translations: "Oh Babua, to protect the rent-free lands of our widows."

[95] Vidhwā (विधवा in Hindi). It is worth noting that "widow" derives from the Indo-European root *h¹widʰéwh²s (nominative), meaning "to be empty." From this we get the Latin *vidua*, "widow, unmarried woman," and the Sanskrit *vidh* (विध), meaning "bereft, destitute." See Don Ringe, *From Proto-Indo-European to Proto-Germanic* (New York: Oxford University Press, 2006), pp. 58, 61–62; also 121, 302.

[96] Dictionaries generally use the spelling *rāṇṛ* (राँड़). See R. S. McGregor, *Oxford Hindi–English Dictionary* (New York: Oxford University Press, 1993), p. 858; and Das, *Hindi Sabdasaragara*, p. 4144. The latter provides the following definition: "१. जिसका पति मर गया हो और पुनर्विवाह न हुआ हो। विधवा। बेवा। २. रंडी। वेश्या। कसबी।" (1. [She] whose husband has died and who has not remarried. Widow. 2. Prostitute [followed by two additional words for "prostitute"].) This is not simply a modern usage: the term was often employed to describe a wanton woman or prostitute in bhakti-sant poetry; see e.g. Kumkum Sangari, "Mirabai and the Spiritual Economy of Bhakti," part II, *Economic and Political Weekly* 25, 28 (July 14, 1990): 1545.

[97] Harsh Mander, "Living with Hunger: Deprivation among the Aged, Single Women and People with Disability," *Economic and Political Weekly* 43, 17 (April 26–May 2, 2008): 92, 94. The interviews were conducted in eight villages, two in Orissa and three each in Rajasthan and Andhra Pradesh. Kamala ended up earning money by brewing illicit liquor.

that between mainly older, "respectable" widows, on the one hand, and younger and bolder, and perhaps less "respectable," widows on the other. Recall one of the cases with which we began this chapter, the dispute between Neaz Begum and Shah Begum from 1852, and the distinction that was later made by John Coke, commanding at Moradabad in 1859, between first and second wives – the latter regarded as temporary marriages involving "kept" women – among Afghan infantry and cavalrymen.

It is here that our tale of military pension "reform" bumps up against the canonical history of modern India, regarding the phenomenon of *satī* ("suttee," lit. "chaste woman" but colloquially understood as widow-immolation) and its regulation in the early nineteenth century and eventual abolition in 1829.[98] In the wake of the 1829 abolition, anxieties about the increasing population of widows, especially young widows with no obvious means of support, fueled a mid nineteenth-century reformist urge to allow widow remarriage in Bengal. Too many women, it seems, were opting for, or (more likely) being forced into, a life of prostitution, as their own and their late husbands' families were either unable or unwilling to support them. As Ishwar Chandra Vidyasagar argued, during his campaign for passage of the Hindu Widows Remarriage Act of 1856, "[e]arly marriages also give rise to another dreadful evil, almost all these girls, after marriage, remain at home one, two, or three years; and during this time, numbers are left widows without having enjoyed the company of their husbands a single day. These young widows being forbidden to marry, almost without exception, become prostitutes."[99]

~ ~ ~

Looking back on the legal proceedings over the marital status of the women connected to the Company's military establishment, one cannot help but be struck by the increasing insensitivity of officials charged with the adjudication of family pensions. Indeed, it almost seems like the civil "left hand" of British administration was unaware what the military "right hand" was up to, and vice versa. How is it, one might ask, that a

---

[98] For exemplary detailed social and cultural historical analyses of *satī*, see Anand A. Yang, "Whose Sati? Widow Burning in Early 19th Century India," *Journal of Women's History* 1, 2 (Fall 1989): 8–33; and Lata Mani, "Contentious Traditions: The Debate on Sati in Colonial India," *Cultural Critique* 7, 2 (Autumn 1987): 119–156.

[99] Vidyasagar quoted in Subal Chandra Mitra, *Isvar Chandra Vidyasagar: A Story of His Life and Work* (Calcutta: Sarat Chandra Mitra, New Bengal Press, 1902), p. 88. According to Mitra, he based this assessment on the authority of Major Wilkinson, former resident of Nagpur, who claimed a local brahman as his informant. For the full passage, see *A Collection of the Proceedings which Led to the Passing of Act XV of 1856*, comp. Narayan Keshav Vaidya (Bombay: Mazagaon Printing Press, 1885), 14–16. See also Ishwar Chandra Vidyasagar, *Hindu Widow Marriage*, ed. and trans. Brian A. Hatcher (New York: Columbia University Press, 2012), esp. the conclusion, pp. 202–206.

government so visibly concerned with the fate of Hindu widows that it passed the Sati Abolition Act in 1829 and the Widows Remarriage Act of 1856 could, almost in the same breath, be prepared to challenge the legality of second marriages of numerous Hindu women married to the native soldiery – and thereby render those women mistresses, "kept women," concubines, and prostitutes, and their sons and daughters bastard children, in the eyes of the state? A partial answer to this question is that at the eleventh hour the government came to its senses and upheld the legality of second marriages for Hindu women: the Court of Directors in London determined in September 1855 that such marriages – known in military circles as *sagāī* – were legal,[100] thus putting a halt to many of the fraud prosecutions carried out by pension paymasters, especially in the Dinapore office.

The cessation of fraud prosecutions notwithstanding, the increasingly haughty tone of moral condemnation that suffused the pension paymasters' correspondences with superiors in Calcutta regarding family relationships in the 1850s, most of which hinged in one way or another on the question of marital legitimacy, is noteworthy. Veteran officers – most famously Charles Napier, until November 1850 commander in chief in India – occasionally recorded their surprise at the high-handed insensitivity of the paymasters' recommendations and the alacrity with which the accounts office and the military secretary to the governor general in Calcutta agreed with them. Napier, as noted earlier, was appalled at the idea that the Company Army would turn its back on an elderly pensioner who had suckled her late sister's child from infancy and who was naturally regarded by that child as his mother and had stated as much on his family pension roll before being killed in 1842 during the disastrous retreat from Kabul, simply because she was, in strict biological terms, his aunt and not mother.[101]

Napier's frustrations with this type of nitpicky bean counting being deployed by Dalhousie and his ilk, which was symptomatic in his view of the wider failure of the new breed to sympathize with the ordinary soldier, was shared by many senior officers of long service. His criticisms of the Dalhousie regime, published posthumously in 1853, were considered prophetic after 1857. Napier's views were also shared by those on the receiving end of official haughtiness. A particularly eloquent example of this is a memorandum written by Shaik Hidayat Ali of the Bengal

---

[100] As noted earlier, the Sudder Dewanny Adawlut had determined in January 1854 that the analogous Muslim marriage ceremony of *nikāh* was legal.
[101] See the earlier discussion regarding the case of Soodhoo, "mother" of Mayaram Tewarry, nos. 118–120 of April 26, 1850, and 158–159 of June 14, 1850, MC.

Police Battalion on January 30, 1858. The high-ranking Hidayat Ali, whose official title was "Subadar & Sirdar Bahadoor," described in considerable detail the array of evidence that a mutinous sentiment had been growing in the Bengal army since the Afghanistan campaign. Of special significance was his sense that "native" soldiers had, over the decades, become reluctant to share their true feelings with their officers. Ironically, given the focus of this chapter, Hidayat Ali attributed this reluctance to a change in marriage patterns – but of British officers:

> In former times the Officers used to keep native women and constantly had the Native Officers and Sepoys in their society and did more to please them[.] These women exercised a good deal of influence in the Regiment[.] This was all in accordance with the feeling of the Sepoys. By acting in this way the officers did good service to the Govt because they became better acquainted with the character of their men and with what was going on in the lines[.] In latter times this has not been the case[.] It appeared to me the officers who have been appointed to the service within the last twenty years are better educated than the officers of former times were[.] I think more books have been published. Now the officers marry English ladies and there is less in common between the officers & Sepoys[.] Of late years the Sepoys have not confided in their officers. The consequence of all this has been that when the Mutiny broke out the officers were misinformed as to its extent[.][102]

The claim that the increasing numbers of British women in India in the early nineteenth century – brought on so-called "fishing fleets" in ironic reference to their marital aspirations – were responsible for the gradual distancing of British men from Indian society, thus creating the social conditions for 1857, is an old one and has long since been subject to historical investigation and, to some degree, nuanced critique.[103]

---

[102] "Statement of Sirdar Bahadoor Subdr Hidayat Ali of the Bengal Police Bn [Battalion] on the causes of the Mutiny," trans. T. Rattray, Captain, nos. 639–40 of April 30, 1858, MC (see pp. 322–333 of the proceedings volume). This version departs from a later and much longer version published by K. K. Datta, "A Contemporary Account of the Indian Movement of 1857–59," *Journal of the Bihar Research Society* 36 (September–December 1950): 96–133, most notably in that it excludes Ali's reflections on the effect of British officers marrying British wives (compare the quoted passage with pp. 111–112). Datta alludes in his introduction to the earlier version quoted here, "which has not yet been traced."

[103] See e.g. Margaret Macmillan, *Women of the Raj* (New York: Thames & Hudson, 1988), esp. pp. 10ff.; and more recently Joan Mickelson Gaughan, *The "Incumberances": British Women in India, 1615–1856* (Delhi: Oxford University Press, 2013), esp. chapter 15, "Of Clay and Porcelain." For a captivating study of the pre-1830s world in which British–Indian marriages were more commonplace, see Ghosh, *Sex and the Family in Colonial India*. The general critique, or conventional wisdom today, is that the arrival in droves of British women in India after about 1800 was less a cause of racial distance than a symptom. See also the perceptive comments in Maya Jasanoff, "The Unknown Women of India," *New York Review of Books*, December 18, 2008.

Hidayat Ali was, it would seem, one of if not the first to articulate this logic. Overly simplistic though his reasoning may have been, he is a reminder that, for many observers, Indian women were integral to the successful functioning of the British Indian Army. That the British managed to alienate so many of these women with shortsighted pension "reforms" in the 1850s must, in retrospect, be regarded as a signal achievement, perhaps comparable to their having offended so many Hindu and Muslim soldiers with the introduction of the anomalously greased cartridges.

The evidence adduced in this chapter notwithstanding, it is difficult to know the thoughts and emotions of those on the receiving end of pension fraud allegations. The heartfelt 1853 petition of Persaud Singh and Doman Singh to Dalhousie – discussed earlier in the case of Gangia, mother to Atmaram Sepoy, for whom they had served as sureties – affords a glimpse of this. It is even more difficult to gain access to the reactions of the numerous women as they were being told that they were not wives but (at best) mistresses. No doubt they too shared the emotional and financial distress of Persaud Singh and Doman Singh, and the incredulity of Napier. But unlike Napier they did not have the luxury of retiring to England. They would have been stunned by the allegation that they had engaged in fraudulent behavior, but their incredulity would have been sharpened by desperation and dishonor. Many of them were carted off to prison to serve short but demeaning terms, often accompanied by hefty fines or forced labor. Faced with this prospect, some simply fled, disappearing into the countryside – perhaps assisted (if they were lucky) by the unwillingness of sympathetic magistrates to pursue them. If we can hear the echo of their voices, it is in the songs sung by village women in the decades to come.

5 Conclusions, Reflections

In 1955 a new Hindi novel appeared, set amid the turmoil of 1857, entitled *Sānjh kā Sūraj* (*The Setting Sun*). The author, Omprakash Sharma (1924–1998), was a well-known writer of cheap and immensely popular "*jāsūsī*" (crime, detective, espionage) page-turners. Sharma began this particular tale at Meerut on the morning of May 9 when (as he described it) seven cavalrymen were stripped of their uniforms, placed in irons, and marched off to prison.[1] He then shifted the scene to the evening, when

> [f]rom behind the curtains and walls, the soldiers [of the prisoners' regiments] endured the rebuke of their mothers and sisters. What's more, the women called *bāzārū*[2] also taunted the soldiers as they strolled through the lanes below. One fellow heard one woman call to another from the balcony of their brothel, saying – "Hey, just look at these young men, seven of their brothers are lying in the foreigners' dungeon. Have they sacrificed their youth? Should these men strut about with their chests held high like lions?"
>
> पर्दों और दीवारों के पीछे से सैनिकों ने माँ और बहनों के उलाहने सुने। और तो और बाज़ारू कही जाने वाली स्त्रियों ने भी नीचे गलियारे में चलते सैनिकों को ताना दिया। किसी एक ने अपने कोठे के छज्जे पर सुनकर दूसरी को सम्बोधित करके कहा – "अरि जरा इन जवां मर्दों का तो देख, इन्हींके सात भाई फिरंगू की काल कोठरी में पड़े है। बलिहारी है इनकी जवानी की, क्या शेर की तरह सीना तानकर चल रहे है?"

Later that night the cavalrymen took the fateful decision "to kill their white officers" and gallop to Delhi.

---

[1] Omprakash Sharma, *Sānjh kā Sūraj* (The Evening Sun) (Delhi-Shahdara: Saraswati Sahakar, 1955), pp. 2–3. Sharma takes other liberties with the historical details – for example, he identifies the imprisoned men's regiments as the 2nd and 3rd Light Cavalries. I am grateful to Kailash Jha for bringing this novel to my attention and to Dalpat Rajpurohit for additional information about this underappreciated writer. As Rajpurohit notes (personal communication, July 3, 2024), *jāsūsī* writers like Sharma are largely, and unjustly, ignored in scholarly writing. Exceptions include Laura Brueck, "Bhais Behaving Badly: Vernacular Masculinities in Hindi Detective Novels," *South Asian Popular Culture* 18, 1 (2020): 29–46, and Tanvi P. Patel, "Emerging Crimewallahs: Modern Developments in South Asian Crime Fiction" (PhD dissertation, University of Washington, 2010).

[2] Denizens of the bazaar, yet another euphemism for prostitutes.

The opening pages of Sharma's *Sānjh kā Sūraj* confirm that a century after the "Mutiny," the women of Meerut were firmly lodged in the popular historical imagination. Curiously, however, Sharma departs from the usual refrain that the women in question were prostitutes. While the soldiers were certainly tormented by the *bāzārū* who flung barbed remarks down at them from their brothel balconies, they were also stung by the reproachful glances of their own wives and daughters. Given the previous chapters' discussion of the identity of the women of Meerut, the historian may be forgiven for wondering about Sharma's narrative choice here – or, rather, his sources. Had he read Dehlvi's *Dāstān-e Ghadr*? Was he aware of the Mughal courtier's phrasing about the "respectable" women whose men were imprisoned? Or perhaps he had internalized Savarkar's 1909 account of "the first war of Indian independence," in which the mention of prostitutes of Meerut is elided in favor of an almost prudish allusion to the "womenfolk of the town" – despite Savarkar's explicit reference to Cracroft Wilson's account of the "frail ones" of the Meerut bazaar.[3]

The timing of the release of Sharma's *Sānjh kā Sūraj* is noteworthy given that just two years later, in 1957, a state-sponsored historical sourcebook appeared that included a translation into English of Dehlvi's account of the cavalrymen's descent into the maelstrom of violence at Meerut.[4] Despite the appearance of this sourcebook in 1957, the dramatic power of Wilson's version is such that until now only one historian has noted the key discrepancy between his and Dehlvi's characterization of the women of Meerut. That historian is Rajat Kanta Ray, in a 2003 study entitled *The Felt Community: Commonalty and Mentality before the Emergence of Indian Nationalism*. For Ray, the Meerut explosion into violence was important because it pointed to the

---

[3] See the discussion in Chapter 2. Sharma was born and raised in Meerut, so it is also possible that his characterization of the women was based on local oral tradition that percolated down over the generations since 1857.

[4] Rizvi and Bhargava, *Freedom Struggle in Uttar Pradesh*, vol. 1, pp. 4042–4047. See the discussion in the Entr'acte chapter. The editors also include here the relevant excerpt from Wilson's 1858 report describing the "frail ones of the Meerut bazaar," along with the deposition by Golab Jaun in "Depositions Taken at Meerut, by Major G. W. Williams, Superintendent of Police, N.W.P.," p. 23 (introduced in Chapter 2). Also included in this section of the sourcebook is an excerpt from a memoir of the uprising in Awadh by Martin Richard Gubbins, *An account of the Mutinies in Oudh and of the Siege of the Lucknow Residency; with some observations on the condition of the Province of Oudh and on the causes of the mutiny of the Bengal Army* (London: Richard Bentley, 1858), p. 100, which notes in passing the premature uprising at Meerut ("mercifully ordered in our favour by a gracious Providence," thus siding with the exculpatory "premature uprising" theory self-servingly promoted by Carmichael-Smyth). These accounts were among those that constituted *Freedom Struggle*'s chapter 6, "The Conspiracy."

place of gender inversion in stimulating rebellious passion. Ray argued that historians should understand the rhetorical appeals to religion in danger, whether Hindu or Muslim, as mid nineteenth-century expressions of *felt* patriotism – or more precisely, that whether "[f]aith or patriotism, the heartfelt emotion behind it is identical."[5] After quoting Wilson's "frail ones" account, Ray turned to Dehlvi to make the point that "[i]t would appear from the account of the sepoys that the 'ladies' were not necessarily all courtesans."[6] He added, quoting Williams' official "Narrative" (drawn from the depositions), that some of the sepoys had their families living with them [in the cantonment lines] at the time and that they were (quoting Williams) "left totally unprovided for" and "wandered about the city for some days, houseless and homeless, and at last scattered in various directions in search of food and shelter."[7]

The historicity of the women of Meerut and their gendered taunts are crucial to Ray's emotions-centered framework: "The offensive imagery of inversion of the role of men and women was a psychological device to incite the former to assert their manhood."[8] Further, the fact that it was not only disreputable "courtesans" who engaged in the gender-inverting ridicule of the soldiers served to reinforce the total social condemnation of the men, making their emotional crisis all the more painful. Whereas Sharma, a novelist, does not identify his sources – after all, the guild to which he belongs establishes its claim to authenticity via a "reality effect,"[9] in the face of which footnotes only serve to undermine the suspension of disbelief – the historian Ray is scrupulous in doing so. Indeed, for Ray, the fact that there are two *independent* accounts of the catalyzing role of the Meerut women in transforming the nonviolent mutiny into a violent revolt is of immense significance, as it affords an almost unimpeachable historicity to the women and the emotional power of their taunts.[10]

---

[5] Ray, *Felt Community*, p. 359.
[6] Ray, *Felt Community*, p. 407. Note that Ray interprets Wilson's use of the euphemism "frail ones" as "courtesans."
[7] Precisely how many women were actually kept in the "native lines" of the cantonment is impossible to say, but it seems to have been a fairly common practice. See e.g. 1100 of April 29, 1859 Military Proceedings, NAI (New Delhi), describing a Punjabi regiment in Moradabad (where Wilson was posted prior to the mutiny-revolt there). Recall that for Williams, the fact that the families of the native soldiery were left destitute by the revolt militated against the claim that the revolt was the result of a premeditated conspiracy (see Chapter 2).
[8] Ray, *Felt Community*, pp. 505–506n257.
[9] Roland Barthes, "The Reality Effect" (first published in 1968), in R. Barthes, *The Rustle of Language*, trans. R. Howard (Berkeley: University of California Press, 1989), pp. 141–148.
[10] This is not to minimize the degree to which historians themselves respond to literary impulses. Indeed, the fact that more than one recent historian has unconsciously

But here it is necessary – or, at the very least, an opportune moment – to revisit the question posed in the Entr'acte discussion of Zahir Dehlvi's narrative: Were the accounts by Dehlvi and Wilson, in fact, *independent*? Recall that Dehlvi's account of the cavalrymen's explanation to the emperor appears in a memoir written a full fifty years after the events in question. One might reasonably ask whether Dehlvi had, during those fifty years, come across Wilson's account – or accounts derivative of Wilson's that were reproduced in the variety of histories produced during the intervening decades, and that this influenced his reconstruction or recollection of the interview with the men of the 3rd Light Cavalry with the Mughal emperor on the morning of May 11. This seems unlikely, especially given other key differences in the details of the accounts – particularly with respect to which men are being asked (or forced) to wear anklets or bangles.[11] Wilson, it will be recalled, wrote that the women of Meerut shamed the men of the 3rd Light Cavalry by invoking the image of their imprisoned brethren "ornamented with anklets," a reference to the iron shackles placed on them during the infamous "ironing parade" of May 9. By contrast, Dehlvi's women insisted that the men "take these [their own] bangles and wear them" and, in exchange, hand over their weapons so that they, the women, could liberate their imprisoned men.

There is also the obverse possibility that Wilson's account was based, directly or indirectly, on Dehlvi. In the Entr'acte, I suggested the likelihood that Wilson heard the story of the Meerut women from the 29th Native Infantry, posted at Moradabad, which he visited on May 13 upon receiving news of the Meerut revolt. However, though they never were in

---

internalized the invented language of Flora Annie Steel's fictional characters as a primary source for what *actually transpired* at Meerut on the night of May 9–10 (see Chapter 2) is evidence of the degree to which their own craft has an important if too-often underrecognized literary dimension. Historians will, naturally, disagree on whether this is a good thing or a bad thing. See, of course, the work of Hayden White, esp. *The Fiction of Narrative: Essays on History, Literature, and Theory, 1957–2007*, ed. Robert Doran (Baltimore: The Johns Hopkins University Press, 2010); and on the skeptical response of historians, and a response to the response, see Frank Ankersmit, "Hayden White's Appeal to the Historians," *History and Theory* 7, 2 (1998): 182–193.

[11] Here it is worth noting that when correcting and sharpening my translation of the account, I had the opportunity to ask Shamshur Rahman Faruqi about this very question, that is, whether it was possible Dehlvi based his account on or was influenced in his recollection of the events by the evolving English-language historiography about the women, which originally derived from Wilson. Faruqi was skeptical, adding: "It is most unlikely that Zahir's account is drawn from the hastily composed reports of Englishmen who didn't have much Urdu anyway. One obvious example is 'prostitutes' and 'frail' ... [Further,] Savarkar was an obscure individual in 1909 when his book first came out. Zahir's book was published in 1910 [*sic*: 1914]. I don't think Zahir had any English at all, nor was he the kind of scholar to look for sources, remote or not so remote." Personal communication, June 16, 2017.

the same place at the same time, Dehlvi's route after fleeing the Mughal capital took him through Wilson's Moradabad District before he ultimately settled in nearby Rampur in April 1858. Inasmuch as Wilson was headquartered in Moradabad till early June, one might ask whether his "frail ones" narrative was somehow based on comments that Dehlvi was making as a refugee from Delhi. It is possible, for example, that Dehlvi related the cavalrymen's response to the Mughal emperor to his hosts or acquaintances while en route to Rampur, or in Rampur itself, and that that information eventually made its way to Wilson's ears. According to his *Dāstān*, Dehlvi and his family lived and worked in Panipat for four or five months, from early or mid-October 1857 to February/March 1858. He had ample occasion to tell the story of the emperor's interview with the men of the 3rd Light Cavalry. Likewise in Rampur, where he and his family settled in April 1862. On one occasion, upon his arrival in Jhajjar, Dehlvi states explicitly that he recounted "the series of events" that led to his flight from Delhi. His uncle, seeing the bedraggled condition of Dehlvi and his brother and brother-in-law, immediately brought them into the house and told his wife,

"See the state my nephews have been reduced to. My sister Badshah Begum underwent such hardships to bring them up. Now they are caught in such a sorry state." Mumami [Dehlvi's aunt] also started crying and asked us to describe the series of events that had brought us here. We told her everything.[12]

A similar situation occurred in Bareilly, just after Dehlvi and his friend Jung Baaz, a Mughal cavalryman, had been saved from execution as suspected British spies. After freeing them, their savior, Mir Fateh Ali, who had served as the head of the royal porters in Delhi, asked Dehlvi to "narrate my circumstances." Jung Baaz explained how they came to be there.

For his part, in early June Wilson left Moradabad for Meerut. The 29th Native Infantry had risen up on June 2 and taken over Moradabad. Meerut cantonment became Wilson's headquarters while he spent the next four months (till mid-October) "engaged in collecting revenue, punishing rebels, and restoring order, &c, &c." (para. 48) in the Meerut Division. His responsibilities also included directing intelligence operations and keeping roads open on the eastern side of the division, between Meerut and the Ganges. After mid-October Wilson shifted to Aligarh and from that point until mid-May 1858, he commanded a small cavalry unit that operated in the triangle between Aligarh, Bareilly, and

---

[12] Dehlvi, *Dastān-e Ghadr*, trans. Safvi, p. 148.

Farrukhabad, mainly rescuing stray British refugees and combating rebel forces. He finally returned to Moradabad, which by then had been restored to British control, on May 12, 1858. Wilson submitted his report seven months later, on December 24, 1858, from Calcutta (where he had shifted in preparation for his retirement to sheep farming and politics in Canterbury, New Zealand).

Thus, it is clear that at no point did Dehlvi's and Wilson's paths cross. The closest they would have come to each other was in the first two weeks of October. Dehlvi had settled briefly in Panipat (early October 1857 to early March 1858) and Wilson was collecting revenue in the adjacent Meerut Division (early June to mid-October 1857). A later near overlap was when Dehlvi had settled in Rampur (after April 1858) and Wilson had returned to Moradabad (May 1858).

Of course, physical overlap was not necessary: Even if Wilson did not hear the account of the Meerut women directly from Dehlvi, he might have heard it second or third hand from those who had learned it from Dehlvi. Or it is possible that Wilson heard similar accounts from others escaping Delhi. After all, Zahir Dehlvi and his family were not the only refugees escaping the Mughal capital after September 1857. Many – including, especially, members of the Mughal court – were fanning out across Hindustan in search of safe harbor in the months following the rebellion, and many of them would have repeated the cavalrymen's story pinning the blame for their actions on the women of the cantonment bazaar.

In sum, one cannot rule out the possibility that Dehlvi's and Wilson's accounts were "genetically" related. Or, even if they were independently generated, it is possible that Wilson first heard the account from the men of the 29th Native Infantry and then later came to know of Dehlvi-esque versions that would have only confirmed in his mind the veracity of the original tale.

The Women of the Meerut Bazaar

The other, and to my mind more likely, scenario is that the two accounts were independently generated – that is, that Dehlvi heard his version from the courtiers gathered in the palace on the morning of May 11, who had heard it from the cavalrymen themselves during their interview with the emperor; and that Wilson heard it from the men of the 29th Native Infantry, whom he had visited in their lines on May 13 and who had been receiving reports of the events in Meerut over the previous two days. Insofar as the accounts possessed a common point of origin, it was the "event" itself – that is, in the impact upon the men of the withering taunts of the women of Meerut.

This returns us to the original question: *Who were these women?* Were they prostitutes or were they wives? The novelist Sharma (1955) and the historian Ray (2003) offer compromise positions. The former, Sharma, tells his readers that the female tormenters included both prostitutes and wives (and sisters); the latter, Ray, is only willing to go so far as to allow the possibility, and then only in an endnote, that they did not all appear to be "courtesans."

Alas, the question cannot be answered definitively. We are too far removed in time. The hearsay evidence, while likely confirmatory, tells a story that feels almost "too good to be true." Clearly many historians have found the story compelling. The present study does offer some important clues in the form of circumstantial evidence. Chapter 3, "Frail Ones," reveals that a kind of informal understanding prevailed between prostitutes and the police in the 1850s. Prostitutes do not appear to have been subject to police persecution – indeed, far from it. They even aided the police in their pursuit of criminals. This is a far cry from the official hostility and discursive demonization prostitutes would come to experience in the wake of the Contagious Diseases Acts of 1868.[13] If anything, when prostitutes appeared in police records in the 1850s, it was as victims of crime, especially grievous crime, and the authorities seem to have gone out of their way to capture and prosecute the perpetrators – or, at least, to have made a show of doing so. This complicates the image of bazaar prostitutes as fomenters of violence against the British – the mysterious case of "Mees Dolly" notwithstanding. In light of Chapter 3, then, the identification of the Meerut women of May 9–10, 1857 as prostitutes, "frail ones," feels unsatisfactory – or at the very least insufficient. In short, for the historian as detective, they lack motive.

By contrast, Chapter 4, "... Women Whose Men," reveals the increasingly fraught relations in the mid-1850s between the wives (and sisters, mothers, and daughters) of soldiers on the one hand, and officials in the pension paymaster office on the other. A significant number of women were accused by the pension establishment of being "fraudulent" – usually on the basis of a revised and overly strict doctrine of what was considered legitimate marriage and parentage. It is not difficult to conclude from this that a distrust of the cantonment authorities was building among the wives and other female relatives of Indian soldiers in the Bengal Army. It is worth noting, too, that this pension-centered discontent was memorialized in Bhojpuri song about the 1857 rebellion, in a region long associated with robust *pūrbiā* sepoy recruitment.

---

[13] See Ballhatchet, *Race, Sex and Class under the Raj*; and Philippa Levine, *Prostitution, Race, and Politics*. On discursive demonization, see Mitra, *Indian Sex Life*.

We might conclude from this that Dehlvi's account is the one to be trusted, and that the women in question were wives (and other close female relations) – that is, to paraphrase Dehlvi, the women in question were those whose men (*wursā*) were imprisoned. At first glance, such a conclusion is appealing, not least because it seems to resist what became a colonial discourse of sexuality according to which all Indian women were deemed, reflexively, a species of prostitute.[14] But as politically appealing as such a conclusion may be, it would conceal much about the fluid nature of marriage relationships at midcentury – or, more precisely, it would posit too stark an opposition between marriage and prostitution. This may feel unsettling, like a version of the radical claim that all marriage is a form of prostitution. Rather, it simply points to a continuum with marriage on one end, prostitution on the other, and forms of informal (frequently illicit) love and temporary contract marriage and concubinage in between.[15] Chapter 4 offers more insights here. Some of the marriages that were subject to scrutiny by Company paymasters in the 1850s involved soldiers who had established quasi-legal secondary relationships (or "marriages") with women in the cantonment towns in which they were quartered. This was especially the case in the western reaches of the Bengal Presidency, on the edge of the Punjab. Recall the 1852–1853 dispute between the younger Neaz Begum and the elderly Shah Begum, both married to the late Mahomed Noor Khan, rissaldar or captain in the Bengal 3rd Light Cavalry, supplemented by the 1859 commentary by Colonel John Coke regarding the tendency of Afghan soldiers from the Punjab to marry "concubines" who were regarded as either (or perhaps both) "kept women" and "wives."[16] Indeed, this kind of contractual relationship may have prevailed between the "Cashmerian" Golab Jaun and Dr. Smith, noted in the depositions collected by G. W. Williams, superintendent of police for the North-Western Provinces. (Smith, it will be recalled from Chapter 2, ignored Golab Jaun's warning on May 10 that the troops were about to revolt. She and Smith later watched the mob assemble around the house; Smith was eventually killed but Golab Jaun escaped in a covered sedan chair or "dooly" sent by her mother from the sadr bazaar.)

---

[14] Cf. Mitra, *Indian Sex Life*.
[15] As the poet Alok Dhanwa puts it, in a riposte to those steeped in tradition, "how terrified you are when a woman fearlessly wanders in search of her identity among prostitutes and wives and lovers!" (कितना आतंकित होते हो / जब स्त्री बेख़ौफ़ भटकती है / ढूंढती हुई अपना व्यक्तित्व /एक ही साथ वेश्याओं और पत्नियों / और प्रेमिकाओं में !). "Bhāgī Huī Laṛakiyām" (Runaway Girls), in Alok Dhanwa, *Duniyā Rōz Bantī Hai* (The World is Made Every Day) (Patna: Rajkamal Prakashan, 2015), p. 41. I thank Sonal Singh for alerting me to this poem.
[16] See Chapter 4, pp. 134–135, 148.

Did Smith, then, regard Golab Jaun as a kind of wife? This is unlikely, given the increasingly stark boundary line of race that – from Smith's countrymen's point of view – would have militated against a formal marriage by the 1850s. But would Golab Jaun have regarded Smith as "her man," her "protector," her *wāris* (singular of *wursā*, to use Dehlvi's term)? Very possibly. In the English translation of her official deposition, she refers to Smith as "my master." We do not have access to the original notes from the deposition and thus cannot know what Urdu term she used. However, a secondary meaning of the term *wāris* is "owner, master."[17] Further, the detail about the sedan chair sent by her mother in the sadr bazaar implies that she was of considerable means and respectability. She added that, "[a]s I passed, they wished to kill me, but hearing I was a woman, allowed me to pass." This suggests that the curtains were down, concealing her person from view. As a high-status concubine, she was also a "veiled woman" – the term for which could, conceivably, have been *masturāt*, another term used by Dehlvi to describe the Meerut women on the night of May 9–10, 1857.

So we may update Omprakash Sharma and Rajat Kanta Ray's characterizations and suggest that while some of the women at Meerut were wives, others were lovers and mistresses, others prostitutes, and others still were concubines – and some were shadings of all three.[18]

Words and Deeds

At this point, the reader might wonder why any of this matters. Fine, the women of Meerut started the revolt, and these women were in a complex

---

[17] S. W. Fallon, *A New Hindustani-English dictionary, with illustrations from Hindustani literature and folk-lore* (Banaras, London: Trubner and Co., 1879), p. 1182, s.v. وارث ; and Steinglass, *A Comprehensive Persian-English Dictionary*, p. 1449, s.v. وارث .

[18] The perspicacious Flora Steel hints at such a continuum in her "Mutiny novel," *On the Face of the Waters* (1896), discussed in Chapter 2. A third of the way into the tale, and just before the fateful cry of "*We of the bazaar kiss no cowards!*" ricochets through Meerut's "lane of lust," Steel introduces the elderly brothel-keeper Nargeeza, the "recognized head of the recognized regimental women," whose soldier-lover had "la[in] in jail for ten years." It was on his account, Steel tells us, that Nargeeza choreographed the mass refusal of sex by the "girls and women" under her roof, the very refusal that ultimately drove the cavalrymen of Meerut headlong into the madness of revolt a few pages later. For Steel, this "new woman" agency transcended race: Tara, a key Indian character of the novel, announces "women do not forget, white or black." Steel, *On the Face of the Waters*, pp. 187–188, 190–191, and (Tara's remark) p. 460. For an illuminating assessment of the novel as a "fraught negotiation of the models presented by colonial adventure writers and New Woman novelists," see LeeAnne Marie Richardson, "*On the Face of the Waters:* Flora Annie Steel and the Politics of Feminist Imperialism," in Brenda Ayers (ed.), *Silent Voices: Forgotten Novels by Victorian Women Writers* (Westport, CT: Praeger, 2003), pp. 119–138.

relationship of mutual obligation with their men. So what? Women have been blamed – or credited – for all manner of cataclysmic events in human history, since ... well, forever (for starters, see Genesis 3:12). Does it really make any difference in the so-called grand scheme of things that it was women who, in Meerut on the night of May 9, 1857, turned what was a nonviolent mutiny into a violent revolt? After all, surely the more salient fact is that there was a revolt at all, that Indians rose up in heroic resistance to British rule – and that the beginnings of a felt nationalism can be traced to this moment. Further, the scrupulous historian would insist that even if women's humiliating taunts were the spark, the kindling had long since been laid. (Here it is impossible to avoid the combustibility rhetoric used by the likes of Carmichael-Smyth, Cracroft Wilson, Flora Steel, George MacMunn, and P. J. O. Taylor.) According to the 20–20 clarity of historiographical hindsight, the revolt would not have spread so quickly, let alone turned into a broad-based armed rebellion, had there not been a host of issues that had, over a protracted period, generated increasing popular and elite dissatisfaction with and disaffection for British rule – and not simply among the Indian soldiery. These factors have long since been noted in 1857 historiography, most famously with respect to the notorious "Doctrine of Lapse" inaugurated in 1849 by Governor General Dalhousie (but with significant precedents in the early 1840s), which culminated in the pensioning off of Rani Lakshmibai and annexation of Jhansi in 1853, the refusal to recognize the Maratha Peshwa Bajirao II's 1827 adoption of the Nana Saheb and consequent rejection of his claim to a royal pension (also in 1853), and the even more consequential dethroning of Nawab Wajid Ali Shah and annexation of Awadh in 1856. Also frequently cited in countless histories are longer-term instances of official indifference to if not disdain for Indian religion and culture, such as the 1829 ban on "Suttee," the Hindu Widow's Remarriage Act of 1856, Macaulay's 1835 "Minute on Education" and its privileging of Anglicist policies and the founding of Western-style educational institutions at the expense of the Orientalist episteme, and the "Liberal Charter" of 1813 opening Company territory to what was increasingly perceived as officially sanctioned missionary activity – leading inexorably to proselytizing in the very ranks of the native soldiery. The historiography also lays emphasis on the anxieties over religion, culture, and sovereignty that were further stoked among the soldiery by penny-pinching alterations to military policy, including the gradual reduction of "batta" (*bhatta*, travel allowance) pay for foreign deployment, beginning in the 1840s and exacerbated by the aforementioned annexation policy and the acquisition of Punjab as Company territory after 1849. The final straw, according to the standard narrative, was the introduction in late 1856 of the greased cartridges to accommodate the new Enfield rifled musket.

Feminist historians might offer the rejoinder that of course it matters that women played a key role in setting events in motion in Meerut, given their chronic underrepresentation in Indian historical narratives – especially in contrast to the key roles ascribed to them in other global-historical revolutionary moments.[19] A rejoinder to this cry for revision might be that female agency at Meerut has long been acknowledged – indeed, it became a veritable staple of Mutiny historiography, as Chapter 2 demonstrates. However, it is surely noteworthy that despite the iconic role of women at Meerut, no one has bothered (until now) to examine, let alone interrogate, the constellation and evolution of that staple narrative, especially the way the women of Meerut ricocheted into and out of literary (as in fictional) portrayals of 1857. Their catalytic role was simply taken as fact, as a point of departure – to be noted and left behind.

Viewed in these terms, the micro-historical focus on events in Meerut does more than simply add detail to a long-accepted narrative. For starters, Chapter 2 reveals the key role of literary fiction (and journalism) in shoring up what ultimately is taken to be historical "fact," even as it (along with the Entr'acte chapter) brings into focus the thorny question of who, precisely, the legendary women of Meerut were. Further, the widening of the micro-historical lens in Chapters 3 and 4 sheds long-overdue light on the lived experience of both cantonment prostitutes and military wives (and sisters, mothers, and daughters) and, moreover, points to some problems with the received historiographical wisdom concerning women in colonial India. Mention has already been made of the unexpected posture of cantonment prostitutes vis-à-vis the Raj, a far cry from the picture presented in postcolonial historiography, an

---

[19] To cite only two examples from the capacious literature on the Russian Revolution: Barbara Evans Clements, "Working-Class and Peasant Women in the Russia Revolution, 1917–1923," *Signs* 8, 2 (Winter 1982): 215–235; Laurie Stoff, *They Fought for the Motherland: Russia's Women Soldiers in World War I and the Revolution* (Lawrence: University Press of Kansas, 2006). The literature is even more vast and of greater duration for the French Revolution, but of particular interest is the catalyzing role and subsequent ideological reverberations of the march of the women of Paris to Versailles in October 1789; see e.g. Suzanne Desan, "Gender, Radicalization, and the October Days: Occupying the National Assembly," *French Historical Studies* 43, 3 (2020): 359–390. As a side note, one cannot help but wonder if the dramatic quality of the march on Versailles was an inspiration for the highly imaginative reenactment of the 1917 "Storming of the Winter Palace" in 1920 by Nikolai Evreinov, itself the inspiration for the storming scene in the 1928 film, *October: Ten Days that Shook the World* by Sergei Eisenstein and Grigoriy Aleksandrov.

image of relentless *tawāif*/prostitute immiseration and oppression over the course of the nineteenth century. Instead, the picture that emerges is one of significant prostitute agency in cantonment towns and, moreover, a perception in the wake of 1857 (and not only in the British imaginary, if Omprakash Sharma is any guide) that the prostitute presided over the soldier's sense of honor and sexual prowess. Similarly, the access afforded by this study (in Chapter 4) to the wives of Indian soldiers necessarily complicates the received wisdom about the perceived affronts to Indian cultural sensibilities by Company social and legal reform in the early and mid nineteenth century, particularly with respect to the promulgation of the Hindu Widows' Remarriage Act of 1856. A close reading of military records not only reveals that soldiers and surviving family members (especially widows) were alienated by the claims of their fraudulent legal status but also suggests that the legal recognition of widow remarriage by the Calcutta Legislative Council might well have been welcomed by Indian soldiers and "camp followers" in the Bengal Army.[20] In any case, a virtue of Chapter 4 is that camp followers finally get their day in the sun (see Figure 5.1).

These discordant historiographical notes serve as an entrée to a broader metahistorical issue. Historians of 1857 frequently make note of how quickly the revolt spread into a broad-based rebellion. Less remarked upon is how quickly historical analysis of the revolt takes on a *counterrevolutionary* tone.[21] The reasons for this are, at one level, obvious: British observers were anxious to understand how the violence that was unleashed May 10 quickly became "viral" – to employ an early twenty-first-century idiom.[22] Interested observers, "old India hands" as they were sometimes called, were quick to offer "I told you so" critiques,

---

[20] The devil is, of course, in the details. As Chapter 4 makes clear, types of widow remarriage varied widely. Whether the developments around the military pensions were a factor in the 1856 legislation is, it seems to me, an open question – especially given the involvement of the *nizāmat adālat* in adjudicating the legality of military marriages. For his part, Ishvarchandra Vidyasagar was likely aware of "war widows" given his involvement in creating annuity funds for widows and orphans, but there is no indication that the family pension controversies in the army informed his reformist efforts concerning the *śāstric* legality of widow marriage. (Email communication with Brian Hatcher, June 23, 2013.) See also Vidyasagar's two Bengali/Sanskrit works of 1855, *Vidhavā Vivāh*, known today as *Hindu Widow Marriage*, trans. Brian Hatcher (New York: Columbia University Press, 2012).

[21] "Counterrevolutionary" should not be understood in conventional left vs. right terms, but rather in terms of continuity vs. discontinuity. For discussion, see Eelco Runia, "Into Cleanness Leaping: The Vertiginous Urge to Commit History," *History and Theory* 49, 1 (2010): 1–20; also Runia's *Moved by the Past: Discontinuity and Historical Mutation* (New York: Columbia University Press, 2014).

[22] Though building on a disease discourse of long standing.

Figure 5.1 "Qr Mr Sergeant" and "Camp Followers," detail of "Line of march of a Bengal regiment of infantry in Scinde," by George Edward Madeley, scroll painting, probably 1845
Note: The Yale Center for British Art online catalogue entry includes the following note with respect to the dating of this scroll painting: "Though dated 1830 in Abbey, the more likely date of publication is 1845. A description of the publication appears in the 'Literary notices' of the *Naval and Military Gazette* of Nov. 22, 1845." The entire scroll may be viewed at https://collections.britishart.yale.edu/catalog/orbis:3087986 (last visited January 17, 2025).
Source: Rare Books and Manuscripts, DS485.B48 L56 1845+, Yale Center for British Art.

some of the more conspiracy-minded of whom also pointed to ominous signs that preceded the explosion of violence: most famously the circulation of chapatis across parts of north India. However, these kinds of discussions rapidly gave way to more developed, historically informed debates about who or what was to blame for the cataclysm: that is, was it the fault of the military or civil authorities? Thus some critics pointed to the aforementioned longer-term official developments around "Lapse" and the official meddling in Indian cultural norms, while others pointed to the issues around *batta* allowances and the greased cartridge. And, of course, there were those who were adamant in insisting that a preconcerted conspiracy was behind the rebellion. These points have long since been noted and have of necessity found their way into this narrative study. But overlooked is how these historicizing gestures invariably situate May 10, 1857 as part of a longer process, a waystation en route to a "durational" view of 1857 that begins in the early 1800s and ends with the formal abolition of the Company and Queen Victoria's Proclamation, the Government of India Act of 1858. This historicizing-cum-contextualizing impulse has even proceeded to the point where leading imperial historians have tended to downplay the significance of 1857 itself, situating it as one (albeit large) revolt among many against the institutionalization of Company rule during the first six decades of the nineteenth century.[23]

Lost amid this drumbeat of continuity is the fact that something radically discontinuous occurred on May 10, 1857, namely, that the vast majority of the men of the 3rd Light Cavalry and 20th Native Infantry, joined by a large segment of the 11th Native Infantry, took a profoundly unexpected step, a step that caught the authorities – and even themselves – completely off guard. In fact, the story the cavalrymen told of the tongue-lashing they were subjected to by the women of Meerut may be read as the soldiers explaining to themselves how a kind of madness overtook them in the heat of the moment, even as they recognized the righteousness of their cause. That they chose to gallop to Delhi and elevate the Mughal emperor as the figurehead of their revolt appears, in this light, as an attempt to legitimize and even historicize their having crossed the Rubicon – in other words, to restore balance in the wake of having taken a "vertiginous" leap into the unknown.[24] In making sense of their actions, shamefacedly shifting the blame onto women when accused of having engaged in rash behavior by Bahadur Shah Zafar, the men of the 3rd Light Cavalry began a process of narrativization that continues to this day.

Am I implying here that the story about the Meerut women is not true, that the event described by Wilson and Dehlvi did not really happen, that the cavalrymen simply invented it to ease their collective conscience? Not at all. The mysterious women of Meerut may well have done precisely

---

[23] Without a doubt the most compelling version of this is C. A. Bayly's *Indian Society and the Making of the British Empire* (Cambridge: Cambridge University Press, 1989), chapter 4, see esp. pp. 169–171, 178–181. The work of Gautam Bhadra ("Four Rebels of 1857") and Ranajit Guha, (*Elementary Aspects of Peasant Insurgency in Colonial India*) are important exceptions in this regard – though it must also be noted that the Marxian-Gramscian framework that undergirds the latter serves to impose its own evolutionary telos. Guha, thus, is far more adept at tracking the prose of counterinsurgency and the subaltern modalities of insurgency than he is at identifying the metahistorical tendency toward continuity in history, whether "elitist" or "subaltern."

[24] *Pace* Runia, "Into Cleanness Leaping."

what the soldiers claimed. Clearly humiliation was in the air,[25] and what with the stripping and shackling of the eighty-five men, that humiliation was rife with a gendered symbolism that all but cried out for subversive, biting commentary. Who better to deliver it than the women themselves? In the end, we cannot know precisely what occurred. But there is no doubt that the voices of the past are trying to tell us something.

---

[25] And it was an atmosphere that lingered. It bears asking to what degree it contributed to the gendered discourse that characterized late nineteenth-century British assertions about the effeminate Bengali; cf. Mrinalini Sinha, *Colonial Masculinity: The "Manly Englishman" and the "Effeminate Bengali" in the Late Nineteenth Century* (Manchester: Manchester University Press, 1995).

Appendix 1: Prostitutes in Criminal Judicial Proceedings, Oriental and India Office Collection, London

Prostitute victims

Date	Place	District	Division	Name of victim	Murder	Wounding	Theft	Sentence	Motive and Comments
n.d. 1855	Delhi	Delhi	Delhi	Jowala Devee, prostitute	X		X	executed	motive theft: sepoy hanged, 3 other sepoys implicated but released
n.d. 1855	Tarpoora village	Jhansi	Saugor	Musstt. Raheemun		X		imprisoned 5 years labor	motive jealous rage; sepoy was spurned lover, he bit off her nose and upper lip
Mar 14, 1855	Meerut Kotwalee	Meerut	Meerut	Musstt. Hyat Buksh, prostitute		X		6 months with Rs 200 fine	motive unknown; quarrel, Mussee Ollah broke Hyat Buksh's arm
Mar 17, 1855	Agra Kotwalee	Agra	Agra	Musst. Beeba Jan, prostitute	X			not captured	motive unknown; chowkidar dismissed
Mar 17, 1855	Meerut Cant.	Meerut	Meerut	prostitute			X	released for want of proof	motive theft; culprits not named
Jun 16, 1855	Sirdhana	Meerut	Meerut	prostitute		X	attempted	not captured	motive theft; culprits unknown
Jul 8, 1855	Goruckpoor Kotwalee	Goruckpoor	Benares	prostitute	X		X	1 hanged, another transported	motive theft; two men not sepoys the culprits
Aug 22, 1855	Russulgunge, Coel	Allyghur	Meerut	Musstt. Motee, Tuwaif			X	not captured	motive theft, culprits "thieves" not ID'd
Sep 25, 1855	Furruckabad city	Furruckabad	Agra	Musst. Bujio, prostitute	X			captured but unpunished	motive probably theft; culprits local men, not sepoys; magstr. very upset by outcome, Kotwal implicated. Detailed follow-up
Oct 7, 1855	Jubbulpore city	Jubbulpore	Saugor	Mussumat Bussuntee, prostitute		X	X	imprisoned for life	motive theft; local miscreant the culprit; magstr. very concerned; hand amputated
Dec 31, 1855	Meerut Cant.	Meerut	Meerut	prostitute	X			not captured	motive apparent case of jealousy; culprit unknown

(cont.)

Date	Place	District	Division	Name of criminal	Murder	Wounding	Theft	Sentence	Comments
Feb 4, 1856	Kydgunge, Allahabad	Allahabad	Allahabad	Mussumat Hydree, prostitute	X			sentenced to be hanged	motive theft; culprit notorious poisoner; escaped in 1857, recaptured
Jul 6, 1856	Bhoropoor	Etawah	Agra	Mussumat Chutteeree, prostitute	X			caught, punished?	motive enmity between client and third part; prostitute killed with him over land dispute
Jul 11, 1856	Futtehghur	Furruckabad	Agra	Bilaso, prostitute	attempted			absconded, reward offered	motive jealousy; Madaree sepoy was spurned suitor

Prostitute criminals

Date	Place	District	Division	Name of criminal	Murder	Wounding	Theft	Sentence	Comments
n.d. 1855	unknown village/town	Jounpore	Benares	Mistress from Oudh	X			escaped with brother	so-called "brother" of mistress murdered the client; reward offerred, Rs. 200
n.d. 1855	Delhi	Delhi	Delhi	prostitute			X	unknown	stolen property recovered in her house

Source: Bengal Criminal Judicial Proceedings, 1855–1856. See Chapter 3 for specific references.

Appendix 2: Pension Fraud Cases, 1850–1857 (a Selection)

File nos.	PPM office	Pensioner	Name of decedent soldier	Decedent's regt.	Decedent's rank	Date of death	Place of death	Claimed relationship	"Actual" relationship	Punishment
97 of Feb 22, 1850	Meerut/Haupper	Gainea	Seearam Doobay	36th NI	Sepoy	Jan 13, 1849	Punjab	Wife/widow	Wife/widow	Deprived pension in favor of father
205 of Apr 10, 1850	Lucknow/Cawnpore	Rhusseea alias Rupeen	Mundraj Sing	47th NI	Sepoy	Feb 10, 1846	Punjab	Mother	Aunt	Deprived pension, wife will apply for pension
112 & 113 Apr 26, 1850	Lucknow/Cawnpore	Sewbundee	(unnamed)	5th LC	Sepoy/Trooper	1842	Afghanistan?	Mother	Brother's wife/aunt	Deprived pension, potential prosecution
112 & 113 Apr 26, 1850	Lucknow/Cawnpore	Seamlall Awasthee	(unnamed)	30th NI	Sepoy	1842	Afghanistan?	Son	Adopted son	Deprived pension, potential prosecution
118–120 Apr 26, 1850	Lucknow/Cawnpore	Soodhoo	Mayaram Tewarry	54th NI	Havildar	Jan 1842	Afghanistan	Mother	Aunt	Deprived pension
207 Aug 9, 1850	Lucknow/Cawnpore	Tackoorah	Mirwan & Rambuccus Sing	54th NI & 5th LI	Sepoy & Trooper	Jan 1842	Afghanistan	Mother	Mother of both soldiers	Deprived pension for collecting two pensions
214–216 Aug 16, 1850	Allahabad	Uggoura	Soobah Pandeh	37th NI	Sepoy	Jan 10, 1842	Afghanistan	Mother	Grandmother	Deprived pension
151 Aug 21, 1850	Meerut/Haupper	Luchmee	Goor Sing Newar	SB	Naick	1842	Afghanistan	Wife/widow	Unmarried	Deprived pension
168–170 Nov 22, 1850	Allahabad	Bukhtah	Ramloll Misser	53rd NI	Sepoy	1843	not stated	Mother	Aunt	Deprived Pension
192–194 Jan 3, 1851	Allahabad	Isree Sing	Sewdial Sing	27th NI	Havildar	1843?	not stated	Son	Nephew	Deprived pension, 2 years prison, Rs. 25 fine or labor
192–194 Jan 3, 1851	Allahabad	Issurdeen Opudeah	Ramgolaum Sing	35th LI	not stated	1844?	not stated	Son	Nephew	Deprived pension, 1 year prison, Rs 20 fine or labor
203–205 Jan 10, 1851	Meerut/Haupper	Mera	Bhola	16th NI	Sepoy	Jan 11, 1842	Afghanistan	Mother	Aunt	Deprived pension
203–205 Jan 10, 1851	Meerut/Haupper	Seeteah	Luckea	HM 44th F	Classie	Jan 11, 1842	Afghanistan	Wife/widow	Wife/widow	Pension will stop, should have gone to son

Case	Location	Name	Name 2	Regiment	Rank	Date	Place	Relation 1	Relation 2	Outcome
112 & 113 Jan 24, 1851	Allahabad	Bheer Sing	Pulwan Sing	37th NI	Sepoy	1843?	not stated	Son	Nephew	Deprived pension, 6 months prison, Rs. 20 fine
211 & 212 Feb 7, 1851	Meerut/Hauppper	Ruheeman alias Goolsun	Jehangeer Beg	54th NI	Sepoy	1844?	not stated	Wife/widow	Mother	Deprived pension
211 & 212 Feb 7, 1851	Meerut/Hauppper	Meer Surwarally Sahebdad Khan	not stated	not stated	Sepoy	1842?	Afghanistan?	Father	Oldest brother	Deprived pension, prosecuted for fraud
211 & 212 Feb 7, 1851	Meerut/Hauppper	Raisha	not stated	not stated	Sepoy	1840?	Afghanistan?	Son	Nephew	Deprived pension, prosecuted for fraud
156 & 157 Apr 19, 1851	Allahabad	Ramun alias Buktah	Koonjul Sing	41st Regt	Havildar	Feb 10, 1846	Punjab	Wife/widow	Sister-in-law	Deprived pension
102–104 Jul 25, 1851	Allahabad	Jubber Sing	Gujraj Sing	16th Gr	Sepoy	not stated	not stated	Mother	Aunt	Deprived pension
380 & 381 Aug 8, 1851	Lucknow/Cawnpore	Adhar Sing	Hurree Sing	VR	Sepoy	1842?	Afghanistan?	Son	Nephew	Deprived pension
380 & 381 Aug 8, 1851	Lucknow/Cawnpore	Shaick Ibrahim	Jehwar Sing	53rd NI	Sepoy	not stated	not stated	Father	Uncle	Deprived pension
210–212 Sep 19, 1851	Lucknow/Cawnpore	Teeajun	Shaik Peer Buccus	51st NI	Sepoy	not stated	not stated	Son	Nephew	Pension cancelled
154 & 155 Sep 26, 1851	Lucknow/Cawnpore	Brinjkhar	not named	33rd NI	Havildar	not stated	not stated	Mother	"Not at all related"	Pension denied
100–102 May 14, 1852	Allahabad	Noorbeeebee	Sewdit Sing	16th NI	Sepoy	not stated	not stated	Mother	Sister-in-law	Deprived pension
100–102 May 14, 1852	Allahabad	Hiria and Lutchmun	Fazar Ali	37th NI	Sepoy	not stated	not stated	Mother	Imposter	Deprived pension and absconded
98–100 May 28, 1852	not stated	Moonia	Sewdeen	S&M	Havildar	Jul 1837	Road to Tibet	Wife and son	Wife and son	Both awarded compassionate pensions
160 & 161 Jun 18, 1852	Meerut/Hauppper	Surwur Ally	Bhowanny Deen	37th NI	Sepoy	1842	Afghanistan	Wife/widow	Sister-in-law	Deprived pension
160 & 161 Jun 18, 1852	Meerut/Hauppper		Furase Ully/Ally	54th NI	Sepoy	not stated	not stated	Father	Brother	Deprived pension, tried for fraud but acquitted

(cont.)

File nos.	PPM office	Pensioner	Name of decedent soldier	Decedent's regt.	Decedent's rank	Date of death	Place of death	Claimed relationship	"Actual" relationship	Punishment
160 & 161 Jun 18, 1852	Meerut/ Haupper	Sahibdad Khan	Dullail Khan	1st Irr. Cav	Sowar (?)	1840	not stated	Son	Nephew (adopted son)	Deprived pension
158–160 Aug 27, 1852	Lucknow/ Cawnpore	Chilliah	Routeeram	59th NI	Sepoy	1825?	Burma?	Daughter	Niece	Deprived pension
158 & 159 Oct 15, 1852	Allahabad	Moongeea	not stated	not stated	Havildar	1842?	not stated	Wife/ widow	Not related	Denied pension, 6 months prison, Rs. 50 fine
133–137 Oct 22, 1852	Allahabad	Purrowtee	Bohaudeen Tewarrah	37th NI	Sepoy	1844?	Afghanistan?	Father	Uncle	Deprived pension
133–137 Oct 22, 1852	Allahabad	Soorsur Buccs	Gyah Deen	48th NI	Sepoy	1841?	Afghanistan?	Son	Nephew	Deprived pension
230–235 Dec 14, 1852	Lucknow/ Cawnpore	Gous Mahomed	Kurrum Allee	5th NI	Sepoy	1842	Afghanistan?	Father	Older brother	Deprived pension
230–235 Dec 14, 1852	Lucknow/ Cawnpore	Doorgapersaud Doobey	Sewahram Doobey	5th NI	Sepoy	1844?	Afghanistan?	Father	Brother	Deprived pension
230–235 Dec 14, 1852	Lucknow/ Cawnpore	Bussunt Sing	Wuzeer Sing	27th NI	Sepoy	1844?	Afghanistan?	Father	Uncle	Deprived pension, awaiting trial
230–235 Dec 14, 1852	Lucknow/ Cawnpore	Bahadoor Sing	Rossum Sing	57th NI	Sepoy	1842?	Afghanistan?	Father	Brother	Deprived pension, 7 years prison
230–235 Dec 14, 1852	Lucknow/ Cawnpore	Puhar Sing	Maharaj Sing	37th NI	Sepoy	1843?	Afghanistan?	Father	Brother	Deprived pension, 7 years prison
207–209 Dec 23, 1852	Dinapore/ Benares	Kissoon Misser	Sewruttee Misser	54th NI	Sepoy	not stated	not stated	Son	not stated	Deprived pension, fined and imprisoned
156 Feb 4, 1853	Meerut/ Haupper	Meermanee	Bolai Havildar	54th NI	Havildar	not stated	not stated	Wife/ widow	Never married	Deprived pension
156 Feb 4, 1853	Meerut/ Haupper	Saunkoor	Ram Singh	1st Brig HA	Gun Lascar	not stated	not stated	Wife/ widow	Never married	Deprived pension

Ref/Date	Station	Claimant	Soldier	Unit	Rank	Date	Place	Relation	Other relation	Outcome
156 Feb 4, 1853	Meerut/Haupper	Jeedunee	Sudha	1st Brig HA	Syce	not stated	not stated		Sister	Deprived pension
156 Feb 4, 1853	Meerut/Haupper	Soomeriah	Kunnye	1st Brig HA	Syce	not stated	not stated	Wife/widow	Never married	Deprived pension
95 & 96 Feb 11, 1853	Barrackpore?	Moona	(1) Emam Bux (2) Rujjub	30th NI	Sepoy	Feb 2, 1846	Punjab	Wife, mother	Wife, mother	Deprived pension, Emam Bux rec'd pension
130–132 Feb 11, 1853	Meerut/Haupper	Shah Begum, Neaz Begum	Mahomed Noor Khan	3rd LC	Ressaldar	Oct 20, 1842	Afghanistan	1st & 2nd wives	1st & 2nd wives	Senior wife will receive pension
179 & 180 Mar 18, 1853	Dinapore/Benares	Jumnie/Jumnee	Kalka Sing	26th NI	Sepoy	1843?	Afghanistan?	Daughter	Illegitimate daughter	Pension continued but notice issued to prohibit in future cases
134–136 May 20, 1853	Dinapore/Benares	Chuttoor Sing	Oograh Sing	41st NI	Sepoy	1846?	China	Father	Lived with the mother	Deprived pension
130–132 Jul 8, 1853	Dinapore/Benares	Punnah	Aumunt Sing	54th NI	Sipahee	1842?	Afghanistan?	Wife/widow	Mistress	Deprived pension, 6 months prison, Rs. 20 fine
143–145 Jul 8, 1853	Dinapore/Benares	Chundee	Moosahib Khan	5th LC	Trooper	1843?	Afghanistan?	Wife/widow	Sister-in-law	Deprived pension, 2 months prison
143–145 Jul 8, 1853	Dinapore/Benares	Brij Lall	Sewgolam	5th LC	Syce	1842?	Afghanistan	Son	Nephew	Deprived pension
138–142 Jul 8, 1853	Dinapore/Benares	Cheejah	Dulloo Sing	35th NI	Sepoy	1842?	Afghanistan	Mother	Sister	Deprived pension, 4 months prison, Rs. 80 fine
139 Jul 22, 1853	Dinapore/Benares	Rutton	Cassee Misser	5th NI	Jemadar	1842?	Afghanistan	Wife/widow	Mistress	Deprived pension
127 Sep 30, 1853	Cawnpore	Jodah	Soobratie Khan	7th Bombay NI	Sepoy	not stated	not stated	Father	Master	Deprived pension, 6 six months prison
162–164 Oct 21, 1853	Dinapore/Benares	Ramkulleeah	Seochurrun	1st Eur. LI	Tent Lascar	1841?	Afghanistan	Wife/widow	Mistress	Deprived pension
188–189 Nov 25, 1853	Dinapore/Benares	Goorsahoy	Susuhoy Govalla	60th NI	Naick	1844?	Afghanistan?	Son	Nephew	Deprived pension and to be tried

(cont.)

File nos.	PPM office	Pensioner	Name of decedent soldier	Decedent's regt.	Decedent's rank	Date of death	Place of death	Claimed relationship	"Actual" relationship	Punishment
188–189A Nov 25, 1853	Dinapore/Benares	Shaick Mahomed	Shaick Fursoo	54th NI	Sepahee	1844?	Afghanistan?	Father	Brother	Deprived pension and to be tried
188–189A Nov 25, 1853	Dinapore/Benares	Gungoo	Atruck Sing	30th NI	Sepahee	1844?	Afghanistan?	Mother	Sister-in-law	Deprived pension and to be tried
188–189A Nov 25, 1853	Dinapore/Benares	Anoop	Gopaul Pandy	38th LI	Jemadar	1844?	Afghanistan?	Daughter	Daughter-in-law	Deprived pension and to be tried
188–189A Nov 25, 1853	Dinapore/Benares	Dooktee	Acbrut (Achuwut) Sing	15th NI	Havildar	1844?	Afghanistan?	Wife/widow	Sister-in-law	Deprived pension and to be tried
188–189A Nov 25, 1853	Dinapore/Benares	Nunkee	Gopee Sohar	60th NI	Sepahee	1844?	Afghanistan?	Mother	Mother by adoption	Deprived pension and to be tried
188–189A Nov 25, 1853	Dinapore/Benares	Jellybeeah	Ramdeen Patuck	53rd NI	Sepahee	1843?	Afghanistan?	Mother	Aunt	Deprived pension (see also 176 of May 26, 1854)
188–189A Nov 25, 1853	Dinapore/Benares	Ruchree	Ramoogeah Misser	61st NI	Sepahee	1847?	Punjab?	Wife/widow	Sister-in-law	Deprived pension and to be tried
188–189A Nov 25, 1853	Dinapore/Benares	Gunga Azil	Munnee Sing	43rd LI	Sepahee	1844?	Afghanistan?	Mother	Mother by "adoption"	Deprived pension and to be tried
189 Nov 25, 1853	Dinapore/Benares	Gangia	Atmaram	#? NI	Sepoy	1842/	Afghanistan	Mother	Sister-in-law	Deprived pension
190–193 Nov 25, 1853	Allahabad	Kutwaree	Soorjoo Sing	27th NI	Havildar	not stated	not stated	Wife/widow	Brother's wife/widow	Deprived pension, 3 years prison
228 & 229 Dec 9, 1853	Dinapore/Benares	Bujoo Misser	Bhurrosah Misser	67th NI	Sipahee	1827?	Burma?	Father	Uncle	To be tried and deprived pension
228 & 229 Dec 9, 1853	Dinapore/Benares	Ooraha	Mhraj Sing	60th NI	Sipahee	1844?	Afghanistan?	Wife/widow	Sister-in-law	To be tried and deprived pension

Number & Date	Station	Claimant	Soldier	Regiment	Rank	Date	Location	Father	Uncle	Outcome
228 & 229 Dec 9, 1853	Dinapore/Benares	Babuchund Singh	Demaj/Demagh Sing	65th NI	Sipahee	1827?	Burma?	Father	Uncle	To be tried and deprived pension
225–227 Dec 16, 1853	Dinapore/Benares	Seespal Sing	Seetaram Sing	72nd NI	Sipahee	1849?	Punjab	Son	Nephew	Deprived pension
166 & 167 Mar 24, 1854	Dinapore/Benares	Jussee	Puram Sing	43rd LI	Sepahee	not stated	not stated	Mother	Sister-in-law	Struck off pension roll (Jussee died in 1852)
168 & 169 Mar 24, 1854	Dinapore/Benares	Brealeah or Rikaba	Gridharry Sing	54th NI	Sepoy	1844?	Afghanistan?	Mother	Sister-in-law	Struck off pension roll (Brealeah/Rikaba had died)
170–172 Mar 24, 1854	Dinapore/Benares	Luchmunnee	Gunga Sing	43rd LI	Sepoy	1844?	Afghanistan?	Mother	Sister	Deprived pension, and "absconded"
180–184 Mar 31, 1854	Dinapore/Benares	Kewnlee	Koomail Tewary	65th NI	Sipahee	1828	Burma?	Wife/widow	Sister-in-law	Deprived pension, ran away
182–184 Mar 31, 1854	Dinapore/Benares	Bhagoo	Ogra Sing	16th NI	Sipahee	1842?	Afghanistan?	Mother	Sister	Deprived pension, gone missing
182–184 Mar 31, 1854	Dinapore/Benares	Biswasee	Achumbeet Sing	26th LI	Sipahee	1842?	Afghanistan?	Wife/widow	Sister-in-law	Deprived pension
160 Apr 15, 1854	Dinapore/Benares	Luchmunnea	Rambit Sing	54th NI	Sepahee	1844?	Afghanistan?	Wife/widow	Sister-in-law	Deprived pension
161 Apr 15, 1854	Dinapore/Benares	Nimbassa	Bulgobind Sing	5th NI	N/A	1844?	Afghanistan?	Mother	Aunt	Deprived pension
162 Apr 15, 1854	Dinapore/Benares	Mohit Sing	Augin Sing	VR	Sepoy	1844?	Afghanistan?	Son	Nephew	Deprived pension
163 Apr 15, 1854	Dinapore/Benares	Lugan	Bugwan Sing	VR	Sepoy	1843?	Afghanistan?	Mother	Aunt	Deprived pension and to be tried
164 Apr 15, 1854	Dinapore/Benares	Lall Beeherrie	Sewburrut	30th NI	Naick	1843?	Afghanistan?	Son	Nephew	Deprived pension
179–182 May 26, 1854	Dinapore/Benares	Talleewindee	Ghureeb Pandy	53rd NI	Sepahee	Mar 19, 1844	Afghanistan?	Mother	Sister-in-law	Deprived pension and to be tried
164 & 165 Jul 7, 1854	Dinapore/Benares	Punkooree	Hunsraj Sing	54th NI	Sipahee	1844?	Afghanistan?	Wife/widow	Sister-in-law	Deprived pension
206 & 207 Jul 21, 1854	Meerut/Haupper	Mewah	Emam Khan	8th LC	Trooper	Nov 1848	Punjab	Wife/widow	Imposter	Deprived pension and granted to actual wife

(cont.)

File nos.	PPM office	Pensioner	Name of decedent soldier	Decedent's regt.	Decedent's rank	Date of death	Place of death	Claimed relationship	"Actual" relationship	Punishment
223 Jul 21, 1854	Dinapore/ Benares	Oodassea	Lowton	41st NI	Sipahee	1844?	China	Wife/ widow	Sister-in-law	Deprived pension
233 Jul 21, 1854	Dinapore/ Benares	Nohallee	Kurrug	40th NI	Sepoy	1826?	Burma?	Wife/ widow	Sister-in-law	Deprived pension
234 Jul 21, 1854	Dinapore/ Benares	Kissona	Hurreeram	5th NI	Drummer	1852?	not stated	Wife/ widow	Sister-in-law	Decision pending determination of sagāī legality
120 & 121 Sep 29, 1854	Dinapore/ Benares	Runneea	Gunnase	30th NI	Naick	1843?	Afghanistan?	Wife/ widow	Mistress (sagāī married)	Decision pending determination of sagāī legality
147 & 150 Aug 18, 1854	Meerut/ Haupper	Soogree (and Soogeeah)	not stated	not stated	not stated	not stated	not stated	Wife/ widow	Complex impersonation	Deprived pension
149 Aug 18, 1854	Meerut/ Haupper	Jeynee	Surnam Sing	54th NI	Naick	1842?	Afghanistan	Wife/ widow	Mistress (no marriage)	Deprived pension, based on caste logic
106–108 Sep 22, 1854	Dinapore/ Benares	Parbuteeah & Judoee	Rumphul Opudia	5th NI	Sepoy	1842?	Afghanistan?	Wife/ widow	Complex impersonation	Both deprived pensions
102–104 Sep 29, 1854	Dinapore/ Benares	Munbasee	Ajaib Lalla	30th NI	Havildar	1853?	not stated	Mother	Mother-in-law of brother	Deprived pension, 7 days prison
157 Oct 13, 1854	Dinapore/ Benares	Ramullee	Sohawun Chowbey	43 NI	Sipahee	1828?	Burma?	Wife/ widow	Sister-in-law of brother	Deprived pension
160 Oct 13, 1854	Dinapore/ Benares	Hottoo	Munsour Khan	3rd LC	Trooper?	1843?	Afghanistan?	Mother	Sister	Deprived pension
161 Oct 13, 1854	Dinapore/ Benares	Hunso	Hunnoomun Sing	26th NI	Sepoy	1826?	Burma?	Wife/ widow	Sister-in-law	Deprived pension
179 Dec 1, 1854	Dinapore/ Benares	Emamee	Bubbur Khan	54th NI	Bheestie	1842?	Afghanistan?	Son	Wife's son (his stepson)	Deprived pension
237 Dec 22, 1854	Dinapore/ Benares	Dooleeah	Soobhur	46th (?) NI	Sepoy	1826?	Burma?	Wife/ widow	Wife, then sagāī rewed	Disposition unclear (file stops)

File/Date	Location	Name 1	Name 2	Regiment	Rank	col	col	Relation 1	Relation 2	Outcome
178 Apr 20, 1855	Dinapore/Benares	Jeenut	Meer Jehan	not stated	Klasee	not stated	not stated	Wife/widow	Mistress	Deprived pension, 6 months prison
117 & 118 Aug 3, 1855	Dinapore/Benares	Khyrim (2 different women)	Rosun Khan	not stated	Naick & Sepoy	not stated	not stated	Wives/widows	Wives/widows	No fraud found; book keeping error
173–175 Jul 11, 1856	Dinapore/Benares	Beesah	Teeluck Sing	42nd LI	Havildar	not stated	not stated	Daughter	Sister-in-law	Deprived pension
200 Jan 23, 1857	Dinapore/Benares	Odassee	not stated	not stated	not stated	not stated	not stated	Mother	Sister	Deprived pension

Notes: 1. This table is not an exhaustive list of pension fraud cases. These are cases upon which I took notes during my research in 2012–2013. See Chapter 4 for discussion.

2. A question mark is included when the soldier's date of death is estimated based on the commencement date of the pension.

3. A question mark is included when the soldier's place of death is estimated based on the date of death given in the file or the commencement date of the pension.

4. Most of these cases also resulted in sureties/securities also being punished with fines, dismissal of pensions, and sometimes prison.

Abbreviations: NI = Native Infantry, LI = Light Infantry, LC = Light Cavalry, HA = Horse Artillery, S&M = Sappers and Miners, VR = Volunteer Regiment [Kabul Campaign], HM = Her Majesty's, F = Foot, SB = Sirmoor Battn., Gr = Grenadiers.

1850 = 9 cases
1851 = 14 cases
1852 = 16 cases
1853 = 30 cases
1854 = 27 cases
1855 = 2 cases
1856 = 1 case
1857 = 1 case

Source: Military Consultations and Proceedings, National Archives of India, New Delhi. File numbers provided in the far left column.

Bibliography

Primary Sources

Official Records

India Office Records, British Library (London):
   North Western Provinces Criminal Judicial Proceedings (NWP-CJP).
National Archives of India (New Delhi):
   Military Consultations (MC).
   Military Proceedings (MP).

Note: In general, "consultations" are the original correspondences, enclosures, and associated documents consulted in the Military Committee, sometimes with notations by members of the committee. These are then recorded (by hand) into volumes known as "proceedings." As a result, proceedings volumes often do not contain the entirety of the material in consultations files. I cite both consultations (MC) and proceedings (MP) in this study, especially in Chapter 4. My use of consultations (preferable) as opposed to proceedings depended on what was delivered to my desk in the National Archives of India, New Delhi, in 2012–2013.

Manuscripts and Other Unpublished Primary Source Materials

"An album containing fifty-three drawings depicting occupations," ca. 1815–1820, Lucknow, AL.7970, Victoria & Albert Museum, London.
Joshi, P. C. "Folk Songs of 1857." File no. 216. Archives on Contemporary History. Jawaharlal Nehru University Library, New Delhi.
"Kitāb-i tashrīḥ al-aqvām, an account of origins and occupations of some of the sects, castes and tribes of India." Produced for James Skinner. 1825, Hansi Cantonment, Add. 27255, British Library.
Saunders Correspondence. Vol. 1 (Moradabad, May and June 1857). Mss.Eur.C93. Asia & Africa Collection, British Library, London.
Carmichael-Smyth, Major-General G. *Papers regarding "the Indian Mutiny."* British Library, Asia, Pacific & Africa Collection. Shelfmark V 8828 (b).
Smyth, Colonel G. C. (Carmichael). "Mutiny of the Third Light Cavalry at Meerut." 1858?

Published Primary Sources

'Abd al-Qādir ibn Mulūk Shāh, known as al Badā'ūnī. *Muntakhabu-t-tawarikh*. Vol. 2. Translated by George S. A. Ranking. Calcutta: Asiatic Society of Bengal, 1898, reprint New Delhi: Atlantic, 1990.

A Collection of the Proceedings which Led to the Passing of Act XV of 1856. Compiled by Narayan Keshav Vaidya. Bombay: Mazagaon Printing Press, 1885.

Annals of the Indian Rebellion, containing Narratives of the Outbreaks and Eventful Occurrences, and Stories of Personal Adventures, during the Mutiny of 1857–58. Compiled by N. A. Chick. Calcutta: Sanders, Cones & Co., 1859.

Bacon, Thomas. *First Impressions and Studies from Nature in Hindostan*. Vol. 2. London: Wm. H. Allen and Co., 1837.

Ball, Charles. *The History of the Indian Mutiny*. 2 vols. London: London Printing and Publishing Company, 1858.

Biharilal, Ras. "*Lokgeeton Men Babu Kuar Singh*" (Babu Kuar Singh in Folk Songs). *Bhojpuri* 3, 7 (April 1955).

Broughton, Thomas D., *Letters Written in a Mahratta Camp during the year 1809, descriptive of the character, manners, domestic habits, and religious ceremonies of the Mahrattas*. London: Archibald Constable and Co., 1813.

Buckler, F. W. "The Political Theory of the Indian Mutiny." (1922) Republished in M. N. Pearson, ed., *Legitimacy and Symbols: The South Asian Writings of F. W. Buckler*. Ann Arbor: University of Michigan Press, 1985.

Carey, W. H. *The Mahomedan Rebellion; its Preminitory Symptoms, Outbreak and Suppression; with an Appendix*. Roorkee: Directory Press, 1857.

Cave-Brown, Rev. J. *The Punjab and Delhi in 1857, being a narrative of the measures by which the Punjab was saved and Delhi recovered during the Indian mutiny*. 2 vols. London: Blackwood, 1861.

Crooke, William. "Songs of the Mutiny." *The Indian Antiquary*, part I (April 1911): 123–124, and part II (June 1911): 165–169.

Das, Syamasundar. *Hindi Shabdasagar*. Kashi: Nagari Pracharini Sabha, 1965–1975.

Datta, K. K. "A Contemporary Account of the Indian Movement of 1857–59." *Journal of the Bihar Research Society*, 36 (1950): 96–133.

Dehlavi, Zahir. *Dastan-e-Ghadar: The Tale of the Mutiny*. Translated by Rana Safvi. Gurgaon: Penguin, 2017.

Dehlvi, Zahir. *Dāstān-e-Ghadr*. Lahore: first published in 1914; republished Lahore: Academy Edition, 1955; and Lahore: Sang-i Mīl Publications, 2007.

"Depositions Taken at Meerut, by Major G. W. Williams, Superintendent of Police, N. W. P., 1858." British Library, London.

Dunlop, R. H. W. *Service and Adventure with the Khakee Resallah; or, Meerut Volunteer Horse, during the Mutinies of 1857–58*. London: Richard Bentley, 1858.

Eden, Emily. *Up the Country: Letters Written to Her Sister from the Upper Provinces of India*. Edward Thompson, ed. London: Oxford University Press, 1930.

Fallon, S. W. *A New Hindustani–English dictionary, with illustrations from Hindustani literature and folk-lore*. Banaras, London: Trubner and Co., 1879.

Fanthome, J. F. *Mariam: A Story of the Indian Mutiny.* Benares: The Chandraprabha Press, 1896.
Forrest, G. W. *A History of the Indian Mutiny.* Edinburgh and London: William Blackwood and Sons, 1914.
"The Frail Ones." *Nashville Dispatch.* 13 August 1863.
Freedom Struggle in Uttar Pradesh. Vol. 1. Edited by S. A. A. Rizvi and Moti Lal Bhargava. Lucknow: Information Department, 1957–1961.
Gough, Hugh. *Old Memories.* Edinburgh and London: William Blackwood and Sons, 1897.
Grierson, George A. *Bihar Peasant Life, being a discursive catalogue of the surroundings of the people of that province.* Calcutta: Bengal Secretariat Press, 1885.
Gubbins, Martin Richard. *An account of the Mutinies in Oudh and of the Siege of the Lucknow Residency; with some observations on the condition of the Province of Oudh and on the causes of the mutiny of the Bengal Army.* London: Richard Bentley, 1858.
Indian Mutiny Papers. Vol. 1. Edited by George W. Forrest. Calcutta: Military Department Press, 1893.
Joshi, P. C. "Folk Songs of 1857." In P. C. Joshi (ed.), *Rebellion 1857: A Symposium.* New Delhi: People's Publishing House, 1957.
Junoon. Directed by Shyam Benegal. 1979. 2h 21m.
Kipling, Rudyard. "The Sudder Bazaar." In Rudyard and Beatrice Kipling, *Echoes: By two writers.* Lahore: Civil and Military Gazette Press, 1884.
The Law of India. Vol. 2, *Miscellaneous Laws.* Compiled and edited by Andrew Lyon. Calcutta: Thacker & Spink, 1873.
MacMunn, Sir George. "Mees Dolly (An Untold Tragedy of '57)." *Cornhill Magazine* (September 1927): 327–331.
———. *The Indian Mutiny in Perspective.* London: G. Bell & Sons, 1931.
Malleson, G. B. *The Indian Mutiny of 1857.* London: Seeley and Col., Ltd., 1891.
———. *The Mutiny of the Bengal Army: An Historical Narrative.* London: Bosworth and Harrison, 1858.
McGregor, R. S. *The Oxford Hindi–English dictionary.* New York: Oxford University Press, 1993.
The Memoirs of Field Marshall Sir Henry Wylie Norman. Edited and arranged by Sir William Lee-Warner. London: Smith, Elder, & Co., 1908.
Napier, Charles James. *Defects, Civil and Military of the Indian Government.* 2nd edition. London: Westerton, 1853.
October: Ten Days that Shook the World. Directed by Sergei Eisenstein, 1928. 1hr 40m.
Platts, John T. *A Dictionary of Urdu, Classical Hindi, and English.* London: W. H. Allen & Co., 1884.
Pollok, Fitz-William Thomas. *Fifty Years' Reminiscences of India: A Retrospect of Travel, Adventure and Shikar.* London: Edward Arnold, 1896.
Prasad, Vishwanath. *Kṛṣikōś.* Patna: Bihar Rashtrabhasha Parishad, 1956.
Rag, Pankaj. *1857: The Oral Tradition.* New Delhi: Rupa, 2010.
The Rising: The Ballad of Mangal Pandey. Directed by Ketan Mehta. Yash Raj Films, 2005. 2h 30m.

Savarkar, V. D. *First War of Indian Independence.* First published 1909. 4th underground edition, n.d., pub. Mayuresh.
Scott, Paul. *The Raj Quartet.* New York: Morrow; 1976.
Selections from Indian Journals. Vol. 1, *Calcutta Journal.* Compiled by Satyajit Das. Calcutta: K. L. Mukhopadhyay, 1963.
Sharma, Omprakash. *Sānjh kā Sūraj (The Evening Sun).* Delhi-Shahdara: Saraswati Sahakar, 1955.
Sleeman, W. H. *A Report on the System of Megpunnaism or, The Murder of Indigent Parents for their Young Children (who are sold as Slaves) as it prevails in the Delhi Territories, and the Native States of Rajpootana, Ulwar, and Bhurtpore.* Serampore: Serampore Press, 1839.
Steel, Flora Annie. *On the Face of the Waters.* New York: Macmillan, 1897.
Steingass, Francis Joseph. *A Comprehensive Persian–English dictionary, including the Arabic words and phrases to be met with in Persian literature.* London: Routledge & K. Paul, 1892.
Taylor, P. J. O. *Chronicles of the Mutiny and Other Historical Sketches.* New Delhi: Indus, 1992.
"Mees Dolly." In *A Companion to the "Indian Mutiny" of 1857.* Delhi: Oxford University Press, 1996.
A Star Shall Fall: India 1857. New Delhi: Indus, 1993.
Vidyasagar, Ishwar Chandra. *Hindu Widow Marriage.* Edited and translated by Brian A. Hatcher. New York: Columbia University Press, 2012.
Williams, G. W. "Memorandum on the Mutiny and Outbreak at Meerut in May 1857." British Library, London.
"Narrative of Events Connected with the Outbreak in 1857." British Library, London.
Wilson, H. H. *A glossary of judicial and revenue terms and of useful words occurring in official documents relating to the administration of the government of British India, from the Arabic, Persian, Hindustani, Sanskrit, Hindi, Bengali, Uriya, Marathi, Guzarathi, Telugu, Karnata, Tamil, Malayalam and other languages.* London: Wm. H. Allen and Co., 1855.
Wilson, J. Cracroft. *Narrative of Events attending the Outbreak of Disturbances and the Restoration of Authority in the District of Moradabad, in 1857–58.* London: Anglo-American Times Press, 1871.

Published and Unpublished Secondary Sources

Alavi, Seema. "The Company Army and Rural Society: The Invalid Thanah 1780–1830." *Modern Asian Studies* 27, 1 (1993): 147–178.
The Sepoys and the Company: Tradition and Transition in Northern India, 1770–1830. Delhi: Oxford University Press, 1995.
Ali, Daud. "War, Servitude, and the Imperial Household: A Study of Palace Women in the Chola Empire." In Indrani Chatterjee and Richard Eaton (eds.), *Slavery and Society in South Asian History.* Bloomington: University of Indiana Press, 2006.
Amin, Shahid. *Event, Metaphor, Memory: Chauri Chaura, 1922–1992.* Berkeley: University of California Press, 1995.

Anderson, Robyn. "'The Hardened Frail Ones': Women and Crime in Auckland, 1845–1870." MA thesis, University of Auckland, 1981.

Ankersmit, Frank. "Hayden White's Appeal to the Historians." *History and Theory* 7, 2 (1998): 182–193.

Archer, Mildred. *British Drawings in the India Office Library*. Vol. 1, *Amateur Artists*. London: Her Majesty's Stationery Office, 1969.

Archer, Mildred and Ronald Lightbown. *India Observed: India as Viewed by British Artists 1760–1860*. London: Victoria and Albert Museum, 1982.

Arnold, David. "Poor Europeans in India, 1750–1947." *Current Anthropology* 20, 2 (1979): 454–455.

Arondekar, Anjali. "Without a Trace: Sexuality and the Colonial Archive." *Journal of the History of Sexuality* 14, 1/2 (2005): 10–27.

Bakhtin, Mikhail. *Rabelais and His World*. Translated by Helene Iswolsky. Bloomington: Indiana University Press, 1984.

Barthes, Roland. *The Rustle of Language*. Translated by R. Howard. Berkeley: University of California Press, 1989.

Bayly, C. A. *Indian Society and the Making of the British Empire*. Cambridge: Cambridge University Press, 1989.

Rulers, Townsmen and Bazaars: North Indian Society in the Age of British Expansion 1770–1870. Cambridge: Cambridge University Press, 1983.

"Town Building in North India, 1790–1830." *Modern Asian Studies* 9, 4 (1975): 483–504.

Bakhle, Janaki. *Savarkar and the Making of Hindutva*. Princeton, NJ: Princeton University Press, 2024.

Ballhatchet, Kenneth. *Race, Sex and Class under the Raj: Imperial Attitudes and Policies and their Critics, 1793–1905*. London: Weidenfeld and Nicolson, 1980.

Bhadra, Gautam. "Four Rebels of 1857." In Ranajit Guha (ed.), *Subaltern Studies 4*. Delhi: Oxford University Press, 1984, pp. 276–329.

Brueck, Laura. "*Bhais* Behaving Badly: Vernacular Masculinities in Hindi Detective Novels." *South Asian Popular Culture* 18, 1 (2020): 29–46.

Caddell, Patrick. "The Outbreak of the Indian Mutiny." *Journal of the Society for Army Historical Research* 33, 135 (1955): 118–122.

Chakrabarty, Dipesh and Rochona Majumdar. "Mangal Pandey: Film and History." *Economic and Political Weekly* 42, 19 (May 12–18, 2007): 1771–1778.

Chatterjee, Indrani. "Colouring Subalternity: Slaves, Concubines and Social Orphans in Early Colonial India." In Gautam Bhadra, Gyan Prakash, and Susie Tharu (eds.), *Subaltern Studies X: Writings on South Asian History and Society*. Delhi: Oxford University Press, 1999.

Gender, Slavery, and Law in Colonial India. Delhi: Oxford University Press, 1999.

Chatterjee, Indrani and Sumit Guha. "Slave-Queen, Waif-Prince: Slavery and Social Capital in Eighteenth-Century India." *Indian Economic and Social History Review* 36, 2 (1999): 165–186.

Chaturvedi, Vinayak. *Hindutva and Violence: V. D. Savarkar and the Politics of History*. New Delhi: Permanent Black, 2022.

Cooper, Randolf G. S. "Culture, Combat, and Colonialism in Eighteenth- and Nineteenth-Century India." *The International History Review* 27, 3 (September 2005): 534–549.

Bibliography

Review of D. F. Harding, *Smallarms of the East India Company, 1600–1856*. *Modern Asian Studies* 36, 3 (July 2002): 758–764.
Dalrymple, William. *The Last Mughal: The Fall of a Dynasty, Delhi, 1857*. London: Penguin Viking, 2007.
David, Julian Saul Markham. "The Bengal Army and the Outbreak of the Indian Mutiny." PhD thesis, Department of History, University of Glasgow, 2001.
David, Saul. *The Bengal Army and the Outbreak of the Indian Mutiny*. New Delhi: Manohar Publishers & Distributors, 2009.
The Indian Mutiny: 1857. London: Viking, 2002.
Dening, Greg. *Mr. Bligh's Bad Language: Passion, Power, and Theatre on the Bounty*. Cambridge: Cambridge University Press, 1992.
Desai, Anita. "The Rage for the Raj: How the Festival of India Lost India." *The New Republic* 193, 22 (1985): 26–30.
Desan, Suzanne. "Gender, Radicalization, and the October Days: Occupying the National Assembly." *French Historical Studies* 43, 3 (2020): 359–390.
Dhanwa, Alok. "Bhāgī Huī Laṛakiyāṃ" (Runaway Girls). In Alok Dhanwa, *Duniyā Rōz Bantī Hai (The World is Made Every Day)*. Patna: Rajkamal Prakashan, 2015.
Dirks, Nicholas. "Castes of Mind." *Representations* 37 (Winter 1992): 56–78.
Eaton, Richard. "The Rise and Fall of Military Slavery in the Deccan, 1450–1650." In Indrani Chatterjee and Richard Eaton (eds.), *Slavery and Society in South Asian History*. Bloomington: University of Indiana Press, 2006.
Evans Clements, Barbara. "Working-Class and Peasant Women in the Russia Revolution, 1917–1923." *Signs* 8, 2 (Winter 1982): 215–235.
Fischer-Tiné, Harald. *"Low and Licentious Europeans": Race, Class and White Subalternity in Colonial India*. New Delhi: Orient Longman, 2009.
"'White Women Degrading Themselves to the Lowest Depths': European Networks of Prostitution and Colonial Anxieties in British India and Ceylon Ca. 1880–1914." *Indian Economic and Social History Review* 40 (2003): 163–190.
Fisher, Michael. "Becoming and Making 'Family' in Hindustan." In Indrani Chatterjee (ed.), *Unfamiliar Relations: Family and History in South Asia*. Delhi: Permanent Black, 2004.
Ghosh, Durba. *Sex and the Family in Colonial India: The Making of Empire*. Cambridge: Cambridge University Press, 2006.
Guha, Ranajit. *Elementary Aspects of Peasant Insurgency in Colonial India*. Delhi: Oxford University Press, 1983.
Guha, Sumit. "Slavery, Society, and the State in Western India, 1700–1800," in Indrani Chatterjee and Richard Eaton (eds.), *Slavery and Society in South Asian History*. Bloomington: University of Indiana Press, 2006.
Gupta, Charu. "Writing Sex and Sexuality: Archives of Colonial North India." *Journal of Women's History* 23, 4 (2011): 12–35.
Harding, David F. "Arming the East India Company's Forces." In Alan J. Guy and Peter B. Boyden (eds.), *Soldiers of the Raj: The Indian Army, 1600–1947*. London: National Army Museum, 1997.
Harding, D. F. *Smallarms of the East India Company, 1600–1856*. Vol. 3, *Ammunition and Performance*. London: Foresight Books, 1999.

Smallarms of the East India Company, 1600–1856. Vol. 4, *The Users and Their Smallarms.* London: Foresight Books, 1999.
Hawes, Christopher J. *Poor Relations: The Making of a Eurasian Community in British India, 1773–1833.* London and New York: Routledge, 1996.
Hibbert, Christopher. *The Great Mutiny: India 1857.* New York: Penguin, 1978.
Jacob, T. *Cantonments in India: Evolution and Growth.* New Delhi: Reliance Publishing House, 1994.
Jasanoff, Maya. "The Unknown Women of India." *New York Review of Books,* December 18, 2008.
Kaye, John. *A History of the Sepoy War in India, 1857–1858.* 4 vols. London: W. H. Allen & Co., 1864–1876.
Kolff, Dirk H. A. *Naukar, Rajput and Sepoy: The Ethnohistory of the Military Labour Market in Hindustan, 1450–1850.* Cambridge: Cambridge University Press, 1990.
Kolsky, Elizabeth. *Colonial Justice in British India: White Violence and the Rule of Law.* Cambridge: Cambridge University Press, 2009.
Koselleck, Reinhart. *Futures Past: On the Semantics of Historical Time.* Translated by Keith Tribe. New York: Columbia University Press, 2004.
LeClair, Danield R. "The 'Greased Cartridge Affair': Re-examining the Pattern 1853 Enfield Cartridge and Its Role in the Indian Mutiny of 1857." *International Ammunition Association Journal* 504 (July/August 2015): 98–109.
Lepore, Jill. "Just the Facts, Ma'am: Fake Memoirs, Factual Fictions, and the History of History." *New Yorker* (March 24, 2008), 79–83.
Levine, Philippa. *Prostitution, Race, and Politics: Policing Venereal Disease in the British Empire.* New York: Routledge, 2003.
Macmillan, Margaret. *Women of the Raj.* New York: Thames & Hudson, 1988.
Mahaur, Bhagwan Das. *1857 ke Swadhinta Sangram ka Hindi Sahitya par Prabhav* (The Impact of the 1857 War of Independence on Hindi Literature). Ajmer: Krishna Brothers, 1976.
Majumdar, R. C. *The Sepoy Mutiny and Revolt of 1857,* Calcutta: Firma K. L. Mukhopadhyay 1957.
Mander, Harsh. "Living with Hunger: Deprivation among the Aged, Single Women and People with Disability." *Economic and Political Weekly* 43, 17 (April 26–May 2, 2008): 87–98.
Mani, Lata. "Contentious Traditions: The Debate on Sati in Colonial India." *Cultural Critique* 7, 2 (Autumn 1987): 119–156.
Miers, Suzanne and Igor Kopytoff (eds). *Slavery in Africa: Historical and Anthropological Perspectives.* Madison: University of Wisconsin Press, 1977.
Mishra, Shridhar. *Bhojpuri Lok Sahitya: Sanskritik Adhyayan (Bhojpuri Folk Literature: A Cultural Study).* Allahabad: Hindustani Academy, 1971.
Mitra, Durba. *Indian Sex Life: Sexuality and the Colonial Origins of Modern Social Thought.* Princeton: Princeton University Press, 2020.
Mitra, Subal Chandra. *Isvar Chandra Vidyasagar: A Story of His Life and Work.* Calcutta: Sarat Chandra Mitra, New Bengal Press, 1902.
Naithani, Sadhana. *In Quest of Indian Folktales: Pandit Ram Gharib Chaube and William Crooke.* Bloomington: Indiana University Press, 2006.

Nandy, Ashis. "Final Encounter: The Politics of the Assassination of Gandhi." In Ashis Nandy, *At the Edge of Psychology: Essays in Politics and Culture*. Delhi: Oxford University Press, 1980, 70–98.

Palmer, J. A. B. *Mutiny Outbreak at Meerut in 1857*. Cambridge: Cambridge University Press, 1966.

Patel, Tanvi P. "Emerging Crimewallahs: Modern Developments in South Asian Crime Fiction." PhD dissertation, University of Washington, 2010.

Patterson, Orlando. *Slavery and Social Death: A Comparative Study*. Cambridge, MA: Harvard University Press, 1982.

Peers, Douglas. *Between Mars and Mammon: Colonial Armies and the Garrison State in Early Nineteenth-Century India*. London: I. B. Tauris, 1995.

"Privates off Parade: Regulating Sexuality in the Nineteenth-Century Indian Empire." *International History Review* 20, 4 (1998): 823–854.

"Soldiers, Surgeons and the Campaigns to Combat Sexually Transmitted Diseases in Colonial India." *Medical History* 42, 2 (1998): 137–160.

Pinch, William R. "Prostituting the Mutiny: Sex-slavery and Crime in the Making of 1857." In Crispin Bates (ed.), *Mutiny at the Margins: New Perspectives on the Indian Uprising of 1857*. Volume 1. New Delhi: Sage, 2013, 61–87.

Pinch, William R. *Warrior Ascetics and Indian Empires*. Cambridge: Cambridge University Press, 2006.

Pinch, Vijay [William]. "*Gosain Tawaif*: Sex, Slaves, and Ascetics in Rasdhan, 1800–1857." *Modern Asian Studies* 38, 3 (July 2004): 559–597.

Ranjan, Ritwik. "Postcoloniality and the Two Sites of Historicity." *History and Theory* 56, 1 (2017): 38–53.

Ray, Rajat Kanta. *Exploring Emotional History: Gender, Mentality and Literature in the Indian Awakening*. Delhi: Oxford University Press, 2001.

The Felt Community: Commonalty and Mentality before the Emergence of Indian Nationalism. Delhi: Oxford UPress, 2003.

Richardson, LeeAnne Marie. "*On the Face of the Waters:* Flora Annie Steel and the Politics of Feminist Imperialism." In Brenda Ayers (ed.), *Silent Voices: Forgotten Novels by Victorian Women Writers*. Westport, CT: Praeger, 2003.

Ringe, Don. *From Proto-Indo-European to Proto-Germanic*. New York: Oxford University Press, 2006.

Robinson, Jane. *Angels of Albion: Women of the Indian Mutiny*. London: Viking, 1996.

Runia, Eelco. "Into Cleanness Leaping: The Vertiginous Urge to Commit History." *History and Theory* 49, 1 (2010): 1–20.

Moved by the Past: Discontinuity and Historical Mutation. New York: Columbia University Press, 2014.

Sangari, Kumkum. "Mirabai and the Spiritual Economy of Bhakti." Part II. *Economic and Political Weekly* 25, 28 (14 July 1990): 1464–1475.

Scott, Joan Wallach. *The Politics of the Veil*. Princeton: Princeton University Press, 2010.

Sharma, Mahendra Narain. *The Life and Times of Begam Samru of Sardhana (A.D. 1750–1836)*. Sahibabad: Vibhu Prakashan, 1985.

Sen, S. N. *Eighteen Fifty-Seven*. Calcutta: Government of India, 1957.

Singha, Radhika. *A Despotism of Law: Crime and Justice in Early Colonial India.* Delhi: Oxford University Press, 1998.
"Making the Domestic More Domestic: Criminal Law and the Head of the Household, 1772–1843." *Indian Economic and Social History Review* 33, 3 (1996): 309–343.
Sinha, Mrinalini. *Colonial Masculinity: The "Manly Englishman" and the "Effeminate Bengali" in the late Nineteenth Century.* Manchester: Manchester University Press, 1995.
Sreenivasan, Ramya. "Drudges, Dancing Girls, and Concubines: Female Slaves in the Rajput Polity, 1500–1850." In Indrani Chatterjee and Richard Eaton (eds.), *Slavery & Society in South Asian History.* Bloomington: University of Indiana Press, 2006, pp. 136–161.
Stallybrass, Peter, and Allon White. *The Politics and Poetics of Transgression.* Ithaca, NY: Cornell University Press, 1986.
Stoff, Laurie. *They Fought for the Motherland: Russia's Women Soldiers in World War I and the Revolution.* Lawrence: University Press of Kansas, 2006.
Stokes, Eric. *The Peasant Armed: The Indian Rebellion of 1857.* Oxford: The Clarendon Press, 1986.
Talwar Oldenburg, Veena. "Lifestyle as Resistance: The Case of the Courtesans of Lucknow." In V. Graff (ed.), *Lucknow: Memories of a City.* Delhi: Oxford University Press, 1997.
Tambe, Ashwini. *Codes of Misconduct: Regulating Prostitution in Late Colonial Bombay.* Minneapolis: University of Minnesota Press, 2009.
Thompson, Edward. *The Other Side of the Medal.* London: Hogarth Press, 1925.
Turner, Victor. *The Ritual Process.* Chicago: Aldine, 1969.
Vetch, Robert Hamilton. "Napier, Charles James." In Sidney Lee (ed.), *Dictionary of National Biography.* Vol. 40. London: Smith, Elder & Co., 1894.
Wagner, Kim. *The Great Fear of 1857.* London: Peter Lang, 2010.
Wald, Erica. "Health, Discipline, and Appropriate Behavior: The Body of the Soldier and the Space of the Cantonment." *Modern Asian Studies* 46, 4 (2012): 815–856.
White, Hayden. *The Fiction of Narrative: Essays on History, Literature, and Theory, 1957–2007.* Edited by Robert Doran. Baltimore: The Johns Hopkins University Press, 2010.
White, Luise. *The Comforts of Home: Prostitution in Colonial Nairobi.* Chicago: University of Chicago Press, 1990.
Yang, Anand A. "A Conversation of Rumors: The Language of Popular 'Mentalités' in Late Nineteenth-Century Colonial India." *Journal of Social History* 20, 3 (Spring 1987): 485–505.
Bazaar India: Markets, Society, and the Colonial State in Bihar. Berkeley: University of California Press, 1999.
"Whose Sati? Widow Burning in Early 19th Century India." *Journal of Women's History* 1, 2 (Fall 1989): 8–33.

Index

3rd Light Cavalry
  See also Carmichael-Smyth, Col. George
11th Native Regiment, 3, 6, 11, 50, 80, 192
15th Native Infantry, 153
1857: The Oral Tradition (Rag, 2010), 74
18th Native Infantry, 152
19th native infantry, 43
1st Irregular Cavalry, 135–136
1st Punjab Infantry, 134, 137
20th Native Infantry
  British deaths in Meerut, 11
  female taunts, 6
  mutiny, 1, 3, 50, 64, 80, 161, 192
26th Native Infantry, 154
29th Native Infantry, 120, 121, 182, 183, 184
30th Native Infantry, 160, 168
35th Native Infantry, 155
36th Native Infantry, 136–137
37th Native Infantry, 130, 132
3rd Irregular Cavalry, 133
3rd Light Cavalry
  Delhi, arrival in, 117–118, 121, 183
  depositions, 73
  disarmament, rumours of, 20, 73
  female taunts, 6, 51–52, 80, 119, 148, 149
  firing drill, 3, 10–11, 40–41, 43–46, 50
  firing parade, 44, 46–49
  ironing parade, 10–11, 40, 46, 50
  mutiny, 3, 11, 50, 63, 192
  oath of refusal, 44–45, 73
  prisoner's wives, 126
  sepoys, 42
40th Native Infantry, 165
41st Native Infantry, 167
46th Native Infantry, 155
53rd Native Regiment, 159
54th Native Infantry, 136–137, 141, 152, 163
5th Native Infantry, 140, 155, 167
60th Queen's Royal Rifles, 10
66th Native Infantry, 43

Ainslee, W., 159, 160
Alavi, Seema, 6
Alee, Salub, 140–141
Ali, Baksh, 48
Ali, Corp. Mir Qudrat, 49
Ali, Kudrut, 45, 73
Ali, Mir Fateh, 183
Ali, Peer, 45, 73
Ally, Meer Bahadoor, 135
Angels of Albion (Robinson, 1996), 66
Annals of the Indian Rebellion (Chick, 1859), 64
Astell, H. G., 110, 111–112, 113
Atmaram, 160, 162
Azizan, 58–59, 76

Baaz, Jung, 183
Bahadoor, Mirza Azim Beg Sirdar, 136
Ballhatchet, Kenneth, 97
bazaars. *See* Meerut bazaar; sadr bazaars
Beadon, Cecil, 157–158
Begum, Neaz, 133, 134–135, 139, 186
Begum, Shah, 132–133, 186
Bhadra, Gautam, 4
Bihar Peasant Life (Grierson, 1885), 173
Birch, Lt. Col. R. J. H., 157, 158, 159–160, 162, 167–168, 169
Broughton, Thomas, 36
Brown, Lt, C. L., 169
Buckland, C. F., 166
Bunnoo, 141, 143–144
Bux, Moulla, 1, 19–20, 32, 33

cantonments
  as bases for native army, 2
  Cantonment Joint Magistrates, 5, 21, 36, 71, 75, 105, 152–153, 159
  Enfield cartridge, 9
  mutiny, 9, 16, 41, 51–52, 61–62
  pensions, 127, 130, 133, 171, 185

cantonments (cont.)
  professions, 33–34
  professions, census data, 83–91
  prostitution, 5–6, 61–62, 79, 94, 107–108, 114–115, 189–190
  wives, 126, 148, 181, 186, 190
  See also Meerut cantonment
Carmichael-Smyth, Col. George, 40–42, 45, 48, 120
Carnegy, P., 104
Carpenter, William, 26
Cashmerians
  contractual relationships, 148, 186
  depositions, 70–71, 80
  information nexus, 82–83
  mutiny, rumours of, 69, 70–71
  as occupation, 76–78, 91–93
Chamberlain, Brig. N., 138–139
Chamberlain, Lt. Col. C. T., 135–136
Chatterjee, Bankim Chandra, 14
Chatterjee, Indrani, 114
Chaube, Râmgharîb, 11–12, 15
Cheejah, 155–156, 158–159
Chick, N. A., 64
Coke, Col. John, 134, 137–138, 148, 186
Company army
  bazaar professions by cantonment, census of, 83–91
  British legitimacy, source of, 6
  cartridges, Brown Bess, 10
  cartridges, Enfield, 2–3, 9–10, 46, 48–49
  early mutinies, 3, 9, 10–11, 43, 50
  free transport, 79
  Pattern 1853 Enfield, introduction of, 2–3, 9–10
  Punjabi (Pathan) recruitment, 137–138
  regimental women, 61, 79
  social aspects of, 126
  subsistence allowance, stoppage of, 80
  volunteer force, 2
  See also pensions
"The Company Army and Rural Society" (Alavi, 1993), 6
Contagious Diseases Acts, 5, 97–98, 108, 185
Cookson, R., 105
Craigie, Capt. H. C., 41
Crooke, William, 11–13, 15, 17–18, 37–39

Dalhousie, Gov. Gen. Lord, 152, 158, 160, 161–164, 169–170, 188
Dalrymple, William, 11
Dāstān-e-Ghadr (Dehlvi, 1914), 6, 116, 183
David, Saul, 66
Deen, Bhowanny, 132

Defects, Civil and Military of the Indian Government (Napier, 1853), 164
Dehlvi, Zahir, 5, 6, 116–118, 121, 122–126, 182, 183, 184, 185–186, 191
Depositions Taken at Meerut (Williams, 1858), 1
Devee, Jowala, 102–103, 105–106
Dhanwa, Alok, 186
Dhingra, Madan Lal, 15
Doctrine of Lapse, 13–14, 118, 188
Donnelly, Mrs. Esther, 80
Doobay, Adjoodhea, 161, 162
Doobey, Girdharee, 136–137
Doobey, Seearam, 136–137
Dooktee, 160
Duff, Sarah, 61
Dunlop, R. H. W., 19

Eden, Emily, 129
Eighteen Fifty-Seven (Sen, 1957), 63

Fanthome, J. F., 71
Faruqi, Shamshur Rahman, 182
Felt Community, The (Ray, 2003), 71, 180
First War of Indian Independence (Savarkar, 1908), 58
folk literature, Bhojpuri, 73–74
"Four Rebels of 1857" (Bhadra, 1984), 4
Fraser, S., 110–111
Freedom Struggle in Uttar Pradesh (Rizvi and Bhargava, 1957), 180

Gandhi (Attenborough, 1982), 65
Gandhi. Mahatma, 15, 54
Gangia, 160–162
General Order 1132 (1854), 168–169

Gough, Sir Hugh, 64
Government of India Act (1858), 192
Great Fear of 1857, The (Wagner, 2010), 4–5, 41, 61, 75
Grierson, George, 173
Guha, Ranajit, 4, 16, 192

Hamilton. T. T., 36
Hanso, 154–155
Harcourt, Alfred Frederick Pollock, 26
Harding, David, 10
Hastings, Warren, 31
Hawes, C. J., 78
Hewitt, Maj-Gen William, 41, 45–46
Hibbert, Christopher, 63–65, 72
Hidayat Ali, 176–177
Hindu Widows Remarriage Act (1856), 175, 176, 188, 190

Index

history
  British Raj, 16, 64–65
  continuity and rupture, 114, 192
  and fiction, 56–58, 66, 80, 181, 187
  Indian nationalism, 14–15
  microhistory, 7–8
  military history, 6–7, 17
  satī, 175
  women in, 55
History of the Sepoy War in India, 1857–1858
  (William, 1864–1876), 18, 54–55
Hugo, Victor, 18

Indian Mutiny in Perspective, The
  (MacMunn, 1931), 63
Indian Mutiny of 1857, The (Malleson, 1891), 153
Indian Mutiny: 1857, The (David, 2002), 66

Jaun, Golab, 70–71, 75, 78, 92–93, 148, 186–187
Jewel in the Crown, The (Scott, 1984), 65
Jeynee, 141
Joshi, P. C., 172–173
Judoee, 155
Jumnie, 169

Kaye, John William, 18, 55–56
Khan, Khanazad, 104
Khan, Mahomed, 107
Khan, Mahomed Noor, 133, 186
Khan, Sayyad Ahmad, 14
khangee (khāṅgī), 78, 83, 91, 92
Kipling, Rudyard, 26–27
Kissona, 167
kusbee (kasbī), 78, 83, 91

Levine, Philippa, 95
"Lifestyle as Resistance" (Oldenburg, 1997), 94
lock hospitals, 5, 95, 97, 98
Luchmee, 130–132
Lushington, C. Hugh, 145, 157, 158, 159, 164

Mackinnon, John, 43
MacMunn, Sir George, 33, 57–63, 79, 93, 116, 125
Maginnis, Tom (pseudonym), 60–61
Majumdar, R. C., 63
Mal, Shah, 4
Malleson, George Bruce, 56, 152–153
Mander, Harsh, 174
Mariam: A Story of the Indian Mutiny
  (Fanthome, 1896), 71

marriage
  arranged, 113
  British officers, 177
  Hindu Widows Remarriage Act (1856), 175, 176, 188, 190
  marriage settlement, 77
  nikāh, 84, 165–166
  passes, 36
  pensions, 137, 141–142
  sagāī (sugaee), 31, 165, 166–169, 176
  second marriages, 134, 144, 175, 186–187
  violence, 101
Masters, John, 56
Mayhew, Capt. W. H., 163
"Meerut, 1857" (mutiny song), 17–18
Meerut bazaar
  bazaar women, 53, 63–64, 70–73, 81, 116, 119, 125, 179–180
  disreputable inhabitants, 19, 51–59, 69, 181
  female taunts, 64, 66, 73, 116
  goods and services, 25–26
  as hybrid space, 28–29
  native constabulary, 68
  nonmilitary census, 21–25, 83, 91
  policing, 18–19
  prostitute narrative, 4–6, 53–59
  prostitution, 25, 82, 91
  violence and deaths, 4, 18–19, 20, 93, 116
  See also Cashmerians
Meerut cantonment, 12
  British deaths, 11
  female taunts, 53, 58, 63, 74–75, 80–81, 181, 182, 193
  geography of, 30–31
  humiliation, 11, 50–51, 193
  mutiny, 1, 3, 10–11, 39, 50, 51, 70–71
  native disarmament, rumors of, 19–20, 32–33, 37, 51, 63, 73
  See also Meerut bazaar; prostitution
Meerut mutiny and revolt
  anti-colonial resistance, 16, 38–39
  British analysis of, 13–14, 43, 62–63, 190–192
  British decision making, 39–40
  conspiracy, 4, 13, 32, 56, 62–63, 68–69, 72
  Indian reaction to, 14–16
  Khakee Risallah, 61, 62
  marriage, British officers, 177–178
  massacre, rumors of, 120
  mutiny novels, 56

Meerut mutiny and revolt (cont.)
  mutiny songs, 11–13, 15, 17–18, 37–40, 171–175
  pension holders, disillusionment of, 170–175
  precursors to, 188–189
  regimental servants, 33–37
  Shahabad District, 162
  subaltern studies, 16
  See also Meerut cantonment; sadr bazaars
Mees Dolly, 5, 59–63, 65, 66, 79–80, 93, 116
Mehonee (Mehree), 71
Memoirs of Field Marshall Sir Henry Wylie Norman, The (Lee-Warner, 1908), 60
Misser, Cassee, 140
Misser, Sewnarrain, 153
Mitra, Durba, 5, 95
Mitra, Subal Chandra, 175
Moore, Thomas, 130, 131, 132, 135, 139, 150, 165–166
Moorhouse, Capt. Thomas, 159
"The Mutiny –1857" (mutiny song), 37–40
Mutiny of the Bengal Army, The (Malleson, 1858), 153
Mutiny Outbreak at Meerut in 1857 (Palmer, 1966), 4, 10
mutiny songs, 11–13, 15, 17–18, 37–40, 171–175

Nahallee, 165, 166–167
Napier, Charles, 163–176
Narain, Dhurm, 71, 75
Narrative of Events attending the Outbreak of Disturbances and the Restoration of Authority in the District of Moradabad, in 1857–58 (Wilson, 1871), 52
native regiments. *See* named regiments
Newar, Goor Singh, 130–131, 132
Nightrunners of Bengal (Masters, 1952), 56
Norman, Revd. A. H., 37
Norman, W. Henry, 59–60
Nunkee, 160

Odassee, 169
Old Memories (Gough, 1897), 64
Oldenburg, Veena Talwar, 94
On the Face of the Waters (Steel, 1896), 56–57, 187
Oodassee, 167
Opadia, Ramphul, 155

Palmer, J. A. B., 3–5, 10, 30–31, 33–34, 75
Pandey, Mangal, 3, 67
Pandy, Bahadoor Adheen, 142, 144–147
Pandy, Ghureeb, 159

Papers Regarding "the Indian Mutiny" (Carmichael-Smyth, 1871), 42
Passage to India, A (Lean, 1984), 65
Peasant Armed, The (Stokes, 1986), 4
pensions
  administrative procedures, 149
  authority, appropriation of, 6
  family impersonation, 154–156, 158–164
  family pensions, 126–127, 150–151
  fraud, assertion of, 127–133
  fraud, investigation of, 139–140, 147–150, 151, 153–154, 159, 164–165, 169–170, 185
  General Order 1132 (1854), 168–169
  identification of dependents, 135–140
  moral condemnation, 176
  official malfeasance, 143–146
  paymaster magisterial powers, request for, 155–158
  pensions, 136–137
  surety, misrepresentation of, 142–143
Pinckney, F. W., 103–104
Platt, John, 91
Pollok, Fitz-William Thomas, 34–35
Poor Relations (Hawes, 1996), 78
prostitution
  benevolent paternalism toward, 108–109, 110, 113, 114
  cantonment censuses, 83, 91
  concubines, 77, 94, 114, 134, 148, 167, 175–176, 186, 187
  Contagious Diseases Acts, 5, 97, 108, 185
  free agency, 114–115, 189–190
  judicial records, 97–100
  khangee (khāṅgī), 78, 83, 91, 92
  kusbee (kasbī), 78, 83, 91
  lock hospitals, 5, 95, 97, 98
  official language, obscuration by, 93, 95–97
  police, distrust of, 105–106
  Regulation 7 109–110
  roles, 82, 89–93
  trafficking, 103, 109–114
  violence, against prostitutes, 99–100, 102–103
  violence, official malfeasance, 106–108
  violence, official response to, 103–105, 185
  See also Cashmerians
Punnah, 152–153
Purbuteeah, 155

Rag, Pankaj, 74, 173
Ram, Dhawal, 38–40, 42–43, 50
Ram, Laik, 20
Ray, Rajat Kanta, 71, 180–181, 185
regimental women, 61, 79

Regulation 7, 109–110
"Reports on Sudder Bazars", 22
Richardson, Roland, 64
"The Rising: The Ballad of Mangal Panday" (Khan, 2007), 67
Robinson, Jane, 66
Rohilla, Naick Kesur Singh, 132
Ruggoonauth, 161
Runia, Eelco, 190
Runneea, 168
Russell, W. H., 13
Rutton, 140–147

sadr bazaars
  "Reports on Sudder Bazars", 22
  census data, 83–92
  goods and services, 26–27
  as hybrid space, 27–28, 31–32
  policing of, 20–21, 29
  See also Meerut bazaar
Safvi, Rana, 117
Samru, Begam, 77
Sānjh kā Sūraj (Sharma, 1955), 179–180
Sati Abolition Act (1829), 176
Saul, David, 10
Saunters, Matilda, 120
Savarkar, V.D., 14–16, 58–59
Sen, S.N., 63
Sepoy Mutiny and Revolt of 1857, The (Majumdar, 1957), 63
Service and Adventure with the Khakee Resallah (Dunlop, 1858), 19
Shah, Nawab Wajid Ali, 14, 188
Sharma, Omprakash, 179, 180, 185
Sing, Hunnooman, 154
Singh, Aumunt, 152
Singh, Boodh, 20
Singh, Brij Mohan, 44–45
Singh, Bukhtawur, 71, 76, 92
Singh, Doman, 160–162, 178
Singh, Dulloo, 155, 158
Singh, Kooman, 44–45, 73
Singh, Kuar, 162
Singh, Kunwar, 171
Singh, Mattadin, 46–48
Singh, Persaud, 160–162, 178
Singh, Rundheer, 44–45, 73
Singh, Surnam, 141
Singh, Zalim, 44–45
Singha, Radhika, 109–110
Sirmoor Battalion, 131, 132
Sleeman, Col. William Henry, 110, 161
Smith, Dr. T., 69, 71, 72, 77–78, 92–93, 148, 186–187

Smyth, Col. George, 40–42, 45, 48, 120
Soodhoo, 162–164
Sophie, 71, 72, 75–76, 80, 92, 93
"Songs of the Mutiny" (Crooke, 1911), 11–13
Steel, Flora Annie, 56–58, 80, 181, 187
Steel, J., 36
Stokes, Eric, 4
subaltern studies, 16
Sudder Dewanny Adawlut (chief or central revenue court), 31, 166

Tallewindee, 159–160
Taylor, P. J. O., 33, 63, 65–66, 95–97
Tewarry, Mayaram, 163
The Great Mutiny: India 1857 (Hibbert, 1978), 64
Tombs, F. C., 140–141, 151–152, 154, 155, 156–157, 159, 161, 164–168
Tucker, Lt. Col. H. T., 136

ud-Din, Shams, 58

Vansittart, Henry, 42
Vidyasagar, Ishvarchandra, 190
Vidyasagar, Ishwar Chandra, 175

Wagner, Kim, 4–5, 41, 61, 75
Walker, R., 163, 169
Watson, J. Forbes, 110
Williams, G. W., 1, 18–19, 32–33, 35–36, 44–45, 51, 68–70, 82–83, 186
Wilson, J. Cracroft, 33, 44, 51–53, 69, 73, 82, 116, 120–121, 125, 182–184
wives
  common law, 130–131, 132
  incitement of mutiny, 117–118, 125
  legitimacy of, 119, 125–126, 190
  pensions, 126–127, 135–136
  pensions, assertion of fraudulent claims, 127–133
  pensions, misrepresentation of surety, 142–143
  second wives and concubines, 133–134, 141–142, 148, 152–153, 167–168, 173–175, 178, 186–187
  within native lines, 181
  See also pensions
women, violence against, 101–102
Wylie, William Hutt Curzon, 15
Wyllie, R., 150

Zafar, Bahadur Shah, 117, 192
Zeenut, 71, 75, 92

For EU product safety concerns, contact us at Calle de José Abascal, 56–1°, 28003 Madrid, Spain or eugpsr@cambridge.org.

www.ingramcontent.com/pod-product-compliance
Ingram Content Group UK Ltd.
Pitfield, Milton Keynes, MK11 3LW, UK
UKHW022003250126
467190UK00019B/350